Grammar in Use

GRAMMAR in use

REFERENCE AND PRACTICE
FOR INTERMEDIATE STUDENTS
OF ENGLISH

RAYMOND MURPHY

with Roann Altman

Consultant: William E. Rutherford

CAMBRIDGE
UNIVERSITY PRESS

Published by the Press Syndicate of the University of Cambridge
The Pitt Building, Trumpington Street, Cambridge CB2 1RP
40 West 20th Street, New York, NY 10011-4211, USA
10 Stamford Road, Oakleigh, Melbourne 3166, Australia

First published 1989
Sixth printing 1993

Printed in the United States of America

Library of Congress Cataloging-in-Publication Data
Murphy, Raymond.
Grammar in use.
Contents: [1] Student's book – [2] Answer key.
1. English language – Textbooks for foreign speakers.
2. English language – Grammar – 1950-
3. English language – United States.   I. Altman, Roann.
II. Title
PE1128.M775   1989   428.2'4   88-29951

ISBN 0-521-34843-9 Student's Book : paperback
ISBN 0-521-35701-2 Answer Key : paperback

Illustrations by Daisy de Puthod
Book design by Final Draft, Inc.

CONTENTS

Contents

Conditionals

Passive

Reported speech

Questions

-ing and the infinitive

Articles

Contents

INTRODUCTION

Grammar in Use is a textbook for intermediate students of English who need to study and practice using the grammar of the language. It can be used as a classroom text or for self-study. It will be especially useful in cases where, in the teacher's view, existing course materials do not provide adequate coverage of grammar.

Level

The book is intended mainly for intermediate students (that is, students who have already studied the basic structures of English). It concentrates on those structures which intermediate students want to use but which often cause difficulty. The book will probably be most useful at middle- and upper-intermediate levels (where all or nearly all of the material will be relevant), and can serve both as a basis for review and as a means of practicing new material. The book will also be useful for more advanced students who still make a lot of grammatical mistakes and who need a book for reference and practice.

The book is not intended to be used by beginning-level students.

How the book is organized

The book consists of 124 units, each of which concentrates on a particular point of grammar. Some areas (for example, the present perfect or the use of articles) are covered in more than one unit. In each unit there are explanations and examples (left-hand page) and exercises (right-hand page), except for Unit 112, which is a double unit.

At the beginning of the book the *Contents* pages provide a full list of units, and there is a detailed *Index* at the end for easy reference.

There are also four *Appendixes* at the end of the book: "List of Present and Past Tenses," "Regular and Irregular Verbs," " Spelling," and "Short Forms." It might be useful for the teacher to draw students' attention to these.

Using the book

It is certainly not intended that anyone should work through this book from beginning to end. It is for the teacher to decide what to teach and in what order to teach it, so the book is best used selectively and flexibly.

The book can be used with the whole class or with individual students. When using the book with the whole class, it is suggested that teachers teach the grammar points concerned in whatever way they want. In this case the left-hand page is not used actively during the lesson but serves as a record of what has been taught and can be referred to by the student in the future. The exercises can then be done in class or as homework. Alternatively (and additionally), individual students can be directed to study certain units of the book by themselves if they have particular difficulties not shared by other students in their class.

Answer Key

A separate answer key is available for teachers and self-study users.

Grammar in Use

UNIT 1 Present continuous (**I am doing**)

a Study this example situation:

> Ann is in her car. She is on her way to work.
>
> She **is driving** to work.
>
> This means: She is driving now, at the time of speaking.
>
> This is the *present continuous* tense:
>
> $$\left. \begin{array}{l} \text{I } \textbf{am} \quad (= \text{ I'm}) \\ \text{he/she/(it) } \textbf{is} \quad (= \text{ he's, etc.}) \\ \text{we/they/you } \textbf{are} \quad (= \text{ we're, etc.}) \end{array} \right\} \textbf{driving}$$

We use the present continuous when we talk about something that is happening at the time of speaking:

- Please don't make so much noise. **I'm studying.** (*not* I study)
- "Where is Peggy?" "She's **taking** a bath." (*not* she takes)
- Let's go out now. It **isn't raining** anymore.
- (*at a party*) Hello, Ann. **Are** you **enjoying** the party? (*not* do you enjoy)

b We also use the present continuous when we talk about something that is happening around the time of speaking, but not necessarily exactly at the time of speaking. Study this example situation:

- Tom and Ann are talking and having coffee in a cafe. Tom says: "**I'm reading** an interesting book at the moment. I'll lend it to you when I've finished it."

Tom is not reading the book at the time of speaking. He means that he has begun the book and hasn't finished it yet. He is in the middle of reading it. Here are some more examples:

- Maria **is studying** English at a language school. (*not* studies)
- Have you heard about Brian? He **is building** his own house. (*not* builds)

But perhaps Maria and Brian are not doing these things exactly at the time of speaking.

c We often use the present continuous when we talk about a period around the present. For example: **today, this week, this season**, etc.:

- "**You're working** hard **today**." "Yes, I have a lot to do."
- Tom **isn't playing** football **this season**. He wants to concentrate on his studies.

d We use the present continuous when we talk about changing situations:

- The population of the world **is rising** very fast. (*not* rises)
- **Is** your English **getting** better? (*not* does . . . get)

2

UNIT 1 Exercises

1.1 *Put the verb into the correct form.*

Examples: Please don't make so much noise. I *am studying* (study).
Let's go out now. It *isn't raining* (not/rain) anymore.
Listen to those people. What language *are they speaking* (they/speak)?

1. Please be quiet. I .... (try) to concentrate.
2. Look! It .... (snow).
3. Why .... (you/look) at me like that? Did I say something wrong?
4. You .... (make) a lot of noise. Can you be a little bit quieter?
5. Excuse me, I .... (look) for a phone booth. Is there one near here?
6. (*at the movies*) It's a good movie, isn't it? .... (you/enjoy) it?
7. Listen! Can you hear those people next door? They .... (yell) at each other again.
8. Why .... (you/wear) your coat today? It's very warm.
9. I .... (not/work) this week. I'm on vacation.
10. I want to lose weight. I .... (not/eat) anything today.

1.2 *Complete these sentences using one of these verbs:*

get   become   change   rise   improve   fall   increase

You don't have to use all the verbs and you can use some of them more than once.

Example: The population of the world ...*is rising*........... very fast.

1. The number of people without jobs .... at the moment.
2. He is still sick, but he .... better slowly.
3. These days food .... more and more expensive.
4. The world .... Things never stay the same.
5. The cost of living .... Every year things are more expensive.
6. George has gone to work in Spain. At first, his Spanish wasn't very good, but now it ....
7. The economic situation is already very bad, and it .... worse.

1.3 *Read this conversation between Brian and Steve. Put each verb into the correct form.*

Brian and Steve meet in a restaurant.

Brian: Hello, Steve. I haven't seen you for ages. What (1) *are you doing* (you/do) these days?
Steve: I (2) .... (work) in a department store.
Brian: Really? (3) .... (you/enjoy) it?
Steve: Yeah, it's OK. How about you?
Brian: Well, I (4) .... (not/work) at the moment, but I'm very busy. I (5) .... (build) a house.
Steve: Really? (6) .... (you/do) it alone?
Brian: No, some friends of mine (7) .... (help) me.

UNIT 2 Simple present (**I do**)

a Study this example situation:

Alex is a bus driver. But now he is asleep in bed. So:

He is *not* driving a bus (he is asleep).

But: He **drives** a bus.

This is the *simple present* tense:

I/we/you/they **drive**
he/she/(it) **drives**

We use the simple present to talk about things in general. We are not thinking only about the present. We use it to say that something happens all the time or repeatedly, or that something is true in general. It is not important whether the action is happening at the time of speaking:

- The earth **goes** around the sun.
- Nurses **take care** of patients in hospitals.
- In Canada, most stores **close** at 6:00 p.m.

Remember that we say **he/she/it –s**. Don't forget the **s**:

- I **work** in a bank. Barry **works** in a department store.

b We use **do/does** to make questions and negative sentences:

do I/we/you/they **does** he/she/it } **work**?	I/we/you/they **don't** he/she/it **doesn't** } **work**

- Excuse me, **do** you **speak** English?
- "Would you like a cigarette?"   "No, thanks. **I don't smoke.**"
- **What does** this word **mean**? (*not* What means this word?)
- Rice **doesn't grow** in Alaska.

For questions see also Unit 47.

c We use the simple present when we say how often we do things:

- I **get up** at 8:00 **every morning.** (*not* am getting)
- **How often do** you **go** to the dentist?
- Ann **doesn't go out very often.**
- In the summer, Tom **usually plays** tennis **twice a week.**

d Note that we say "Where **do** you **come** from?" (= Where are you from?):

- Where **do** you **come** from? (*not* Where are you coming from?)
- He **comes** from Japan. (*not* He is coming from Japan.)

UNIT 2   Exercises

2.1 *Put the verb into the correct form.*

Examples: Water ......*boils*................ (boil) at 100 degrees Celsius.
George ...*doesn't go*......... (not/go) to the movies very often.
How many languages ..*do you speak*...... (you/speak)?

1. The swimming pool .... (open) at 9:00 and ....
   (close) at 6:30 every day.
2. What time .... (the banks / close) here?
3. I have a car, but I .... (not/use) it very often.
4. How many cigarettes .... (you/smoke) a day?
5. "What .... (you/do)?"   "I'm an electrical engineer."
6. "Where .... (your father / come) from?"   "He ....
   (come) from Mexico."
7. It .... (take) me an hour to get to work. How long ....
   (it/take) you?
8. I .... (play) the piano, but I .... (not/play) very well.
9. I don't understand the word "deceive." What .... ("deceive" / mean)?

2.2 *Read these sentences and correct them. The English is correct but the information is wrong.*
Write two correct sentences each time.

Example: The sun goes around the earth. *The sun doesn't go around the earth.*
The earth goes around the sun.................................

1. The sun rises in the west.   ....
   ....
2. Mice catch cats.   ....
   ....
3. Carpenters make things from metal.   ....
   ....
4. The Amazon River flows into the Pacific Ocean.   ....
   ....

2.3 *Use these sentences to make questions. Begin your questions with the word(s) in parentheses*
(. . .).

Examples: Tom plays tennis. (How often?) *How often does Tom play tennis?*....
I jog in the morning. (What time / usually?) *What time do you usually jog?*

1. Ann watches television. (How often?)   How often ....
2. I write to my parents. (How often?)   ....
3. I have dinner in the evening. (What time / usually?)   ....
4. Tom works. (Where?)   ....
5. I go to the movies. (How often?)   ....
6. People do stupid things. (Why?)   ....
7. The car breaks down. (How often?)   ....

UNIT 3 Present continuous (**I am doing**) or simple present (**I do**)?

Before you study this unit, study Units 1 and 2.

a Study this explanation and compare the examples:

Present continuous (**I am doing**)	*Simple present* (**I do**)
Use the present continuous to talk about something that is happening at or close to the time of speaking:	Use the simple present to talk about things in general or things that happen repeatedly:

I am
doing

$\leftarrow$ **I do** $\rightarrow$

past *now* *future*	*past* *now* *future*
The water **is boiling**. Could you turn it off, please?	Water **boils** at 100 degrees Celsius.
Listen to those people. What language **are** they **speaking?**	Excuse me, **do** you **speak** English?
"Where's Tom?" "He's **playing** tennis."	Tom **plays** tennis every Saturday.
(*you find a stranger in your room*) What **are** you **doing** here?	What **do** you usually **do** on the weekend?
Maria is in Canada for three months. She**'s learning** English.	What **do** you **do?** (= What's your job?) Most people **learn** to swim when they are children.
Use the present continuous for a *temporary* situation:	Use the simple present for a *permanent* situation:
I'm living with some friends until I can find an apartment. Mary usually has a summer job, but she **isn't working** this summer.	My parents **live** in Boston. They have been there for 20 years. Jack **doesn't work** during the summer. He always takes a long vacation.

b Some verbs are used only in *simple* tenses. For example, you cannot say "I am knowing." You can only say **I know**. Here is a list of verbs that are not normally used in *continuous* tenses (but there are exceptions):

want	like	belong	know	suppose	remember
need	love	see	realize	mean	forget
prefer	hate	hear	believe	understand	seem

have (meaning "possess"; see also Unit 23) **think** (meaning "believe" / "have an opinion")

- **Do** you **like** Rome? (*not* are you liking)
- He **doesn't understand** the problem. (*not* he isn't understanding)
- These shoes **belong** to me. (*not* are belonging)
- What **do** you **think** Tom will do? (= What do you believe he will do?)
- **Do** you **have** a car? (*not* are you having)

but:
- What **are** you **thinking** about? (= What is going on in your mind?)

UNIT 3   Exercises

3.1 *Decide whether the verbs in these sentences are right or wrong. Correct the ones that are wrong.*

Examples: I don't <u>know</u> your telephone number.   *R.I.GH.T.....*
               Please don't make so much noise. I <u>study</u>.   *W.RO.N.G.:-am studying*

1. Look! Somebody is <u>climbing</u> that tree over there.   ....
2. Can you hear those people? What <u>do</u> they <u>talk</u> about?   ....
3. <u>Are</u> you <u>believing</u> in God?   ....
4. <u>Look!</u> That man <u>tries</u> to open the door of your car.   ....
5. The moon <u>goes</u> around the earth.   ....
6. What are you <u>thinking</u> about my idea?   ⱳ r.   ....
7. The government is <u>worried</u> because the number of people
    without jobs <u>is increasing</u>.   ....
8. I'm usually <u>going</u> to work by car.   ⱳ r.   ....

3.2 *Put the verb into the correct form, present continuous (**I am doing**) or simple present (**I do**).*

Examples: Please don't make so much noise. I *am.studying*....... (study).
           How many languages *does.Tom.speak*.... (Tom/speak)?
           Jean *doesn't.speak*..... (not speak) any foreign languages.

1. I .... (not/belong) to a political party.
2. Hurry! The bus .... (come). I .... (not/want) to
    miss it.
3. The Nile River .... (flow) into the Mediterranean.
4. The river .... (flow) very fast today – much faster than usual.
5. .... (it/ever/snow) in India?
6. We usually .... (grow) vegetables in our garden, but this year
    we .... (not/grow) any.
7. A: Can you drive?
    B: No, but I .... (learn).
8. You can borrow my umbrella. I .... (not/need) it right now.
9. I ....(get) hungry. Let's go get something to eat.
10. George is a vegetarian. He .... (not/eat) meat.
11. George says he's 80 years old, but I .... (not/believe) him.
12. Ron is in San Francisco now. He .... (stay) at the Hilton Hotel. He
    usually .... (stay) at the Hilton Hotel when he's in San Francisco.

In these sentences, think about whether the situation is temporary or permanent.

13. My parents .... (live) in Winnipeg. They were born there and have
    never lived anywhere else. Where .... (your parents / live)?
14. She .... (stay) with her sister until she finds somewhere else to live.
15. A: What .... (your father / do)?
    B: He's a teacher, but he .... (not/work) right now.

Present tenses (**I am doing** / **I do**) with a future meaning

a   *Present continuous* with a future meaning

Study this example situation:

This is Tom's schedule for next week.

He **is playing** tennis on Monday afternoon.
He **is going** to the dentist on Tuesday morning.
He **is having** dinner with Ann on Friday.

In all these examples, Tom has already decided and arranged to do these things.

When you are talking about what you have already arranged to do, use the present continuous (**I am doing**). Do *not* use the simple present (**I do**).

- A: What **are** you **doing** tomorrow evening? (*not* what do you do)
  B: **I'm going** to the theater. (*not* I go)
- A: **Are** you **playing** tennis tomorrow?
  B: Yes, but Tom **isn't playing**. He hurt his leg.
- A: Ann **is coming** tomorrow.
  B: Oh, **is** she? What time **is** she **arriving**?
  A: At 10:15.
  B: **Are** you **meeting** her at the station?
  A: I can't. **I'm working** tomorrow morning.

It is also possible to use **going to (do)** in these sentences:

- What **are** you **going to do** tomorrow evening?
- Tom **is going to play** tennis on Monday afternoon.

But the present continuous is usually more natural when you are talking about arrangements. See also Unit 5.

Do *not* use **will** to talk about what you have already arranged to do:

- What **are** you **doing** this evening? (*not* what will you do)
- Alex **is getting** married next month. (*not* Alex will get)

For **will** see Units 6 and 7.

b   *Simple present* with a future meaning

We use the simple present when we are talking about timetables, schedules, etc. (for example, public transportation, movies):

- What time **does** the movie **begin?**
- The train **leaves** Boston at 7:25 a.m. and **arrives** in Washington, D.C., at 3:41 p.m.
- The football game **starts** at 2:00.
- Tomorrow **is** Wednesday.

But we do not usually use the simple present for personal arrangements:

- What time **are** you **meeting** Ann? (*not* do you meet)

UNIT 4 Exercises

4.1 *A friend of yours is planning to go on vacation very soon. You ask him about his plans. Use the words in parentheses (. . .) to make your questions.*
Example: (where / go)? *Where are you going?* ....

1. (how long / stay?) ....
2. (when / leave?) ....
3. (go / alone?) ....

4. (go / by car?) ....
5. (where / stay?) ....

4.2 *Ann is going on vacation. Write sentences about her vacation plans. Use the words in parentheses to write your sentences.*
Example: (go / Hawaii) *She is going to Hawaii.*..

1. (leave / next Friday) She ....
2. (stay / in Hawaii for two weeks) ....
3. (go / with a friend of hers) ....
4. (stay / in a hotel) They ....
5. (go / by plane) ....

4.3 *Tom wants you to visit him, but you are very busy. Look at your schedule for the next few days and explain to him why you can't come.*

Tom: Can you come on Monday evening?
You: Sorry, I'd love to, but *I'm playing volleyball.*
Tom: What about Tuesday evening then?
You: I'm afraid I can't. I (1) ....
Tom: Well, what are you doing on Wednesday evening?
You: (2) ....
Tom: I see. Well, are you free on Thursday evening?
You: I'm afraid not. (3) ....

4.4 *Put the verb into the most appropriate form: present continuous (**I am doing***) or simple present (**I do***).*
Example: We ...*are going*............ (go) to the theater this evening.
          Does the movie begin (the movie / begin) at 3:30 or 4:30?

1. We .... (have) a party next Saturday. Would you like to come?
2. I ....(not/go) away for my vacation next month because I don't have enough money. .... (you/go) away?
3. The concert this evening ....(start) at 8:00.
4. George, is it true that you ....(get) married next week?
5. The art exhibit ....(open) on May 3rd and ....
   (close) on July 15th.
6. What time .... (the next train / leave)?
7. Ann, we .... (go) to the park. .... (you/come) with us?

9

UNIT 5 Going to (I am going to do)

a We use **going to (do)** when we say what we have already decided to do, or what we intend to do in the future:

- A: There's a movie on television tonight. **Are** you **going to watch** it?
  B: No, I'm too tired. **I'm going to make** it an early night.
- A: I hear Ann has won a lot of money. What **is** she **going to do** with it?
  B: I've heard she's **going to travel** around the world.

For the difference between **will** and **going to** see Unit 8. *(will is a stronger intention) but > spontaneous*

b We prefer to use the present continuous (**I am doing**) when we say what someone has *arranged* to do – for example, arranged to meet someone, arranged to travel somewhere. **Going to** is also possible:

- What time **are** you **meeting** Ann? (*or* **are** you **going to meet**)
- **I'm leaving** for Europe on Monday. (*or* **I'm going to leave**)

See also Unit 4a.

c We use **was/were going to** to say what someone intended to do in the past (but didn't do):

- We **were going to take** the train, but then we decided to go by car.
- A: Did Tom take the exam?
  B: No, he **was going to take** it, but then he changed his mind.

d **Going to** also has another meaning. Study this example situation:

The man can't see where he is going. There is a hole in front of him.

He **is going to fall** into the hole.

Here the speaker is saying what he thinks will happen. Of course he doesn't mean that the man intends to fall into the hole.

We use **going to** in this way when we say what we think will happen. Usually there is something in the present situation (the man walking toward the hole) that makes the speaker sure about what will happen.

- Look at those black clouds! It's **going to rain.** (the clouds are there now)
- Oh, I feel terrible. I think **I'm going to be** sick. (I feel terrible now)

UNIT 5 Exercises

5.1 *Say when you are going to do something.*
Example: Have you cleaned the car? (tomorrow)
Not yet. I'm going to clean it tomorrow. ....

1. Have you called Tom? (after lunch)   Not yet. I ....
2. Have you had dinner? (in a little while)   Not yet. ....
3. Have you painted your apartment? (soon)   Not ....
4. Have you fixed my bicycle? (this afternoon)   ....

5.2 *Write questions with* **going to**.
Example: I've won a lot of money. (what / with it?) *What are you going to do with it?*

1. I'm going to a party tonight. (what / wear?)   ....
2. Tom has just bought a painting. (where / hang it?)   ....
3. I've decided to have a party. (who / invite?)   ....

5.3 *Use* **was/were going to**.
Example: Did you travel by train?
No, I was going to travel by train, but I changed my mind. ......

1. Did you buy that jacket you saw in the store window?
   No, I .... , but I changed my mind.
2. Did Sue get married?
   No, she .... , but she ....
3. Did Tom quit his job?
   No, ... , but ....
4. Did Wayne and Sharon go to Greece for their vacation?
   No, ...
5. Did you play tennis yesterday?
   No, ...
6. Did you invite Ann to the party?
   No, ...

5.4 *Say what you think is going to happen in these situations.*
Example: The sky is full of black clouds. (rain) *It's going to rain.* ....

1. Terry is taking his exams tomorrow. He hasn't done any work for them, and he is not very intelligent. (fail)   He ....
2. It is 8:30. Tom is leaving his house. He has to be at work at 8:45, but the trip takes 30 minutes. (be late)   ....
3. There is a hole in the bottom of the boat. It is filling up with water very quickly. (sink) It ....
4. Ann is driving. There is very little gas left in the tank. The nearest gas station is a long way from here. (run out of gas)   ....

UNIT 6 Will (1)

a We use **will** ('**ll**) when we decide to do something at the time of speaking:
- Oh, I left the door open. **I'll go** and shut it.
- "What would you like to drink?"   "**I'll have** some coffee, please."
- "Did you call Ann?"   "Oh no, I forgot. **I'll do** it now."
- I'm too tired to walk home. I think **I'll take** a taxi.

You cannot use the simple present (**I do**) in these sentences.
- **I'll go** and shut it. (*not* I go and shut it)

Do not use **will** to say what someone has already decided to do or arranged to do:
- I can't meet you tomorrow because my parents **are coming** to see me. (*not* my parents will come) ~~not "will come"~~ → T.K. says into system conditional

The negative of **will** is **won't** (or **will not**):
- Receptionist: I'm afraid Mr. Wood can't see you until 4:00.
  You: Oh, in that case I **won't** wait.

We often use **I think I'll . . .** or **I don't think I'll . . .** when we decide to do something:
- **I think I'll stay** home this evening.
- **I don't think I'll go** out tonight. I'm too tired.

b We often use **will** in these situations:

> *Offering* to do something:
> - That bag looks heavy. **I'll help** you with it. (*not* I help)
> - "I need some money."   "Don't worry. **I'll lend** you some."
>
> *Agreeing* or *refusing* to do something:
> - A: You know that book I lent you? Can I have it back?
> - B: Of course. **I'll bring** it back this afternoon. (*not* I bring)
> - I've asked John to help me, but he **won't.**
> - The car **won't** start. (= the car "refuses" to start)
>
> *Promising* to do something:
> - Thank you for lending me the money. **I'll pay** you back on Friday. (*not* I pay)
> - I **won't tell** Tom what you said. I promise.
> - I promise **I'll call** you as soon as I arrive.
>
> *Asking* someone to do something (**Will you . . . ?**):
> - **Will you shut** the door, please?
> - **Will you** please **be** quiet? I'm trying to concentrate.

For **will** see also Unit 7. For **will** and **going to** see Unit 8.

UNIT 6 Exercises

6.1 *Complete the sentences with* **I'll** + *an appropriate verb.*

Example: I'm too tired to walk home. I think *I'll take* a taxi.

1. I'm a little hungry. I think .... something to eat.
2. It's too late to call Tom now. .... him in the morning.
3. "It's a bit cold in this room." "Is it? .... on the heat then."
4. "We don't have any milk." "Oh, we don't? .... and get some."
5. "Did you write that letter to Jack?" "Oh, I forgot. Thanks for reminding me. .... it tonight."
6. "Would you like tea or coffee?" "......................... coffee, please."

6.2 *Use* **I think I'll** ... *or* **I don't think I'll** ... . *Read the situation and then write your sentence.*

Examples: It's cold. You decide to close the window. *I think I'll close the window.*
It's raining. You decide not to go out. *I don't think I'll go out.*

1. You feel tired. You decide to go to bed. I ....
2. A friend of yours offers you a ride home, but you decide to walk.
   Thank you, but ....
3. You arranged to play tennis. Now you decide that you don't want to play.
   ....
4. You were going to go swimming. Now you decide that you don't want to go.
   ....

6.3 *Offer to do things. Tom has a lot of things to do and you offer to do them for him.*

Example: Tom: Oh, I have to clean up. You: *No, that's all right. I'll clean up.*

1. Tom: Oh, I have to get dinner ready. You: No, that's all right. I ....
2. Tom: Oh, I have to do the shopping. You: No, ...
3. Tom: Oh, I have to water the plants. You: ....

6.4 *Agree and promise to do things.*

Example: A: Can you clean the windows? B: Sure, *I'll clean them* this afternoon.
A: Do you promise? B: *Yes, I promise I'll clean them this afternoon.*

1. A: Can you call me later? B: Sure, ... tonight.
   A: Do you promise? B: Yes, ...
2. A: Can you fix the clock? B: Okay, ... tomorrow.
   A: Do ....? B: ....
3. A: Please don't tell anyone. B: All right, I won't tell anyone.
   A: ....? B: ....
4. A: Please don't hurt me. B: Don't worry, ...
   A: ....? B: ....

UNIT 7 Will (2)

a When we talk about the future, we often say what someone has arranged to do or intends to do. Do *not* use **will** in this situation:

- Tom **is playing** tennis on Monday. (*not* Tom will play)
- **Are** you **going to watch** television this evening? (*not* will you watch)

For arrangements and intentions see Units 4 and 5.

But often when we are talking about the future, we are not talking about arrangements or intentions. Study this example:

> Tom: I'm really worried about my exam next week.
> Ann: Don't worry, Tom. You**'ll pass.**
>
> "You**'ll pass**" is not an arrangement or an intention. Ann is just saying what will happen or what she thinks will happen; she is predicting the future. When we predict a future happening or a future situation, we use **will/won't.**

- When you return home, you**'ll notice** a lot of changes.
- This time next year **I'll be** in Japan. Where **will** you **be**?
- When **will** you **find out** your exam results?
- Tom **won't pass** his exam. He hasn't done any work for it.

We often use **will** with these words and expressions:

probably	**I'll probably be** a little late this evening.
(I'm) sure	You must meet Ann. **I'm sure** you**'ll like** her.
(I) bet	**I bet** Carol **will get** the job.
(I) think	Do you think we**'ll win** the match?
(I) suppose	**I suppose** we**'ll see** John at the party.
(I) guess	**I guess** I**'ll see** you next week.

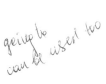

going to can be used too

b **Will** and **shall**

You can say **I will** or **I shall** (**I'll**)

                we will or **we shall** (**we'll**)

- **I will** (or **I shall**) probably **go** to Europe this summer.
- **We will** (or **we shall**) probably **go** to Europe this summer.

Will is more common than **shall**. In speech we normally use the short forms **I'll** and **we'll**:

- **I'll** probably **go** to Europe.

Do not use **shall** with **he / she / it / they / you.**

- **John will help** you. (*not* shall help you)

We use **shall** (not **will**) in the questions **Shall I . . . ?** and **Shall we . . . ?** (for offers, suggestions, etc.):

- **Shall I open** the window? (= Do you want me to open the window?)
- Where **shall we go** this evening?

For **will** see also Units 6, 8, and 9.

14

UNIT 7 Exercises

7.1 *Decide which form of the verb is correct (or more natural) in these sentences. Cross out the one that is wrong.*
Example: Tom isn't free on Saturday. He ~~will work~~ / is working.

1. I will go / am going to a party tomorrow night. Would you like to come too?
2. According to the weather forecast, it will rain / is raining tomorrow.
3. I'm sure Tom will get / is getting the job. He has a lot of experience.
4. I can't meet you this evening. A friend of mine will come / is coming to see me.
5. A: Have you decided where to go for your vacation yet?
   B: Yes, we will go / are going to Italy.
6. Don't worry about the dog. It won't hurt / isn't hurting you.

7.2 *Write questions using* **do you think . . . will . . . .** *Use a verb from the box each time.*

arrive	come	cost	finish	get married	rain	~~pass~~

1. Bill is taking his final exam soon. *Do you think* ....he .*will pass*............. ?
2. I've invited her to the party. Do you ....she ·····························?
3. Jack and Ann are coming over this evening. What time do ·····························
   they······························· ?
4. The weather doesn't look very good. Do ··· ?
5. My car needs to be repaired. How much ·····························?
6. They are in love. Do ·····························?
7. The meeting is still going on. When ·····························?

7.3 *Answer these questions using the words in parentheses (. . .).*
Example: Who do you think will win the prize? (bet/Sue) *I bet Sue will win.*...............

1. What do you think she'll say? (probably / nothing)   She ·····························
2. Where do you think she'll go? (bet / South America)   I ·····························
3. When do you think she'll leave? (think / tomorrow)   I ·····························
4. How do you think she'll go there? (suppose / by plane)   I ·····························
5. When do you think she'll be back? (think / quite soon)   I·····························
6. Do you think you'll miss her? (I'm sure / very much)   Yes, ·····························

7.4 *Read each situation and then write a question with* **shall I?** *or* **shall we?** *In each situation you are talking to a friend.*
Example: It's very hot in the room. The window is shut. *Shall I open the window?*.....

1. Your friend wants you to call him/her later. You don't know what time to call. Ask your friend.   You say: What ·····························
2. You and your friend haven't decided what to have for dinner.
   You say: ·····························
3. You and your friend are going out. You haven't decided whether to go by car or to walk.   You say: ·····························
   or ·····························

UNIT 8 Will or going to?

a *Talking about future actions*

We use both **will** and **going to** to talk about our future actions, but there is a clear difference. Study this example situation:

Helen's bicycle has a flat tire. She tells her father. Helen: My bicycle has a flat tire. Can you fix it for me? Father: Okay, but I can't do it now. **I'll fix** it tomorrow.	**will:** We use **will** when we decide to do something at the time of speaking. The speaker has not decided before. Before Helen told her father, he didn't know about the flat tire.
Later, Helen's mother speaks to her husband. Mother: Can you fix Helen's bicycle? It has a flat tire. Father: Yes, I know. She told me. **I'm going to fix** it tomorrow.	**going to:** We use **going to** when we have already decided to do something. Helen's father had already decided to fix the bicycle before his wife spoke to him.

Here is another example:

- *Tom is cooking when he suddenly discovers that there isn't any salt:*
  Tom: Ann, we don't have any salt.
  Ann: Oh, we don't? **I'll get** some from the store. *(she decides at the time of speaking)*

  Before going out, Ann says to Jim:
  Ann: **I'm going to get** some salt from the store. *(she has already decided)* Can I get you anything, Jim?

b *Saying what will happen (predicting future happenings)*

We use both **will** and **going to** to say what we think will happen in the future:

- Do you think Laura **will get** the job?
- Oh no! It's already 4:00. We**'re going to be** late.

We use **going to** (not **will**) when there is something in the present situation that shows what will happen in the future (especially the near future). The speaker feels sure about what will happen because of the situation now (see also Unit 5d):

- Look at those black clouds. It**'s going to rain.** (the clouds are there *now*)
- I feel terrible. I think **I'm going to be** sick. (I feel terrible *now*)

Do not use **will** in situations like these.

In other situations, use **will** (see also Unit 7):

- Sue **will** probably **arrive** at about 8 o'clock.
- I think George **will like** the present you bought for him.

16

UNIT 8 Exercises

8.1 *Put the verb into the correct form, using* **will** *or* **going to**.

the clue is given by the present cont. the tense (present) is in the question → the same sentence

Examples: A: Why are you turning on the TV?
B: I *'m going to watch*............(watch) the news.

A: Oh, I just realized – I don't have any money.
B: Don't worry – that's no problem. I *'ll lend*......................(lend) you some.

Those clouds are very black, aren't they? I think it *is going to rain*....(rain).

1. A: I've got a terrible headache.
   B: Do you? Wait here and I ....(get) you some aspirin.
2. A: Why are you filling that bucket with water?
   B: I ....(wash) the car.
3. A: I've decided to repaint this room.
   B: Oh, you have? What color ....(you/paint) it?
4. A: Look! There's smoke coming out of that house. It's on fire!
   B: Oh no! I ....(call) the fire department right away.
5. A: The ceiling in this room doesn't look very safe, does it?
   B: No, it looks as if it ....(fall) down.
6. A: Where are you going? Are you going shopping?
   B: Yes, I ....(buy) something for dinner.
7. A: I can't figure out how to use this camera.
   B: It's easy. I ....(show) you.
8. A: What would you like to have – coffee or tea?
   B: I ....(have) coffee, please.
9. A: Has George decided what to do when he finishes school?
   B: Oh yes. Everything is settled. He ....(take) a vacation for a
   few weeks, and then he.........................(start) a computer programming course.
10. A: Did you mail that letter for me?
    B: Oh, I'm sorry. I completely forgot. I ....(do) it now.
11. A: What shall we have for dinner?
    B: I don't know. I can't make up my mind.
    A: Come on, hurry up! Make a decision!
    B: Okay. We...................................(have) chicken.
12. Jack: We need some bread for lunch.
    Ben: Oh, we do? I ....(go) to the store and get some. I feel like
          taking a walk.
    Before he goes out, Ben talks to Jane:
    Ben: I ....(get) some bread. Do you want anything from the store?
    Jane: Yes, I need some envelopes.
    Ben: Okay, I ....(get) you some.
13. *John has to go to the airport to catch a plane. He doesn't have a car:*
    John: Toshi, can you take me to the airport tonight?
    Toshi: Of course I...................................(take) you. I'd be happy to.
    Later that day Eric offers to take John to the airport.
    Eric: John, do you want me to take you to the airport?
    John: No thanks, Eric. Toshi ....(take) me.

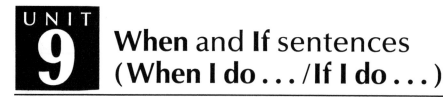

UNIT 9 When and If sentences (When I do... / If I do...)

a Study this example:

> A: What time will you call me tonight?
> B: I'll call you **when I get** home from work.
>
> "I'll call you when I get home from work" is a sentence with two parts: "I'll call you" (the main part) and "when I get home from work" (the **when** part). The sentence is future (*tonight*), but you cannot use **will** or **going to** in the **when** part of the sentence. Instead we use a present tense, usually simple present (**I do**).

- I can't talk to you now. I'll talk to you later when I have more time. (*not* when I'll have)
- **When** the rain **stops**, we'll go out. (*not* when the rain will stop)

The same thing happens after:

while   after   before   until/till   as soon as

- Can you take care of the children **while I am** out? (*not* will be)
- **Before** you **leave**, you must visit the museum. (*not* will leave)
- Wait here **until I come** back. (*not* will come)

b You can also use the present perfect (**I have done**) after **when/after/until**, etc., to show that the first action will be finished before the second:

- **After I've read** this book, you can have it.
- Don't say anything while Tom is here. Wait **until** he **has gone**.

It is often possible to use either the simple present or the present perfect:

- I'll come **as soon as** I **finish**.   *or*   I'll come **as soon as I've finished**.
- You'll feel better **when** you **have**   *or*   You'll feel better **when you've had** something to eat.

c After **if** we also use the simple present (**I do**) for the future:

- It's raining. We'll get wet **if** we **go** out. (*not* if we will go)
- Hurry up! **If** we **don't hurry,** we'll be late. (*not* if we won't hurry)

Be careful not to confuse **when** and **if**.
Use **when** for things that are *sure* to happen:

- *I'm going* shopping this afternoon. **When** I go shopping, I'll buy some food.

Use **if** (not **when**) for things that will *possibly* happen:

- *I might go* shopping this afternoon. **If** I go shopping, I'll buy some food.
- **If** it rains this evening, I won't go out. (*not* when it rains)
- Don't worry **if** I'm late tonight. (*not* when I'm late)
- **If** he doesn't come soon, I'm not going to wait. (*not* when he doesn't come)

UNIT 9   Exercises

9.1 *All the sentences in this exercise are about the future. Put the verbs into the correct form: the future* **will/won't** *or the simple present* (**I do**).

Example: When I .*see*........(see) Tom tonight, I'*ll invite*....(invite) him to our party.

1. Before you .... (leave), don't forget to shut the windows.
2. I .... (call) you as soon as I .... (arrive) in Tokyo.
3. Please don't touch anything before the police ....*come*................. (come).
4. Everyone .... (be) very surprised if he .... (pass) the exam.
5. When you .... (see) Brian again, you .... (not/recognize) him.
6. We .... (not/start) dinner until Karen .... (arrive).
7. .... (you/be) lonely without me while I .... (be) away?
8. If I .... (need) any help, I .... (ask) you.
9. Come on! Hurry up! Ann ....(be) annoyed if we ....(be) late.

9.2 *Make one sentence from two sentences.*

Example: You are going to leave soon. You must visit the museum before that.
You must visit the museum...........before *you leave.*........................

1. I'll find somewhere to live. Then I'll give you my address.
   I ....when ....
2. It's going to start raining. Let's go out before that.
   Let's ....before ....
3. I'm going to do the shopping. Then I'll come straight home.
   .... after ....
4. You'll be in Washington next month. You must come and see me then.
   .... when ....
5. I'm going to finish reading this book. Then I'll get the dinner ready.
   .... when ....
6. We'll make our decision. Then we'll let you know.
   .... as soon as ....

9.3 *Fill in* **when** *or* **if**.

Example: .*If*...... it rains this evening, I won't go out.

1. I'm sorry you've decided to go away. I'll be very sad ....you leave.
2. Tom might call this evening. ....he does, can you take a message?
3. I think he'll get the job. I'll be very surprised ....he doesn't get it.
4. I hope to be there by 10:30. But ....I'm not there, don't wait for me.
5. I'm going shopping. ....you want anything, I can get it for you.
6. I think I'll go home now. I'm feeling very tired. I think I'll go right to bed ....I get home.
7. I'm going away for a few days. I'll call you ....I get back.
8. I want you to come to the party but ....you don't want to come, you don't have to.

UNIT 10 Will be doing and will have done

a First study this example situation:

> Tom is a football fan, and there is a football game on television this evening. The game begins at 7:30 and ends at 9:15. Ann wants to go and see Tom this evening and wants to know what time to come over:
>
> Ann: Is it all right if I come over at about 8:30?
> Tom: No, don't come then. **I'll be watching** the game on TV.
> Ann: Oh. Well, what about 9:30?
> Tom: Yes, that'll be fine. The game **will have ended** by then.

b We use **will be doing** (*future continuous*) to say that we will be in the middle of doing something at a certain time in the future. The football game begins at 7:30 and ends at 9:15. So during this time, for example at 8:30, Tom **will be watching** the match.
Here are some more examples:
- You'll recognize her when you see her. She**'ll be wearing** a yellow hat.
- This time next week I'll be on vacation. **I'll** probably **be lying** on a beautiful beach.

Compare **will be doing** with the other continuous forms:
Bill works every morning from 9 o'clock until noon. So:
- At 10 o'clock yesterday he **was working**. (*past continuous* – see Unit 12)
- It's 10 o'clock now. He **is working**. (*present continuous* – see Unit 1)
- At 10 o'clock tomorrow he **will be working**.

c You can also use **will be doing** in another way: to talk about things that are already planned or decided:
- **I'll be going** downtown later. Can I get you anything?

With this meaning **will be doing** is similar to **am doing** (see Unit 4a):
- **I'm going** downtown later.

We often use **Will (you) be -ing**? to ask about people's plans, especially when we want something or want someone to do something:
- "**Will** you **be using** your bicycle this evening?" "No, you can take it."
- "**Will** you **be passing** the post office when you go out?" "Yes, why?"

d We use **will have done** (*future perfect*) to say that something will already have happened before a certain time in the future. Tom's football game ends at 9:15. So after this time, for example at 9:30, the game **will have ended**. Here are some more examples:
- Next year is Ted and Amy's 25th wedding anniversary. They **will have been** married for 25 years. (Now they have been married for 24 years.)
- We're late. I guess the movie **will** already **have started** by the time we get to the theater.

UNIT 10 Exercises

10.1 *Make sentences with* **will be -ing.**

Example: I'm going to watch television from 9 until 10 o'clock this evening.
So at 9:30 I *will be watching television.* ....

1. Tomorrow afternoon I'm going to play tennis from 3:00 to 4:30. So at 4:00 tomorrow
   I ....
2. Jim is going to study from 7:00 until 10:00 this evening. So at 8:30 this evening
   he ....
3. We are going to clean the apartment tomorrow. It will take from 9 until 11 o'clock. So at
   10 o'clock tomorrow morning ....

10.2 *Write three sentences, one each about the past, present, and future. Bob always reads the
newspaper in the morning. It always takes him half an hour, from 8:00 until 8:30. So:*

1. At 8:15 yesterday morning Bob ....
2. It's 8:15 now. He ....
3. At 8:15 tomorrow morning he ....

10.3 *Ask questions with* **Will you be -ing?**

Example: You want to borrow your friend's bicycle this evening.   (you / use /
your bicycle this evening?)   *Will you be using your bicycle this evening?*

1. You want your friend to give Jean a message this afternoon.
   (you / see / Jean this afternoon?)   ....
2. You want to use your friend's typewriter tomorrow evening.
   (you /use / your typewriter tomorrow evening?)   ....
3. Your friend is going shopping. You want him/her to buy some stamps for you at the post
   office. (you / pass / the post office while you're downtown?)   ....
   ....

10.4 *Use* **will have done.**

Example: Tom and Ann are going to the movies. The movie begins at 7:30, and it is already
7:20. It will take them 20 minutes to get there. When they get there,
(the film/already/start) *the film will have already started.* ....

1. Jim always goes to bed at 11:00. Peter is going to visit him at 11:30 this evening. When
   Peter arrives, (Jim / go / to bed) ....
2. Tom is on vacation. He has very little money and he is spending too much too quickly.
   Before the end of his vacation, (he / spend / all his money) ....
   ....
3. Sue went to Canada from the U.S. almost three years ago. Next Monday it will be exactly
   three years since she arrived. Next Monday (she / be / in Canada / exactly three years) .....
   ....

UNIT 11 Simple past (**I did**)

a Study this example:

> Tom: Look! It's raining again.
> Ann: Oh no, not again. It **rained** all day yesterday too.
>
> **Rained** is the *simple past* tense. We use the simple past to talk about actions or situations in the past.

- I **enjoyed** the party very much.   ■ Mr. Brown **died** ten years ago.
- When I **lived** in Athens, I **worked** in a bank.

b Very often the simple past ends in **-ed**:
- We invit**ed** them to our party, but they decid**ed** not to come.
- The police stopp**ed** me on my way home last night.
- She pass**ed** her exam because she stud**ied** very hard.

For spelling rules see Appendix 3.

But many important verbs are *irregular*. This means that the simple past does *not* end in **-ed**:

leave → **left**   We all **left** the party at 11:00.
go   → **went**   Last month I **went** to Rome to see a friend of mine.
cost → **cost**   This house **cost** $75,000 in 1980.

The past of the verb **be** (**am/is/are**) is **was/were**:

> I/he/she/it **was**   we/you/they **were**
>
> I **was** angry because Tom and Ann **were** late.

For a list of irregular verbs see Appendix 2.

c In simple past questions and negatives we use **did/didn't** + the base form (**do/open**, etc.):

> it rain**ed**   **did** it **rain**?   it **didn't rain**

- Ann: **Did** you **go** out last night, Tom?
  Tom: Yes, I went to the movies. But I **didn't enjoy** it.
- When **did** Mrs. Johnson **die**?   ■ What **did** you **do** over the weekend?
- We **didn't invite** her to the party, so she **didn't come**.
- Why **didn't** you **call** me on Tuesday?

Note that we normally use **did/didn't** with **have**:
- **Did** you **have** time to write the letter?
- I **didn't have** enough money to buy anything to eat.

But we do *not* use **did** with the verb **be** (**was/were**):
- Why **were** you so angry?   ■ **Was** Mark at work yesterday?
- They **weren't** able to come because they were very busy.

For the simple past see also Units 12, 19, and 20.

UNIT 11 Exercises

11.1 *Read a sentence about the present and then write a sentence about the past.*

Example: Carol usually gets up at 7:30. Yesterday *she got up at 7:30.*

1. Carol usually wakes up early. Yesterday morning ....
2. Carol usually walks to work. Yesterday ....
3. Carol is usually late for work. Yesterday ....
4. Carol usually has a sandwich for lunch. Yesterday ....
5. Carol usually goes out in the evening. Yesterday evening ....
6. Carol usually sleeps very well. Last night ....

11.2 *Put one of these verbs in each sentence:*

hurt   teach   spend   sell   throw   fall   catch   buy   cost

Example: I was hungry, so I *bought* ....something to eat at the store.

1. Tom's father ....him how to drive when he was 17.
2. Don ....down the stairs this morning and ....his leg.
3. We needed some money, so we .... our car.
4. Ann .... a lot of money yesterday. She .... a dress that .... $80.
5. Jim .... the ball to Sue, who ....it.

11.3 *Write questions. A friend has just come back from vacation and you are asking about it.*

Examples: where / go? *.Where did you go.?*...
          food / good? *.Was the food good.?*...

1. how long / stay there? ....
2. stay in a hotel? ....
3. go alone? ....
4. how / travel? ....
5. the weather / nice? ....
6. what / do in the evenings? ....
7. meet any interesting people? ....

11.4 *Put the verb into the correct form. Use the simple past.*

Example: I *.didn't go...* (not/go) to work yesterday because I *.wasn't.....* (not/be) well.

1. Tom .... (not/shave) this morning because he .... (not/have) time.
2. We .... (not/eat) anything because we .... (not/be) hungry.
3. I ....(not/rush) because I ....(not/be) in a hurry.
4. She .... (not/be) interested in the book because she .... (not/understand) it.

U N I T 12 Past continuous (**I was doing**)

a Study this example situation:

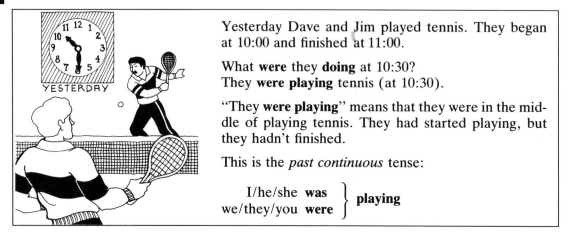

Yesterday Dave and Jim played tennis. They began at 10:00 and finished at 11:00.

What **were** they **doing** at 10:30?
They **were playing** tennis (at 10:30).

"They **were playing**" means that they were in the middle of playing tennis. They had started playing, but they hadn't finished.

This is the *past continuous* tense:

I/he/she **was** ⎫
we/they/you **were** ⎬ **playing**

We use the past continuous to say that someone was in the middle of doing something at a certain time. The action or situation had already started before this time but hadn't finished:

- This time last year I **was living** in Brazil.
- What **were** you **doing** at 10:00 last night?

b The past continuous does not tell us whether an action was finished or not. Perhaps it was finished, perhaps not. Compare:

- Dan **was cooking** dinner. (*past continuous*) = He was in the middle of cooking dinner and we don't know whether he finished cooking it.
- Dan **cooked** dinner. (*simple past*) = He began and finished it.

c We often use the past continuous (**I was doing**) and the simple past (**I did**) together to say that something happened in the middle of something else:

- Dan **burned** his hand while he **was cooking** dinner.
- I **saw** Jim in the park. He **was sitting** on the grass and **reading** a book.
- It **was raining** when I **got** up.
- While I **was working** in the garden, I **hurt** my back.

But to say that one thing happened *after* another, use the simple past.

- Last night Sue was taking a bath when the phone rang. She **got** out of the bathtub and **answered** the phone.

Compare:

- When Helen arrived, we **were having** dinner. (*past continuous*) = We had already started dinner before Helen arrived.
- When Helen arrived, we **had** dinner. (*simple past*) = Helen arrived and then we had dinner.

Note: There are some verbs (for example, **know**) that are not normally used in continuous tenses. For a list of these verbs see Unit 3b.

24

UNIT 12 Exercises

12.1 *Here is a list of some things that Ann did yesterday (and the times at which she did them):*

1.	8:45–9:15	had breakfast	4.	12:45–1:30	had lunch
2.	9:15–10:00	read the newspaper	5.	2:30–3:30	washed some clothes
3.	10:00–12:00	cleaned her apartment	6.	4:00–6:00	watched TV

Now write sentences saying what she was doing at these times:

1. At 9:00 *she was having breakfast.*   4. At 1:00 ....
2. At 9:30 she ....   5. At 3:00 ....
3. At 11:00 ....   6. At 5:00 ....

12.2 *A group of people were staying in a hotel. One evening the fire alarm went off. Use the words in parentheses (. . .) to make sentences saying what each person was doing at the time.*

Example: (Don / take / a bath) *Don was taking a bath.*...

1. (Ann / write / a letter in her room) Ann ....
2. (George / get / ready to go out) George ....
3. (Carol and Dennis / have / dinner) Carol and Dennis ....
4. (Tom / make / a phone call) Tom ....

12.3 *Make sentences from the words in parentheses. Put the verbs into the correct form: simple past (I did) or past continuous (I was doing).*

Example: (I / fall / asleep when I / watch / TV). *I fell asleep when I was watching T.V.*....

1. (the phone / ring / while I / take a shower) The phone ....
2. (it / begin / to rain while I / walk / home) ....
3. (we / see / an accident while we / wait / for the bus) ....

12.4 *Put the verb into the correct form: past continuous or simple past.*

Example: While Tom *was cooking*.. (cook) dinner, the phone ...*rang*........... (ring).

1. George ....(fall) off the ladder while he ....(paint) the ceiling.
2. Last night I ....(read) in bed when suddenly I ....(hear) a scream.
3. .... (you/watch) TV when I called you?
4. Ann .... (wait) for me when I........................ (arrive).
5. I........................(not/drive) very fast when the accident ....(happen).
6. I ....(break) a plate last night. I ....(wash) the dishes when it ....(slip) out of my hand.
7. Tom ....(take) a picture of me while I ....(not/look).
8. We ....(not/go) out because it ....(rain).
9. What ....(you/do) at this time yesterday?
10. I ....(see) Carol at the party. She ....(wear) a new dress.

UNIT 13 Present perfect (I have done) (1)

a Study this example situation:

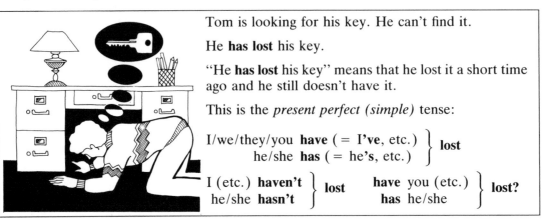

Tom is looking for his key. He can't find it.

He **has lost** his key.

"He **has lost** his key" means that he lost it a short time ago and he still doesn't have it.

This is the *present perfect (simple)* tense:

I/we/they/you **have** (= I've, etc.)
he/she **has** (= he's, etc.) } lost

I (etc.) **haven't**
he/she **hasn't** } lost   **have** you (etc.)
                              has he/she } lost?

We form the present perfect with **have/has** + the *past participle*. The past participle often ends in **-ed** (open**ed**, decid**ed**), but many important verbs are *irregular* (**lost, written, done,** etc.). See Appendix 2.

b When we use the present perfect, there is a connection with the present:
- **I've lost** my key. (= I don't have it *now*.)
- Jim **has gone** to Canada. (= He is in Canada or on his way there *now*.)

c We often use the present perfect to give new information or to announce a recent happening:
- **I've lost** my key. Can you help me look for it?
- Did you hear about Jim? He**'s gone** to Canada.

You can use the present perfect with **just** (= a short time ago):
- "Would you like something to eat?"   "No, thanks. **I've just had** lunch."
- Hello, **have** you **just arrived**?

Use the present perfect with **already** to say something has happened sooner than expected:
- "Don't forget to mail the letter."   "**I've already mailed** it."
- "When is Tom going to start his new job?"   "He **has already started**."

Note that you can also use the simple past (I did / I lost, etc.) in the above situations.
- **I lost** my key. Can you help me look for it?
- "Would you like something to eat?"   "No thanks. **I just had** lunch."
- "Don't forget to mail the letter."   "**I already mailed** it."

d Study the difference between **gone to** and **been to**:
- Beth is on vacation. She **has gone** to Italy. (= She is there now or she is on her way there.)
- Tom is back from his vacation. He **has been** to Italy. (= He was there, but now he has come back.)

(See also Unit 114.)
For the present perfect see also Units 14–19.
For the present perfect and simple past see Units 19–20.

UNIT 13   Exercises

13.1 *You are writing a letter to a friend and giving news about people you both know. Use the words given to make sentences and put the verb into the correct form.*

Example: Phil / find a new job   *Phil has found a new job.*...

Dear Chris,
Lots of things have happened since I last wrote to you.
1. Fred / go / Brazil   Fred ....
2. Jack and Jill / decide / to get married   ....
3. Suzanne / have / a baby   ....
4. Liz / give up / smoking   ....
5. George / pass / his driving test   ....

13.2 *Read the situation and then write an appropriate sentence. Use the verb given.*

Example: Tom is looking for his key. He can't find it. (lose)   *He has lost his key.*.........

1. Sue's hair was dirty. Now it is clean. (wash)   She...
2. Tom weighed 190 pounds. Now he weighs 170. (lose weight)   ....
3. The car has just stopped because there isn't any more gas in the tank. (run out of gas)
   ....
4. This morning Bill was playing football. Now he can't walk and his leg is in a cast.
   (break)   ....

13.3 *Use* **just**. *Answer the questions using the words given.*

Example: Would you like something to eat? (no thank you / I / just / have / dinner)
   No thank you. I've just had dinner....

1. Have you seen John anywhere? (yes / I / just / see / him)   Yes, ...
2. Has Ann called yet? (yes / she / just / call)   ....
3. Would you like a cigarette? (no thanks / I / just / put / one out)   ....

13.4 *Write sentences with* **already**.

Example: Don't forget to mail that letter.   *I've already mailed it.*...........................

1. Don't forget to call Eric.   I ....
2. Why don't you read the paper?   ....
3. Shall I pay the waiter?   No, I ....

13.5 *Fill in* **been** *or* **gone**.

Example: "Where's Amy?"   "She's on vacation. She has .*gone*.... to Italy."

1. Hello! I've just .... to the store. Look at all the things I've bought.
2. Jim isn't here at the moment. He's .... to the store.
3. "Are you going to the bank?"   "No, I've already .... to the bank."

UNIT 14 Present perfect (**I have done**) (2)

a   Study this example conversation:

> Dave: **Have** you **traveled** a lot, Jane?
> Jane: Yes, **I've been** to 47 different countries.
> Dave: Really? **Have** you ever **been** to China?
> Jane: Yes, **I've visited** China twice.
> Dave: What about India?
> Jane: No, **I've** never **been** to India.
>
> JANE'S LIFE
> past ⇨ present
>
> When we talk about a period of time that continues up to the present, we use the present perfect. Jane and Dave are talking about the places Jane has visited in her life (which is a period continuing up to the present).

Here are some more examples:
- "**Have** you **read** *Hamlet?*"   "No, I **haven't read** any of Shakespeare's plays."
- How many times **have** you **been** to the United States?
- Susan really loves that movie. She**'s seen** it eight times.
- Carlos **has lived** in Argentina all his life. (*or* Carlos **has** always **lived** in Argentina.)

We often use **ever** and **never** with the present perfect:
- **Have** you **ever eaten** caviar?
- We **have never had** a car.

We often use the present perfect after a *superlative* (see Unit 100d):
- What a boring movie! It's **the most boring** movie **I've ever seen**.

b   You have to use the present perfect with **This is the first time . . .**, **It's the first time . . .**, etc. Study this example situation:
- Ron is driving a car. He is very nervous and unsure because it's his first time behind the wheel of a car. You can say:
  This is the first time he **has driven** a car. (*not* drives)
- *or*:   He **has never driven** a car **before**.

Here are some more examples:
- Kathy has lost her passport again. **It's the second time** she **has lost** it.
- **Is this the first time** you**'ve been** in the hospital?

c   Use the present perfect to say that you have never done something or that you haven't done something during a period of time that continues up to the present:
- **I have never smoked.**
- **I haven't smoked for three years.** (*not* I don't smoke for . . .)
- **I haven't smoked since September.** (*not* I don't smoke since . . .)
- Jill **hasn't written** to me **for nearly a month**.
- Jill **has never driven** a car.

For the difference between **for** and **since** see Unit 19b.

UNIT 14 Exercises

14.1 *You are asking someone about things she has done in her life. Use the words in parentheses (. . .) to make your questions.*

Example: (you ever / be / to China?) *Have you ever been to China?* ....

1. (you ever / be / to South America?) ....
2. (you / read / any English novels?) ....
3. (you / live / in this town all your life?) ....
4. (how many times / you / be / in love?) ....
5. (what's the most beautiful country you / ever / visit?) ....

   ....
6. (you ever / speak / to a famous person?) ....

14.2 *Complete the answers to these questions. Use the verb in parentheses.*

Example: Is it a beautiful painting? (see) Yes, *it's the most beautiful painting I've ever seen.*

1. Is it a good movie? (see) Yes, it's the best ....
2. Is it a long book? (read) Yes, it's the ....
3. Is she an interesting person? (meet) Yes, she's the most ....

14.3 *Write questions and answers as shown in the example.*

Example: Jack is driving a car, but he's very nervous and not sure what to do.
   You ask: *Is this the first time you've driven a car?* ....
   Jack: *Yes, I've never driven a car before.* ....

1. Len is playing tennis. He's not very good and doesn't know the rules.
   You ask: Is this the first time ....
   Len: Yes, I've ....
2. Sue is riding a horse. She doesn't look very confident or comfortable.
   You ask: ....
   Sue: ....
3. Marie is in Canada. She's just arrived and it's very new to her.
   You ask: ....
   Maria: ....

14.4 *Answer these questions using the words in parentheses.*

Example: When did you last smoke? (for two years) *I haven't smoked for two years.*

1. When did it last rain? (for ages) It .... for ages.
2. When did they last visit you? (since June) They ....
3. When did you last play tennis? (for a long time) ....
4. When did you last eat caviar? (never) ....
5. When did you last drive? (for six months) ....
6. When did you last go to Puerto Rico? (never) ....
7. When did she last write to you? (since last summer) ....

UNIT 15
Present perfect (**I have done**) (3)

a Study this example:

> Tom: **Have** you **heard** from George?
> Ann: No, he **hasn't written** to me lately.
>
> We use the present perfect when we talk about
> a period of time that continues up to the
> present. Tom and Ann are talking about the
> period between a short time ago and now. So
> they say "**have** you **heard**" and "he **hasn't
> written**."

Here are some more examples:

- **Have** you **seen** my umbrella? I can't find it anywhere.
- Everything is going fine. We **haven't had** any problems **so far**.
- We've **met** a lot of interesting people **in the last few days**.
- Fred **has been** sick a lot **in the past few years,** hasn't he?
- I **haven't seen** Maria **recently**. Have you?

For sentences with **for** and **since** see Unit 18.

b We often use the present perfect with **yet** (see also Unit 103). **Yet** shows that the speaker is expecting something to happen. Use **yet** only in questions and negative sentences:

- **Has** it **stopped** raining **yet**?
- I **haven't told** them about the accident **yet**.

You can also use **yet** with the simple past:

- **Did** it **stop** raining **yet**?
- I **didn't tell** them **yet**.

(See also Unit 20.)

c We use the present perfect with **this morning / this evening / today / this week / this semester**, etc. (when these periods are not finished at the time of speaking):

- I've **had** five cups of coffee **today**. (Perhaps I'll have more before the day is over.)
- **Has** Ann **had** a vacation **this year**?
- I **haven't seen** Tom **this morning. Have** you?
- Liz **hasn't studied** very much **this semester**.
- Bill is calling his girlfriend again. That's the third time he's **called** her **this evening**.

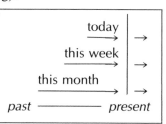

d We also use the *present perfect continuous* (**I have been doing**) when we talk about a period of time continuing up to the present:

- I **haven't been feeling** very well **lately**.

For the present perfect continuous see Units 16–18.

For the present perfect and simple past see Units 19–20.

UNIT 15 Exercises

15.1 *Make questions with the words given.*

Example: (you / hear / from George recently?) *Have you heard from George recently?*

1. (you / read / a newspaper lately?) ....
2. (you / see / Lisa in the past few days?) ....
3. (you / play / tennis lately?) ....
4. (you / eat / anything today?) ....
5. (you / see / any good movies lately?) ....
6. (you / take / your vacation yet?) ....

15.2 *Answer the questions in the way shown.* Use **yet**.

Example: Have you seen the new film at the local cinema?
      I haven't seen it yet................, but *I'm going to see it.*........................

1. Have you eaten at the new Japanese restaurant?
   I .... yet, but I'm ....
2. Have you bought a car?
   I .... , but I ....
3. Has Jerry asked Diana to marry him?
   He ....

15.3 *Complete the sentence.* Use **so far**.

Examples: I saw Tom yesterday, but *I haven't seen him so far*......... today.
          It rained a lot last week, but *it hasn't rained much so far*..... this week.

1. We ate a lot yesterday, but we .... much so far today.
2. It snowed a lot last winter, but it .... so far this winter.
3. I played tennis a lot last year, but .... this year.
4. She worked hard last semester, but .... this semester.
5. I watched television last night, but .... tonight.
6. My favorite baseball team won a lot of games last season, but they ....
   many games so far this season.

15.4 *Read the situation and then finish the last sentence.*

Example: Ron is calling Jill again. He has already called her twice this evening.
      It's the third *time he has called her this evening.*................................

1. You're late again. You've already been late once this week.
   It's the second .... this week.
2. The car has broken down. It has already broken down twice this month.
   It's the ....
3. Ann has just finished drinking a cup of tea. She has already had four cups this morning.
   It's the fifth ....

UNIT 16 Present perfect continuous (I have been doing)

a Study this example situation:

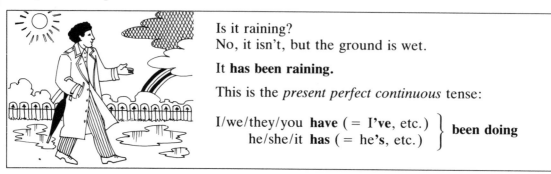

Is it raining?
No, it isn't, but the ground is wet.

It **has been raining.**

This is the *present perfect continuous* tense:

I/we/they/you **have** (= **I've**, etc.)
he/she/it **has** (= **he's**, etc.) } **been doing**

We use the present perfect continuous when we talk about an action that began in the past and has recently stopped or just stopped. Here are some examples:

- You're out of breath. **Have** you **been running**?
- Why are your clothes so dirty? What **have** you **been doing**?
- **I've been talking** to Tom about your problem, and he thinks . . .

b We also use the present perfect continuous to ask or say how long something has been happening. This time the action or situation began in the past and is still happening or has just stopped. Study this example:

It is raining now. It began to rain two hours ago, and it is still raining.

It **has been raining for two hours.**

We often use the present perfect continuous in this way, especially with **how long, for**, and **since**.

Here are some more examples:

- **How long have** you **been studying** English?
- They've **been waiting** here **for over an hour**.
- **I've been watching** television **since 2:00**.
- George **hasn't been feeling** very well **lately**.
- **Have** you **been working** hard **today**?

You can also use the present perfect continuous (with **how long, for,** and **since**) for actions repeated over a period of time:

- She **has been playing** tennis **since she was eight**.
- **How long have** you **been smoking**?

For more information about the present perfect + **since/for**, see Units 18–19. For the difference between the present perfect simple and present perfect continuous, see Units 17–18.

UNIT 16 Exercises

16.1 *Read the situation and then write a sentence with the present perfect continuous (**I have been doing**).*

Example: Carlos is out of breath. (he / run) *He has been running.*...........................

1. Jane is very tired. (she / work / hard) ....
2. Bob has a black eye, and Bill has a cut lip. (Bob and Bill / fight) ....
3. George has just come back from the beach. He is very red. (he / lie / in the sun)

    ....
4. Janet is hot and tired. (she / play / tennis) ....

16.2 *Ask a question for each situation.*

Example: Your friend's hands are covered with grease. (you / work / on the car?)
Have you been working on the car?...........................

1. You see a little boy. His eyes are red and watery. (you / cry?)

    ....
2. You have just arrived to meet your friend, who is waiting for you. (you / wait / long?)

    ....
3. Your friend comes in. Her face and hands are very dirty. (what / you / do?)

    ....

16.3 *Say how long something has been happening.*

Example: It is raining now. It began raining two hours ago.
It has been raining................. for two hours.

1. Kevin is studying. He began studying three hours ago.
    He .... for three hours.
2. I'm learning Spanish. I started learning Spanish in December.
    I .... since December.
3. Ann is looking for a job. She began looking six months ago.
    .... for six months.
4. Mary is working in Toronto. She started working there on January 18th.
    .... since January 18th.
5. Mark smokes. He started smoking five years ago.
    .... for five years.

16.4 *Ask questions with **how long**.*

Example: It is raining. *How long has it been raining?*...........................

1. Sue is reading *War and Peace*. How long ....
2. Mike plays chess. How ....
3. Jim sells washing machines. ....
4. Linda is living on Main Street. ....

33

UNIT 17
Present perfect continuous (**I have been doing**) or present perfect simple (**I have done**)?

a Study these example situations:

Ann's clothes are covered in paint. She **has been painting** the ceiling.

Has been painting is the *present perfect continuous* tense.

We are interested in the action. It does not matter whether something has been finished or not. In the example, the action has not been finished.

The ceiling was white. Now it's blue. She **has painted** the ceiling.

Has painted is the *present perfect simple* tense.

This time, the important thing is that something has been finished. We are interested in the result of the action, not in the action itself.

Here are some pairs of examples:

Tom's hands are very dirty. He **has been fixing** the car.
You**'ve been smoking** too much lately. You should smoke less.

The car is working again now. Tom **has fixed** it.
Somebody **has smoked** all my cigarettes. The packet is empty.

b We use the *continuous* form to say how long something has been happening:

Ann **has been writing** letters **all day**.
How long have you **been reading** that book?
Jim **has been playing** tennis **since 2:00**.

We use the *simple* form to say how much we have done, how many things we have done, or how many times we have done something:

Ann **has written ten letters** today.

How many pages of that book **have** you **read**?
Jim **has played** tennis **three times** this week.

See Unit 18 for more information about the present perfect and **how long?**

c Some verbs are not used in the continuous form, for example **know**. You have to say **have known** (*not* have been knowing). For a list of these verbs see Unit 3b.

UNIT 17 Exercises

17.1 *Read the situation and then write two sentences, one with the present perfect simple (**I have done**) and one with the present perfect continuous (**I have been doing**).*

Example: Tom is reading a book. He started two hours ago, and he is on page 53.
(he / read / for two hours) .*He has been reading for two hours.*...............
(he / read / 53 pages so far) .*He has read 53 pages so far.*........................

1. Linda is from Canada. Now she is traveling around Europe. She began her trip three months ago.
(she / travel / around Europe for three months) ....
(she / visit / six countries so far) ....
2. Sue is a tennis champion. She began playing tennis when she was 11 years old. Now she has just won the national championship for the fourth time.
(she / play / tennis since she was 11) ....
(she / win / the national championship four times) ....
3. Bill and Andy make films. They started making films together when they left college.
(they / make / films since they left college) ....
(they / make / ten films since they left college) ....

17.2 *Imagine that you are talking to a friend. Read the situation and ask a question beginning in the way shown.*

Example: Your friend is studying Arabic. How long *have you been studying Arabic?*

1. Your friend is waiting for you. How long ....
2. Your friend writes books. How many books ....
3. Your friend writes books. How long ....
4. Your friend is fishing by the river. How many fish ....
....

17.3 *Put the verb into the correct form: present perfect simple (**I have done**) or continuous (**I have been doing**).*

Examples: I ....*have lost*............... (lost) my key. Can you help me look for it?
You look tired. .*Have you been working* (you/work) too hard?

1. Look! Somebody .... (break) that window.
2. I .... (read) the book you gave me, but I ....
.... (not/finish) it yet.
3. "Sorry I'm late." "That's all right. I .... (not/wait) long."
4. Hello! I .... (clean) the windows. So far I
.... (clean) five of them and there are two more to do.
5. There's a strange smell in here. .... (you/cook) something?
6. My brother is an actor. He .... (appear) in several movies.

UNIT 18 Present perfect (**I have done** / **I have been doing**) with **how long, for, since**

a Study this example situation:

Bob and Alice are married. They got married exactly 20 years ago, so today is their 20th wedding anniversary.

They **have been** married **for 20 years**.

We use the present perfect to say how long something has existed or how long something has been happening.

They **are** married. { **How long have** they **been** married?
They **have been** married **for 20 years.**

b We use the present perfect continuous (**I have been doing**) to say how long something has been happening. Note that the action is still happening now.
- **I've been studying** English **for a long time**.
- Sorry I'm late. **Have** you **been waiting long**?
- It**'s been raining since I got up** this morning.

Sometimes the action is a repeated action (see also Unit 16b):
- Liz **has been driving for ten years.**
- **How long have** you **been smoking?**

The continuous (**I have been doing**) or the simple (**I have done**) can be used for actions repeated over a long period:
- **I've been collecting** / **I've collected** stamps since I was a child.

c We use the simple (**I have done**) for situations that exist for a long time (especially if we say **always**). Note that the situation still exists now.
- My father **has always worked** hard. (*not* has always been working)

We use the continuous for situations over a shorter time. Compare:
- John **has been living** in Caracas **since January.**
- John **has always lived** in Caracas.

d Some verbs (for example **be, have, know**) are not normally used in the continuous (see Unit 3b for a list and Unit 23 for **have**):
- How long **have** Bob and Alice **been** married?
- Sue **has had** a cold for the past week. (*not* has been having)
- Bill and I **have known** each other since high school.

e Do not use the simple present (**I do**) or present continuous (**I am doing**) to say how long something has been happening:
- **I've been waiting** here for an hour. (*not* I am waiting)
- How long **have** you **known** Jane? (*not* do you know)

UNIT 18 Exercises

18.1 *Are these sentences right or wrong? Correct the ones that are wrong.*

Examples: How long have Bob and Alice been married?   *RIGHT*
  I know Bob for five years.   *WRONG - have known*

1. Sue and Alan are married since July.   ....
2. It is raining all day.   ....
3. How long has George been unemployed?   ....
4. Have you always been living in this house?   ....
5. How long does Ken have a beard?   ....
6. How long do you know Ann?   ....
7. She has been sick for a long time.   ....

18.2 *Write questions with* **how long**?

Examples: Jim is studying Chinese.   *How long has he been studying Chinese?*
  I know Bob.   *How long have you known Bob?*

1. My sister is married.   How long ....
2. Carol is on vacation.   How long ....
3. I live in Australia.   ....
4. It is snowing.   ....
5. Jack smokes.   ....
6. I know about her problem.   ....
7. Robert and Jill are looking for an apartment.   ....
8. Diana teaches English in Brazil.   ....
9. Dennis is in love with Liz.   ....
10. John has a car.   ....

18.3 *Read a sentence and then write another sentence with* **since** *or* **for**.

Example: I know Bob. (for five years)   *I have known Bob for five years.*

1. Jack lives in Chicago. (since he was born)   Jack ....
2. Mary is unemployed. (since April)   Mary ....
3. Ann has a bad cold. (for the last few days)   ....
4. I want to go to the moon. (since I was a child)   ....
   ....
5. My brother is studying languages in college. (for two years)   ....
   ....
6. Tim and Jane are working in Peru. (since February)   ....
   ....
7. My cousin is in the army. (since he was 18)   ....
   ....
8. They are waiting for us. (for half an hour)   ....
   ....

UNIT 19

Present perfect with **how long**; simple past with **when**; since and for

a   Use the *simple past* (**I did**) to ask or say *when* something happened:
- A: **When did** it **start** raining?
- B: It **started** raining **at one o'clock / an hour ago**.
- A: **When did** Joe and Carol first **meet**?
- B: They first **met when they were in college / a long time ago**.

Use the *present perfect* (**I have done / I have been doing**) to ask or say *how long* something has been happening (up to the present):
- A: **How long has** it **been raining**?
- B: It's **been raining since one o'clock / for an hour**.
- A: **How long have** Joe and Carol **known** each other?
- B: They've **known** each other **since they were in college / for a long time**.

b   **Since** and **for**

We use both **since** and **for** to say how long something has been happening:
- I've been waiting for you **since 8 o'clock.**
- I've been waiting for you **for two hours.**

We use **since** when we say the beginning of the period (**8 o'clock**).
We use **for** when we say the period of time (**two hours**).

	since	**for**	
8 o'clock	1977	two hours	a week
Monday	Christmas	ten minutes	five years
May 12	lunchtime	three days	a long time
April	we arrived	six months	ages

- She's been working here **since April**. (= from April until now)
  She's been working here **for six months**. (*not* since six months)
- I haven't seen Tom **since Monday**. (= from Monday until now)
  I haven't seen Tom **for three days**. (*not* since three days)

We do not use **for** in expressions with **all** (**all day / all morning / all week / all my life**, etc.):
- I've lived here **all my life**. (*not* for all my life)

c   Note the structure **How long has it been since ... ?**:
- A: **How long has it been since** you had a vacation?
- B: **It's been** (= it **has** been) **two years since** I had a vacation. (= I haven't had a vacation for two years.)
- **It's been ages since** Aunt Helen visited us. (= She hasn't visited us for ages.)

UNIT 19 Exercises

19.1 *Write questions with* **how long** *and* **when.**

Example: It is raining. (how long / it / rain?) *How long has it been raining?*
(when / it / start / raining?) *When did it start raining?*

1. Ann is studying Italian.
   (how long / she / study / Italian?) ....
   (when / she / begin / studying Italian?) ....
2. I know Tom.
   (how long / you / know / Tom?) ....
   (when / you / first / meet / Tom?) ....
3. Glen and Mary are married.
   (how long / they / be / married?) ....
   (when / they / get / married?) ....

19.2 *Put in* **since** *or* **for.**

Example: Tom and I have known each other ...**for**......... six months.

1. It's been raining .... I got up this morning.
2. Randy's father has been a policeman .... 20 years.
3. Have you been studying English .... a long time?
4. .... Christmas, the weather has been quite mild.
5. Janet has been on vacation .... three days.
6. That's a very old car. I've had it .... ages.

19.3 *Make a new sentence beginning in the way shown.*

Examples: I know Liz. I first met her six months ago. I have *known her for six months.*
It's been raining since 2:00. It started *raining at 2:00.*

1. Maria's sick. She got sick three days ago. She has ....
2. We have been married for five years. We got ....
3. Jim has a beard. He grew it ten years ago. He has ....
4. She has been in France for three weeks. She went ....
5. He has had his new car since February. He bought ....

19.4 *Imagine that two people are talking. Make sentences with* **It's ... since ...**

Example: A: Do you take a vacation very often? (no / five years)
B: *No, it's been five years since I took a vacation.*

1. A: Do you eat in restaurants very often? (no / six months)
   B: No, it ....
2. A: Does it snow here very often? (no / years)
   B: No, ...
3. A: Do you go swimming very often? (no / a long time)
   B: ....

UNIT 20 Present perfect (**I have done**) or simple past (**I did**)?

a It is often possible to use the present perfect (**I have done**) or the simple past (**I did**):
- ■ I've **lost** my key. **Have you seen** it anywhere?
- *or:* I **lost** my key. **Did you see** it anywhere?

But do *not* use the present perfect to say *when* something happened (for example, **yesterday, two years ago, when I was a child**, etc.). Use a *past* tense in these sentences:
- ■ I **lost** my key **yesterday**. (*not* have lost)
- ■ **Did you see** the movie on TV **last night**? (*not* have you seen)
- ■ I **ate** a lot of candy **when I was a child**. (*not* have eaten)

Use a past tense to ask **when** or **what time** something happened:
- ■ **What time did** they **arrive**? (*not* have they arrived)
- ■ **When were** you born? (*not* have been born)

b Do *not* use the present perfect (**I have done**) for happenings and actions that are not connected with the present (for example, historical events):
- ■ The Chinese **invented** printing. (*not* have invented)
- ■ How many symphonies did Beethoven **compose**? (*not* has . . . composed)

c Now compare these sentences:

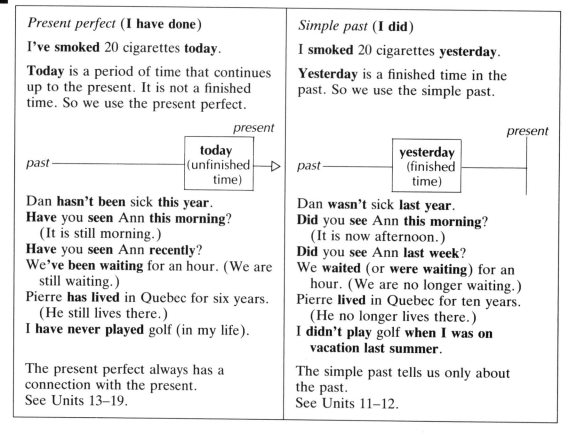

Present perfect (**I have done**)	*Simple past* (**I did**)
I've smoked 20 cigarettes **today**.	I **smoked** 20 cigarettes **yesterday**.
Today is a period of time that continues up to the present. It is not a finished time. So we use the present perfect.	**Yesterday** is a finished time in the past. So we use the simple past.
Dan **hasn't been** sick **this year**. **Have** you **seen** Ann **this morning**? (It is still morning.) **Have** you **seen** Ann **recently**? **We've been waiting** for an hour. (We are still waiting.) Pierre **has lived** in Quebec for six years. (He still lives there.) I **have never played** golf (in my life).	Dan **wasn't** sick **last year**. **Did** you see Ann **this morning**? (It is now afternoon.) **Did** you see Ann **last week**? We **waited** (or **were waiting**) for an hour. (We are no longer waiting.) Pierre **lived** in Quebec for ten years. (He no longer lives there.) I **didn't play** golf **when I was on vacation last summer**.
The present perfect always has a connection with the present. See Units 13–19.	The simple past tells us only about the past. See Units 11–12.

40

UNIT 20   Exercises

20.1   Are the underlined parts of these sentences right or wrong? Correct the ones that are wrong.

Examples: Have you heard? Suzanne <u>has gotten</u> married! *RIGHT*......
             The Chinese <u>have invented</u> printing. *WRONG: invented*

1. Who <u>has written</u> the play *Hamlet*? ....
2. Aristotle <u>has been</u> a Greek philosopher. ....
3. Ow! I've <u>cut</u> my finger. It's bleeding. ....
4. My grandparents <u>got</u> married in Montreal. ....
5. Einstein was the physicist who <u>has developed</u> the theory of relativity. ....
6. Abraham Lincoln <u>was</u> President of the U.S. from 1861 to 1865. ....
7. The U.S. <u>has bought</u> Alaska from Russia in 1867. ....
8. Jill <u>bought</u> a new car two weeks ago. ....
9. <u>Have you visited</u> many museums when you were in Paris? ....
10. <u>When did you give</u> up smoking? ....
11. My bicycle isn't here. Somebody <u>has taken</u> it. ....
12. <u>I haven't eaten</u> anything yesterday <u>because</u> <u>I haven't been</u> hungry. ....

20.2   Make sentences using the words given.

Examples: (I / smoke / 20 cigarettes yesterday) *I smoked 20 cigarettes yesterday.*
             (how many cigarettes / you / smoke / today?)
             How many cigarettes have you smoked today?

1. (I / be / sick twice so far this year)   I ....
2. (how many times / be / you / sick last year?)   How many times ....
3. (I / not / drink / any coffee so far today)   ....
4. (he / be / late three times this week)   ....
5. (how many games / the team / win / last season?)   ....
   ....
6. (how many games / the team / win / so far this season?)   ....
   ....

20.3   Put the verb into the correct form: present perfect (**I have done**) or simple past (**I did**).

Example: I ...*didn't play*......... (not/play) golf when I was on vacation last summer.

1. Mr. Clark .... (work) in a bank for 15 years. Then he gave it up.
2. George lives in Athens. He .... (live) there all his life.
3. Bob and Alice are married. They .... (be) married for 20 years.
4. When we were on vacation, the weather .... (be) terrible.
5. The weather .... (be) very nice lately.
6. My grandfather died 30 years ago. I .... (never/meet) him.
7. I don't know Carol's husband. I .... (never/meet) him.

Past perfect (**I had done**)

a Study this example situation:

I went to a party last week. Tom went to the party too. Tom went home at 10:30. So, when I arrived at 11:00, Tom wasn't there.

When I arrived at the party, Tom wasn't there. He **had gone** home.

This is the *past perfect (simple)* tense:

I/he/she (etc.) **had** (= I'**d** / he'**d** / she'**d**, etc.) **gone**
I/he/she (etc.) **hadn't gone**
had you/he/she (etc.) **gone**?

We form the past perfect with **had** + the *past participle* (**gone/opened/written**, etc.). For irregular past participles see Appendix 2.

Sometimes we talk about something that happened in the past:
- I **arrived** at the party.

We use the past perfect to say that something had already happened before this time:
- **When I arrived** at the party, Tom **had** already **gone** home.

Here are some more examples:
- When I got home, I found that someone **had broken** into my apartment and **had stolen** my fur coat.
- George didn't want to come to the movies with us because he **had** already **seen** the film twice.
- It was my first time in an airplane. I was very nervous because I **had never flown** before.

b The past perfect (**I had done**) is the past of the present perfect (**I have done**). Compare these situations:

Present	*Past*
I'm not hungry. I'**ve** just **had** lunch.	I wasn't hungry. I'**d** just **had** lunch.
The house is dirty. We **haven't cleaned** it for weeks.	The house was dirty. We **hadn't cleaned** it for weeks.

c Compare the past perfect (**I had done**) and the simple past (**I did**):
- "Was Tom there when you arrived?" "**No**, he **had** already **gone** home."
- *but*: "Was Tom there when you arrived?" "**Yes**, but he **went** home soon afterward."
- Ann **wasn't** home when I **called** her. She **was** at work.
- *but*: Ann **had** just **gotten** home when I **called** her. She **had been** at work.

For the past perfect continuous see Unit 22.

42

UNIT 21 Exercises

21.1 *Complete these sentences using the verbs in parentheses (. . .). You went back to your home town after many years, and you found that many things were different.*

Example: Most of my friends were no longer there. They *had left* .... (leave).

1. My best friend, Kevin, was no longer there. He .... (go) away.
2. The local movie theater was no longer open. It .... (close) down.
3. Mr. Johnson was no longer alive. He .... (die).
4. I didn't recognize Mrs. Johnson. She .... (change) a lot.
5. Bill no longer had his car. He .... (sell) it.

21.2 *Complete these sentences as in the example. Use the verb in parentheses.*

Example: Mr. and Mrs. Davis were in an airplane. They were very nervous as the plane took off because they (never / fly) *had never flown before.* ....

1. The woman was a complete stranger to me. (never / see) I .... before.
2. Margaret was late for work. Her boss was very surprised. (never / be / late) She ....
....
3. Jane played tennis yesterday – at least she tried to play tennis. She wasn't very good at it because she (never / play) ....
4. It was Carl's first driving lesson. He was very nervous and didn't know what to do. (never / drive) He ....

21.3 *Make sentences using the words in parentheses.*

Example: I wasn't hungry. (I / just / have / lunch) *I had just had lunch.* ....

1. Tom wasn't home when I arrived. (he / just / go / out) ....
2. We arrived at the theater late. (the movie / already / begin) ....
3. They weren't eating when I went to see them. (they / just / finish / their dinner)
....
4. I invited Ann to dinner last night, but she couldn't come. (she / already / make plans / to do something else) ....
5. I was very pleased to see Diane again after such a long time. (I / not / see / her for five years) ....

21.4 *Put the verb into the correct form: past perfect (**I had done**) or simple past (**I did**).*

Examples: "Was Tom there when you arrived?" "No, he *had gone* ..... (go) home."
"Was Tom there when you arrived?" "Yes, but he *went* .... (go) home soon afterward."

1. The house was very quiet when I got home. Everybody .... (go) to bed.
2. I felt very tired when I got home, so I ....(go) straight to bed.
3. Sorry I'm late. The car .... (break) down on my way here.
4. There was a car by the side of the road. It .... (break) down and the driver was trying to repair it. So we .... (stop) to see if we could help.

UNIT 22 Past perfect continuous (I had been doing)

a Study this example situation:

Yesterday morning I got up and looked out the window. The sun was shining, but the ground was very wet.

It **had been raining**.

It wasn't raining when I looked out the window; the sun was shining. But it **had been raining**. That's why the ground was wet.

Had been raining is the *past perfect continuous* tense:

I/he/she (etc.) **had** (= **I'd**/**he'd**/**she'd**, etc.) **been doing**

Here are some more examples:
- When the boys came into the house, their clothes were dirty, their hair was a mess, and one had a black eye. They **had been fighting**.
- I was very tired when I arrived home. **I'd been working** hard all day.

b You can use the past perfect continuous to say how long something had been happening before something else happened:
- The soccer game had to be stopped. They **had been playing** for half an hour when there was a terrible storm.
- Ken **had been smoking** for 30 years when he finally gave it up.

c The past perfect continuous (**I had been doing**) is the past of the present perfect continuous (**I have been doing**). Compare:

Present	*Past*
How long **have** you **been waiting**? (until now)	How long **had** you **been waiting** when the bus finally came?
He's out of breath. He **has been running**.	He was out of breath. He **had been running**.

d Compare the past perfect continuous (**I had been doing**) with the past continuous (**I was doing**):
- When I looked out the window, it **had been raining**. (= It wasn't raining when I looked out; it had stopped.)
- When I looked out the window, it **was raining**. (= Rain was falling at the time I looked out.)

e Some verbs (for example, **know**) cannot be used in the continuous form. See Unit 3b for a list of these verbs.

For the past perfect simple see Unit 21.

UNIT 22 Exercises

22.1 *Read the situation and then write a sentence.*

Example: The two boys came into the house. One had a black eye and the other had a cut lip. (they / fight) *They had been fighting.*..

1. Tom was watching TV. He was feeling very tired.
   (he / study / hard all day) He ....
2. When I walked into the room, it was empty. But it smelled of cigarettes.
   (somebody / smoke / in the room) Somebody......................................
3. When Mary came back from the beach, she looked very red from the sun.
   (she / lie / in the sun too long) ....
4. The two boys came into the house. They had a football, and they were both very tired.
   (they / play / football) ....
5. Ann woke up in the middle of the night. She was frightened, and she didn't know where she was. (she / dream) ....

22.2 *Read the situation and then write a sentence.*

Example: We began playing football. After half an hour there was a terrible storm.
   We *had been playing for half an hour* when *there was a terrible storm.*....

1. The orchestra began playing at the concert. After about ten minutes a man in the audience suddenly began shouting.
   The orchestra .... for about ten minutes when ....
   ....
2. I had arranged to meet Sue in a cafe. I arrived and began waiting. After 20 minutes I realized that I had come to the wrong cafe.
   I .... when I ....
3. Mr. and Mrs. Jenkins went to live in the south of France. Six months later Mr. Jenkins died. They .... when ....

22.3 *Put the verb into the correct form: past perfect continuous (**I had been doing**) or past continuous (**I was doing**).*

Examples: Sue was leaning against the wall, out of breath. *She had been running.* (run).
   I tried to catch Sue but I couldn't. She *was running* (run) very fast.

1. Jim was on his hands and knees on the floor. He .... (look) for his contact lens.
2. We .... (walk) along the road for about 20 minutes when a car stopped and the driver offered us a lift.
3. When I arrived, everyone was sitting around the table with their mouths full. They .... (eat).
4. When I arrived, everyone was sitting around the table and talking. Their mouths were empty but their stomachs were full. They .... (eat).
5. When I arrived, Ann .... (wait) for me. She was annoyed because I was late, and she .... (wait) for a very long time.

45

UNIT 23 Have and have got

a **Have** / **has** / **had** = *possess*, but we also use **have** for other things (for example, family relationships):

- We **have** a new car.
- I **have** a brother and two sisters.
- Tom **has** a headache / a cold / the flu / etc.
- When she was a child, she **had** long blonde hair.

In questions use **do** / **does** / **did**:

- How many brothers and sisters **do** you **have**?
- **Does** Ann **have** a car?
- **Did** you **have** a car when you lived in California? (*not* had you a car)

In negative sentences use **don't** / **doesn't** / **didn't**:

- I **don't have** any money.
- Ann **doesn't have** any brothers or sisters.
- I wanted to call you, but I **didn't have** your number. (*not* I hadn't your number)
- He **didn't have** a watch, so he didn't know what time it was.

b **Have got** / **has got**

You can use **have got** / **has got** rather than **have** / **has** alone:

- We've **got** a new car. (= We have a new car.)
- Tom **has got** a headache. (= Tom has a headache.)

The question and negative forms are:

- **Have** you **got** a headache? (= do you have)
- **Has** she **got** any brothers or sisters? (= does she have)
- I **haven't got** any money. (= I don't have)
- Ann **hasn't got** a car. (= Ann doesn't have)

But don't use **got** for the *past*:

- When she was a child, she **had** long blonde hair. (*not* she had got)

c **Have** for *actions*

We also use **have** for a number of actions (especially eating and drinking):

have breakfast / lunch / dinner / a meal / a cup of coffee / a cigarette / etc.
have a good time / a nice day / etc.   **have** a party (= give a party)
have a look (at something)   **have** a baby (= give birth to a baby)

(You *cannot* use **have got** in these expressions.)

- I always **have** a big breakfast in the morning. (*not* have got)
- **Did** you **have** a good time last night?
- We're **having** a party on Saturday. Would you like to come?
- What time **does** Ann usually **have** lunch?

UNIT 23 Exercises

23.1 *Make negative sentences with* **have**. *Some sentences are present* (**can't**) *and some past* (**couldn't**).

Examples: I can't make a phone call. (any change)   *I don't have any change.*
          (or: I haven't got any change.)
          I couldn't read the notice. (my glasses)   *I didn't have my glasses.*

1. I can't climb up onto the roof. (a ladder)   I ....
2. We couldn't visit the museum. (enough time)   We ....
3. He couldn't find his way to our house. (map)   ....
4. She can't pay her bills. (any money)   ....
5. I couldn't make an omelette. (any eggs)   ....
6. I can't get into the house. (my key)   ....
7. They couldn't take any photographs. (a camera)   ....
8. We couldn't go out in the rain. (an umbrella)   ....

23.2 *Complete these questions with* **have**. *Some are present and some are past.*

Examples: Excuse me, ...*do you have*......... a light, please?
          ...*Did you have*......... a lot of friends when you lived in Greece?

1. Why are you holding your mouth like that? .... a toothache?
2. .... enough time to answer all the questions when you took your exam last week?
3. I need a stamp for this letter. .... any?
4. "It started to rain when I was walking home."   "Did it? .... an umbrella?"
5. "................................... the time, please?"   "Yes, it's ten after seven."
6. .... your own room when you were a child?

23.3 *Complete these sentences using the expressions below. Put the verb into the correct form where necessary.*

have a baby	**have a good time**	**have a party**
have a look	**have a good flight**	**have a nice day**
have a cigarette	~~**have a nice lunch**~~	**have something to drink**

1. Tom has just come back from a restaurant. You say: Hi, Tom.   *Did you have*
   a nice lunch? ....
2. We .... last week. It was great – we invited lots of people.
3. Thank you for shopping here, and .... !
4. Suzanne took six months off her job when she ....
5. Excuse me, can I .... at your newspaper, please?
6. You meet Ann at the airport. She has just arrived. You say: Hello, Ann.
   .... ?
7. I don't usually smoke, but I was feeling nervous, so I ....
8. If you're thirsty, why don't you .... ?
9. I haven't seen you since you came back from vacation.   .... ?

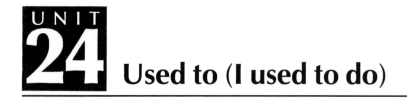

UNIT 24
Used to (I used to do)

a Study this example situation:

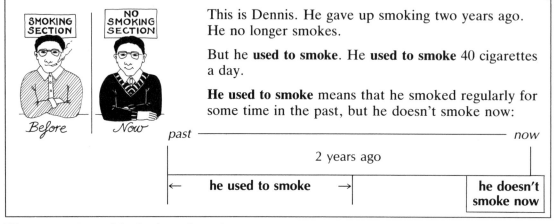

This is Dennis. He gave up smoking two years ago. He no longer smokes.

But he **used to smoke**. He **used to smoke** 40 cigarettes a day.

He used to smoke means that he smoked regularly for some time in the past, but he doesn't smoke now:

We use **used to** with the *base form* (**used to do / used to smoke**, etc.) to say that something happened regularly in the past but no longer happens:

- I **used to play** tennis a lot, but now I'm too lazy.
- "Do you go to the movies very often?"   "Not now, but I **used to**."
- Sue **used to travel** a lot. These days she doesn't go away very often.

We also use **used to** for past situations (that no longer exist):

- We **used to live** in a small village, but now we live in Milan.
- This building is now a furniture store. It **used to be** a movie theater.
- Do you see that hill over there? There **used to be** a castle on that hill.
- I've started drinking tea lately. I never **used to like** it before.
- Ann **used to have** long hair, but she cut it some time ago.

b **Used to** + base form is always past. There is no present. You cannot say "I use to do." For the present, use the simple present (**I do**). Compare the present and past:

past	he **used to smoke**	we **used to live**	there **used to be**
present	he **smokes**	we **live**	there **is**

c The normal question form is **did...use to...?**:

- **Did** you **use to eat** a lot of candy when you were a child?

The negative form is **didn't use to...** (*or* never used to)

- Jim **didn't use to go** out very often until he met Jill. (*or* never used to go out)

d Be careful not to confuse **I used to do** and **I am used to doing** (see Unit 59). The structures and meanings are different:

- **I used to live** alone. (= I lived alone but I no longer live alone.)
- **I am** used to living alone. (= I live alone and don't find it strange or new because I've been living alone for some time.)

UNIT 24   Exercises

24.1 *Complete each sentence with* **used to . . .**

Example: Dennis doesn't smoke anymore, but he *used to smoke*...... 40 cigarettes a day.

1. The baby doesn't cry so much now, but she .... every night.
2. She .... my best friend, but we aren't friends anymore.
3. We live in Barcelona now, but we .... in Madrid.
4. Now there's only one cafe in the village, but there .... three.
5. When I was a child I .... ice cream, but I don't like it now.
6. Now Tom has a car. He .... a motorcycle.

24.2 *Write some sentences about a man who changed his lifestyle. Ron stopped doing some things and started doing other things:*

He stopped { studying hard
going to bed early
running three miles every morning   He started { smoking
staying out late
spending a lot of money

Make sentences like these:
Examples: *He used to study hard.*...
 He never used to smoke, or He didn't use to smoke.......

1. ....
2. ....
3. ....
4. ....

24.3 *Write sentences about the present. Remember there is no present tense of* **used to.**

Examples: Ron used to study hard, but now *he doesn't study very hard.*............
 Ron didn't use to smoke, but now *he smokes.*................................

1. Mark used to play tennis a lot, but now ....
2. Mary never used to drink coffee, but now ....
3. Jill didn't use to be fat, but now ....
4. Jack didn't use to go out much, but now ....

24.4 *Ask some questions. Mr. Park is an old man now. You are asking someone what he used to do when he was younger.*

Example: I know he doesn't smoke now, but *did he use to smoke*........................ ?

1. I know he doesn't play the piano now, but .... ?
2. I know he isn't very rich now, but .... ?
3. I know he doesn't go out very often these days, but .... ?
4. I know he doesn't dance these days, but .... ?
5. I know he doesn't have many friends now, but .... ?

UNIT 25 Can, could, and be able to

a We use **can (do)** to say that something is possible or that someone has the ability to do something. The negative is **can't (cannot)**.

- You **can see** the ocean from our bedroom window.
- **Can** you **speak** any foreign languages?
- I'm afraid I **can't come** to your party next Friday.

Be able to is possible instead of **can**, but **can** is more usual:

- **Are** you **able to speak** any foreign languages?

But **can** has only two forms: **can** (*present*) and **could** (*past*). So sometimes you have to use **be able to**:

- I **haven't been able to sleep** recently. (**can** has no present perfect)
- Sue might not **be able to come** tomorrow. (**can** has no infinitive)
- I'm very busy today, but I should **be able to meet** with you tomorrow.

b **Could** and **was able to**

Sometimes **could** is the past of **can**. We use **could** especially with these verbs:

see	hear	smell	taste	feel	remember	understand

- When we went into the house, we **could smell** something burning.
- She spoke in a low voice, but I **could understand** what she was saying.

We also use **could** to say that someone had the general ability to do something:

- My grandfather **could speak** five languages.
- When Joe was 16, he **could run** 100 meters in 11 seconds.

But if you mean that someone *managed* to do something *in one particular situation*, you have to use **was/were able to** (not **could**):

- The fire spread through the building very quickly, but everyone **was able** (= managed) **to escape**. (*not* could escape)
- They didn't want to come with us at first, but finally we **were able** (= managed) **to persuade** them. (*not* could persuade)

Compare **could** and **was able to** in this example:

- Jack was an excellent tennis player. He **could** beat anybody. (= He had the ability to beat anybody.)
- But once he had a difficult game against Bob. Bob played very well, but in the end Jack **was able to** beat him. (= He managed to beat him *in this particular game*.)

The negative **couldn't** is possible in all situations:

- My grandfather **couldn't swim**.
- We tried hard but we **couldn't persuade** them to come with us.

For **can** see also Unit 30. For **could** see also Units 26 and 30.

50

UNIT 25   Exercises

25.1   *Use* **can** *or* **be able to**. *Sometimes it is possible to use either; sometimes only* **be able to** *is possible.*

Examples: George has traveled a lot. He *can (or is able to).* speak four languages.
I haven't *been able to* sleep very well lately.

1. Tom .... drive, but he doesn't have a car.
2. I can't understand Martin. I've never .... understand him.
3. I used to .... stand on my head, but I can't do it now.
4. Ask Ann about your problem. She should .... help you.

25.2   *Complete the sentence with* **could . . .**

Example: I can't sing now, but I .... *could sing* .... very well when I was a child.

1. He can't play tennis very well now, but he .... fairly well when he was younger.
2. She can't run very fast now, but when she was in school she .... faster than anyone else.
3. I can't swim very far these days, but ten years ago I .... from one side of the lake to the other.

25.3   *Answer the questions with* **was/were able to**.

Example: Did you persuade them?
Yes. It was difficult, but we *were able to persuade them.* ....

1. Did they find your house?
Yes. It took them a long time, but they ....
2. Did you win the match?
Yes. It wasn't easy, but I ....
3. Did the thief escape?
Yes. The police officer chased the thief, but he ....

25.4   *Complete each sentence with* **could, was/were able to,** *or* **couldn't.**

Examples: My grandfather was very clever. He *could (or was able to)* speak five languages.
I looked everywhere for the book, but I ... *couldn't* .... find it.
The fire spread quickly, but everyone ... *was able to* .... escape.

1. He had hurt his leg, so he .... walk very well.
2. She wasn't at home when I called, but I .... contact her at her office.
3. I looked very carefully, and I .... see a figure in the distance.
4. They didn't have any tomatoes in the first store I went to, but I .... get some in the next store.
5. My grandmother loved music. She .... play the piano very well.
6. The boy fell into the river, but fortunately we .... rescue him.

51

UNIT 26 Could (do) and could have (done)

a Study this example:

What do you want to do this evening?

We could go to the movies.

Dan: What do you want to do this evening?
Sue: We **could go** to the movies.

We use **could (do)** in a number of ways. Sometimes it is the past of **can (do)** (see Unit 25), but sometimes it has a *present* or *future* meaning. For example, we sometimes use **could** to talk about possible future actions, especially when we make suggestions:

"When you go to New York, you **could stay** with Linda."

Can is also possible in these sentences. ("We **can** go to the movies.")
Could is more unsure than **can**.

We also use **could** to talk about possible future happenings:
- There **could be** another rise in the price of gas soon. (= It is possible that there will be.)

Sometimes **could** means **would be able to**:
- Why doesn't Tom apply for the job? He **could get** it.
- I don't know how she works 14 hours a day. I **couldn't do** it.

b The past of **could (do)** is **could have (done)**. We use **could have (done)** to say that we had the ability or the opportunity to do something but did *not* do it:
- We didn't go out last night. We **could have gone** to the movies, but we decided to stay home. (We had the opportunity to go out, but we didn't.)
- Why did you stay at a hotel in New York? You **could have stayed** with Linda. (You had the opportunity to stay with her but you didn't.)
- Why didn't Tom apply for the job? He **could have gotten** it. (He had the ability to get it.)

We also use **could have (done)** to say something was a possibility but *didn't* happen:
- He was lucky when he fell off the ladder. He **could have hurt** himself.

c Here are some examples of **couldn't have (done)**. "I **couldn't have done** something" = I wouldn't have been able to do it if I had wanted or tried to do it:
- When I went to New York last year, I decided not to stay with Linda. Later I found out that she was away while I was there, so I **couldn't have stayed** with her anyway.
- The hockey game was canceled last week. Tom **couldn't have played** anyway because he was sick.

For **could/couldn't** see also Units 25, 27b, 28c, 30.
For **could** in **if** sentences see Units 34–35 and 36c.

UNIT 26 Exercises

26.1 *Make suggestions. Use* **could.**

Example: Where should we go for our vacation? (Mexico) *We could go to Mexico.*

1. What should we have for dinner tonight? (fish) ....
2. When should we go and see Tom? (on Friday) ....
3. What should I give Ann for her birthday? (a book) ....

26.2 *Use* **could have.** *Answer the questions in the way shown.*

Example: "Did you go to the movies?"
"No. We *could have gone to the movies, but we decided not to.*"

1. "Did you go to the concert last night?" "No. We .... "
2. "Did John take the exam?" "No. He .... "
3. "Did you buy a new car?" "No. I .... "

26.3 *Write sentences with* **could** *or* **could have.**

Examples: She doesn't want to stay with Linda. *But she could stay with Linda.*
She didn't want to stay with Linda. *But she could have stayed with Linda.*

1. He didn't want to help us. But he ....
2. He doesn't want to help us. But ....
3. They don't want to lend us any money. But ....
4. She didn't want to have anything to eat. ....

26.4 *First read this information about Ken:*

Ken doesn't know any Spanish.   Ken doesn't know anything about machines.
Ken is very rich and generous.   Ken can't drive.
Ken was sick on Friday night.   Ken was free on Monday afternoon.

A lot of people wanted Ken to do different things last week, but they couldn't contact him. So he didn't do any of these things. Say whether he could have done or couldn't have done these things (if he had known).

Example: His aunt wanted him to drive her to the station.
He couldn't have driven her to the station (because he can't drive).

1. Ann wanted him to come to a party on Friday night.
   He .... because ....
2. Jim wanted him to play tennis on Monday afternoon.
   He ....
3. Sue wanted him to translate a Spanish newspaper article into English.
   .... because ....
4. Jack wanted Ken to lend him $20. ....
5. Ken's mother wanted him to fix her washing machine.
   .... because ....

53

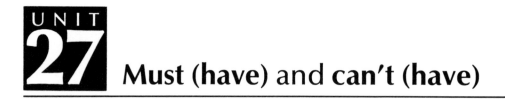

Must (have) and can't (have)

a Study this example situation:

> Liz is a very good tennis player, and not many players beat her. But yesterday she played against Bill and Bill won. So:
>
> Bill **must be** a very good player (otherwise he wouldn't have won).

We use **must** to say we are sure that something is true:

- You've been traveling all day. You **must be** tired. (= I am sure that you are tired.)
- I hear that your exams are next week. You **must be studying** very hard right now. (= I am sure that you are studying.)
- Carol knows a lot about films. She **must like** to go to the movies. (= I am sure she likes to go to the movies.)

We use **can't** to say that we think something is impossible:

- You've just had dinner. You **can't be** hungry already. (= It is impossible that you are hungry.)
- Tom said that he would be here ten minutes ago, and he is never late. He **can't be coming**.

Study the structure:

I/you/he (etc.)	$\begin{Bmatrix} \textbf{must} \\ \textbf{can't} \end{Bmatrix}$	**be** tired/hungry, etc. **be** study**ing**/wait**ing**/com**ing**, etc. **know/like**, etc.

b For the past we use **must have (done)** and **can't have (done)**. Study this example:

> We went to Roy's house last night and rang the doorbell. There was no answer.
> **He must have gone** out (otherwise he would have answered).

- The phone rang, but I didn't hear it. I **must have been** asleep.
- I made a lot of noise when I came home. You **must have heard** me.
- She passed me on the street without speaking. She **can't have seen** me.
- Tom walked into the wall. He **can't have been looking** where he was going.

Study the structure:

I/you/he (etc.)	$\begin{Bmatrix} \textbf{must} \\ \textbf{can't} \end{Bmatrix}$	**have**	**been** asleep/tired, etc. **been** looking/waiting, etc. **gone/done/seen/heard**, etc.

"**Couldn't** have (done)" is possible instead of "**can't** have (done)":

- She **couldn't have seen** me.
- He **couldn't have been looking** where he was going.

For other meanings of **must** and **can't** see Units 25 and 31.

UNIT 27   Exercises

27.1   *Complete these sentences using* **must (have)** ..., **couldn't (have)** ..., *or* **can't (have)** ....

Examples: "Is he American?"   "Yes, *he must be American.* ...."
                  "Did she see you?"   "No, *she can't have seen me.* ...."

1. "Are they married?"   "Yes, they must ...."
2. "Is he serious?"   "No, he can't ...."
3. "Were they in a hurry?"   "Yes, they ...."
4. "Does Ann know a lot of people?"   "Yes, she ...."
5. "Did Tom know about the plan?"   "Yes, he ...."
6. "Do they have much money?"   "No, they ...."
7. "Was she driving carefully?"   "No, she ...."
8. "Are they waiting for somebody?"   "Yes, they ...."

27.2   *Complete these sentences with* **must** *or* **can't** + *an appropriate verb.*

Example: You've been traveling all day. You *must be* .... very tired.

1. Brian has three houses, six cars, a yacht, and a helicopter. He .... a lot of money.
2. (*The doorbell rings.*) I wonder who that is. It ....Jim. He said he would come after 7:00 and it's only 6:30 now.
3. I wonder why Sue isn't at work today. She .... sick.
4. John seems to know a lot about history. He .... a lot of books.
5. Jane's putting on her hat and coat. She .... out.

27.3   *Read each situation and write a sentence with* **must have** *or* **can't have**. *Use the words in parentheses (...).*

Example: The phone rang but I didn't hear it. (I must / be / asleep)
             I must have been asleep....

1. That dress you bought is very good quality. (it must / be / very expensive)
   It must ....
2. I haven't seen Jim for ages. (he must / go / away)   He ....
3. I wonder where my umbrella is. (you must / leave / it on the bus)   ....
   ....
4. Don passed the exam. He didn't study very much for it. (the exam can't / be / very difficult)   ....
5. She knew everything about our plans. (she must / listen / to our conversation)
   ....
6. Dennis did the opposite of what I asked him to do. (he can't / understand / what I said)
   ....
7. When I woke up this morning, the light was on. (I must / forget / to turn it off)
   ...*I must have forgotten*..
8. I don't understand how the accident happened. (the driver can't / see / the red light)
   ....

UNIT 28 May (have) and might (have)

a Study this example situation:

> You are looking for Jack. Nobody knows for sure where he is, but you get some suggestions:
>
> He **may be** in his office. (= perhaps he is in his office)
> He **might be having** lunch. (= perhaps he is having lunch)
> Ask Ann. She **might know**. (= perhaps Ann knows)

We use **may** or **might** to say that something is possible. You can say:
  - He **may be** in his office. *or* He **might be** in his office.
The negative is **may not** and **might not**:
  - Jack **might not be** in his office. (= perhaps he isn't in his office)
  - I'm not sure whether I can lend you any money. I **may not have** enough.
      (= perhaps I don't have enough)
Study the structure:

I/you/he (etc.)	may / might	(not)	be in his office / be having/waiting, etc. / know/have/do, etc.

b To say what was possible in the past, we use **may have (done)** and **might have (done)**:
  - A: I wonder why Ann didn't answer the doorbell.
    B: Well, I suppose she **may have been** asleep. (= perhaps she **was** asleep)
  - A: Why didn't he say hello when he passed us on the street?
    B: He **might have been daydreaming**. (= perhaps he **was daydreaming**)
  - A: I can't find my bag anywhere.
    B: You **might have left** it in the store. (= perhaps you **left** it)
  - A: I wonder why Jill didn't come to the meeting.
    B: She **might not have known** about it. (= perhaps she **didn't know**)
Study the structure:

I/you/he (etc.)	may / might	(not)	have	been asleep / been daydreaming/waiting, etc. / known/left/had, etc.

c You can use **could** instead of **may** or **might**. But with **could** the possibility is smaller:
  - "Where's Jack?"   "I'm not sure. He **could be** in his office, I suppose, but he's not usually there at this time."

For **may** and **might** see also Units 29 and 30.

UNIT 28   Exercises

28.1
Make sentences with **may** *or* **might**. *The first four sentences are present.*

Examples: "Do you know if Jack is in his office?" *"I'm not sure. He may be in his office..."*
"Do you know if Joan likes ice cream?" *"I'm not sure. She might like ice cream."*

1. "Do you know if they are married?" "I'm not sure. They ...."
2. "Do you know if she wants to go?" "I'm not sure. ...."
3. "Do you know if he's telling the truth?" "I'm ...."
4. "Do you know if he has a car?" "I ...."

The next three sentences are past.
Examples: "Do you know if he was serious?" *"I'm not sure. He might have been serious."*
"Do you know if they were looking?" *"I'm not sure. They may have been looking."*

5. "Do you know if she was sick?" "I'm not sure. She ...."
6. "Do you know if she told anybody?" "I ...."
7. "Do you know if they were listening?" " ...."

Use **may not** *or* **might not**.
Example: "Is Jack in his office?" *"I'm not sure. He might not be in his office.........."*

8. "Does she want to go?" " ...."
9. "Is he telling the truth?" " ...."
10. "Are they ready?" " ...."

28.2
Write sentences to explain each situation. Use the words in parentheses (. . .) to make your sentences.

Example: I can't find George anywhere. I wonder where he is.
  a) (he might / go / shopping) *He might have gone shopping.*....................
  b) (he could / play / tennis) *.He could be playing tennis.*........................

1. Look! Sue's going out. I wonder where she's going.
   a) (she may / go / to the theater) ....
   b) (she could / go / to a party) ....
2. Why didn't Tom answer the doorbell? I'm sure he was in the house at the time.
   a) (he may / go / to bed early) ....
   b) (he might not / hear / the bell) ....
3. How do you think the fire started?
   a) (someone may / drop / a cigarette) ....
   b) (it could / be / a short circuit) ....
4. I wonder where Liz was going when you saw her.
   a) (she might / go / to work) ....
   b) (she may / go / shopping) ....
5. George didn't come to the party. I wonder why not.
   a) (he might / have / to go somewhere else) *he might have had to*
   b) (he may not / know / about it) *..may not have known about it*

UNIT 29
May and **might** (future)

a We use **may** or **might** to talk about possible happenings or possible actions in the future. Study these examples:
- ■ I'm not sure where to go on my vacation, but I **may go** to Puerto Rico.
  (= perhaps I will go)
- ■ The weather forecast is not very good. It **might rain** this afternoon.
  (= perhaps it will rain)
- ■ I can't help you. Why don't you ask Tom? He **might be** able to help you.
  (= perhaps he will be able to help)

The negative form is **may not** or **might not**:
- ■ Ann **may not come** to the party tonight. She isn't feeling well.
  (= perhaps she won't come)
- ■ There **might not be** a meeting on Friday because the director is sick.
  (= perhaps there won't be a meeting)

It doesn't matter whether you use **may** or **might**. You can say:
- ■ I **may** go to Italy. *or* I **might** go to Italy.

b There is also a continuous form: **may/might be doing**. Compare this with **will be doing** (see Unit 10a,b):
- ■ Don't call at 8:30. I'**ll be watching** the football game on TV.
- ■ Don't call at 8:30. I **may** (or **might**) **be watching** the football game on TV.
  (= perhaps I'll be in the middle of watching it)

You can also use the continuous (**may/might be doing**) when you are talking about possible plans. Compare:
- ■ I'**m going** to Puerto Rico in July. (for sure)
- ■ I **may** (or **might**) **be going** to Puerto Rico in July. (it's possible)

But you can also say: I **may/might go** to Puerto Rico in July.

c **May as well, might as well**
Study this example:

> A: What do you want to do this evening?
> B: I don't know. Any ideas?
> A: Well, there's a movie on television. It sounds interesting.
> B: **We might as well watch it.** There's nothing else to do.
>
> We use **may/might as well** to say that we should do something, but only because there is no reason not to do it and because there is nothing better to do. **We might as well watch it** means, "Why not watch it? There's nothing better to do."

- ■ You'll have to wait an hour for the next bus, so **you might as well walk**.
- ■ **We may as well go** to the party. We have nothing else to do.
- ■ "Should we have dinner now?"   "**We might as well.**"

For **may** and **might** see also Units 28 and 34c. For **may** only, see Unit 30.

58

UNIT 29 Exercises

29.1 Talk about future plans. You are not sure what is going to happen. Use **may** or **might**.

Example: Where are you going on your vacation? (to Brazil???)
I haven't decided yet, but *I may (or might) go to Brazil.*.....................

1. What kind of car are you going to buy? (a Toyota???)
   I'm not sure yet, but I ....
2. What are you doing this weekend? (go skiing???)
   I don't know for sure, but ....
3. Where are you going to hang that picture? (in the dining room???)
   I haven't made up my mind yet, but ....
4. When is Tom coming to see us? (tomorrow evening???)
   I'm not sure, but ....
5. What's Jill going to do when she graduates? (go to a business college???)
   She hasn't decided yet, but ....

29.2 Talk about possible happenings. Use the word(s) in parentheses (. . .).

Examples: Do you think it will rain this afternoon? (may) *It may rain this afternoon.*
Do you think Ann will come to the party? (might not)
She might not come to the party......................

1. Do you think Bob will be late? (may)   He ....
2. Do you think Amy will be able to find our house? (might not)   She ....
   ....
3. Do you think there'll be a rainstorm tonight? (might)   There ....
   ....
4. Do you think Tony will pass the exam? (may not)   ....
5. Do you think they'll be waiting for us when we arrive? (might)   ....
   ....
6. Do you think it'll snow later? (may)   ....

29.3 Read these situations and make sentences with **may/might as well**.

Example: A friend has invited you to a party. You're not very excited about going, but
there isn't anything else to do. So you think you should go.
You say: *I might as well go. There isn't anything else to do.*.....................

1. You're in a coffee shop with a friend. You've just finished your coffee. You're not in a
   hurry, so you think you should both have another cup.
   You say: We ...*might as well have another cup*... Are you ready for one?
2. Someone has given you a free ticket to a concert. You're not very interested in the
   concert, but you think you should go because you have a free ticket.
   You say: I ...*might as well go*............... It's a shame to waste a free ticket.
3. You invited some friends to dinner, but they haven't come. The dinner has been ready
   for half an hour and you think you should begin without them.
   You say: We ...*might as well start*... I don't think they are coming.

Permission: Can - may ≠ interchangible (range uom. can)

a   *Asking people to do things* (requests)

Could you open the door, please?

We often use **can** or **could** when we ask someone to do something:

Can you wait a moment, please?
Ann, **can you** do me a favor?
Excuse me. **Could you** tell me how to get to the bus station?
Do you think you could lend me some money?
I wonder if you could help me.

We also use **would** to ask someone to do something:

Ann, **would you** do me a favor?
Would you wait here, please?

b   *To ask for something* you can say **Can I have . . . ?/ Could I have . . . ?/ May I have . . . ?**:
- *(in a gift shop)* **Can I have** these postcards, please?
- *(at the dinner table)* **Could I have** the salt, please?

c   *Asking for and giving permission*
*We often use **can, could**, or **may** to ask permission to do something:*
- *(on the telephone)* Hello, **can I** speak to Tom, please?
- "**Could I** use your telephone?" "Yes, of course."
- "**Do you think I could** borrow your bicycle?" "Yes, help yourself."
- "**May I** come in?" "Yes, please do."

To give permission, we use **can** or **may** (but *not* **could**):
- You **can** (or **may**) smoke if you like.

d   We sometimes use **can** or **may** when we *offer* to do things. (**May** is more formal.):
- "**Can I get you** a cup of coffee?" "That's very nice of you."
- *(in a store)* "**May I help you**, ma'am?" "No thank you. I'm being helped."

e   For *offering* and *inviting* we use **Would you like . . . ?** (*not* do you like):
- **Would you like** a cup of coffee? (*not* do you like)
- **Would you like to go** to the movies with us tomorrow evening? (*not* do you like to come)

I'd like (= **I would like**) is a polite way of saying what you want or what you want to do:
- **I'd like** some information about hotels, please.
- **I'd like to try** on this jacket, please.

wish- if you woud south you dont have

UNIT 30 Exercises

30.1 *Read the situation and write what you would say. Use the words given in parentheses (. . .).*

Example: You've got a $20 bill, and you need some change. You ask somebody to help you.
(Can you . . . ?) ..... *Can you change a $20 bill ?* ....

1. You want to borrow your friend's camera. What do you say to him/her? (Could I . . . ?)
   ....
2. You have a car and you want to give somebody a lift. What do you say? (Can I . . . ?)
   ....
3. You have to go to the airport, but you don't know how to get there. You ask a passerby.
   (Could you . . . ?) ....
4. You are telephoning the owner of an apartment that was advertised in a newspaper. You
   are interested in the apartment, and you want to stop by and see it today. (Do you think
   I . . . ?) ....
5. You are at a meeting with your boss. You want to smoke a cigarette. What do you ask
   first? (May I . . . ?) ....
6. You want to leave work early because you have some important things to do. What do
   you ask your boss? (Do you think I . . . ?) ....
7. You want to invite someone to come and stay with you for the weekend. (Would you
   like . . . ?) ....
8. The person in the next room has some music on very loud. How do you ask him politely
   to turn it down? (Do you think you . . . ?) ....

30.2 *Decide how to say what you want to say.*

Examples: You have to carry some heavy boxes upstairs. Ask someone to help you.
Do you think you could give me a hand with these boxes?
A friend has just come to see you in your apartment. Offer him some coffee or
tea. *Can I get you some coffee or tea ?* ....

1. You want your friend to show you how to change the film in your camera. What do you
   say to him/her? ....
2. You're on a train. The woman next to you has finished reading her newspaper. Now you
   want to look at it. What do you say?
   ....
3. You need a match to light your cigarette. You don't have any, but the man sitting next to
   you has some. What do you ask him?
   ....
4. There is a concert tonight and you are going with some friends. You think Mary would
   enjoy it too. Invite her. ....
5. You're in the post office. You want three airmail stamps. What do you say?
   ....
6. You are sitting on a crowded bus. There is an old lady standing. Offer her your seat.
   ....
7. You are having a party next Saturday. Invite your friend Tim.
   ....

UNIT 31 Have to and **must**

a We use **have to (do)** and **must (do)** to say that it is necessary to do something:

- Oh, it's later than I thought. I { **have to** / **must** } go now.
- You { **have to** / **must** } have a passport to visit most foreign countries.

There is sometimes a difference between **must** and **have to**. With **must** the speaker is expressing personal feelings, saying what *he* or *she* thinks is necessary:

- I **must** write to Ann. I haven't written to her for ages. (= The speaker personally feels that he or she must write to Ann.)
- The government really **must** do something about unemployment. (= The speaker personally feels that the government must do something.)

With **have to** the speaker is not expressing feelings. The speaker is just giving facts. For example:

- Karen's eyes are not very good. She **has to** wear glasses for reading.
- I can't meet you on Friday. I **have to** work.

b You use **must** to talk only about the *present* and *future*:

- We **must** go now.
- **Must** you leave tomorrow?

Have to can be used in all forms. For example:

- I **had to** go to the hospital. (*past*)
- I might **have to** go to the hospital. (*base form*)
- **Have** you ever **had to** go to the hospital? (*present perfect*)

Note that we use **do/does/did** with **have to** in questions and negative sentences:

- What **do** I **have to** do to get a driver's license? (*not* "have I to do")
- Why **did** you **have to** go to the hospital? (*not* "had you to go")
- Tom **doesn't have to** work on Saturdays. (*not* "hasn't to work")

c **Mustn't** and **don't have to** are completely different. "You **mustn't** do something" means "it is necessary that you do *not* do it":

- You **mustn't** tell anyone what I said. (= Don't tell anyone.)
- I promised I'd be on time. I **mustn't** be late. (= I must be on time.)

"You **don't have to** do something" means "it is not necessary to do it; you don't need to do it":

- I **don't have to** wear a suit to work, but I usually do.
- She stayed in bed this morning because she **didn't have to** go to work.

d You can use "**have got to**" instead of "**have to**." So you can say:

- I**'ve got to** work tomorrow. *or* I **have to** work tomorrow.

UNIT 31 Exercises

31.1 *Complete these sentences with* **must** *or* **have to** *(in its correct form). Sometimes it is possible to use either; sometimes only* **have to** *is possible.*

Examples: Well, it's 10:00. I *must (or have to)* go now.
Ann wasn't feeling well last night. She ...*had to*.......... leave the party early.

1. You really .... work harder if you want to pass that exam.
2. Some children .... wear uniforms when they go to school.
3. Last night Don suddenly became ill. We .... call the doctor.
4. Ann has .... wear glasses since she was eight years old.
5. I'm afraid I can't come tomorrow. I .... work late.
6. I'm sorry I couldn't come yesterday. I .... work late.
7. Tom may .... go away next week.
8. We couldn't repair the car ourselves. We .... take it to a garage.
9. When you come to Houston again, you .... come and see us.

31.2 *Make questions with* **have to**.

Example: "Tom had to go to the police station."
"Why *did he have to go to the police station?*.............................."

1. "Linda has to leave tomorrow."   "What time exactly ...."
2. "We had to answer a lot of questions on the exam."
   "How many questions ...."
3. "George had to pay a parking fine."   "How much ...."
4. "I have to get up early tomorrow."   "Why ...."

31.3 *Make negative sentences with* **have to**.

Example: "Did they change planes?"
"No, it was a direct flight, so *they didn't have to change planes.*.........."

1. "Did you pay to get into the concert?"
   "No, we had free tickets, so we ...."
2. "Does Jack shave?"   "No, he has a beard, so ...."
3. "Did you get up early this morning?"
   "No, it's my day off, so ...."
4. "Do you work?"   "No, I'm extremely rich, so.............................."

31.4 *Complete these sentences with* **mustn't** *or* **don't/doesn't have to**.

Examples: I don't want anyone to know. You ...*mustn't*.......... tell anyone what I said.
I *don't have to*... wear a suit to work, but I usually do.

1. I can stay in bed tomorrow morning because I .... work.
2. Whatever you do, you .... touch that switch. It's very dangerous.
3. You .... forget what I told you. It's very important.
4. She .... get up so early. She gets up early because she likes to.
5. We .... leave yet. We've got plenty of time.

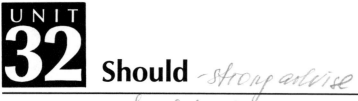

UNIT 32   Should

-strong advise

~ had better do
↓
> stronger

a   Study this example:

> Tom has just come back from the movies:
>
> Ann: Hello, Tom. Did you enjoy the movie?
> Tom: Yes, it was great. You **should go** and see it.
>
> Tom is advising Ann to go and see the movie. "You **should go**" means that it would be a good thing to do. We often use **should (do)** when we say what we think is a good thing to do or the right thing to do.

- The government **should do** something about the economy.
- "**Should** we **invite** Sue to the party?"   "Yes, I think we **should**."

"You should**n't** do something" means that it is not a good thing to do:
- You've been coughing a lot lately. You **shouldn't smoke** so much.
- Tom really **shouldn't** go out. He has too much homework to do.

Should is not as strong as **must**:
- You **should** stop smoking. (= It would be a good idea.)
- You **must** stop smoking. (= It is necessary that you stop.)

b   We often use **should** when we ask for or give an opinion about something. Often we use **I think / I don't think / do you think?**:
- **I think** the government **should do** something about the economy.
- **I don't think** you **should work** so hard.
- "**Do you think I should apply** for this job?"   "Yes, **I think** you **should**."

c   We also use **should** to say something is not "right" or not what we expect:
- The price on this package is wrong. It says 65¢ but it **should be** 50¢.
- Those children **shouldn't be playing**. They **should be** at school.

d   For the past, we use **should have (done)** to say that someone did the wrong thing:
- The party was great. You **should have come**. Why didn't you?
- I feel sick. I **shouldn't have eaten** so much chocolate.
- She **shouldn't have been listening** to our conversation. It was private.

e   We also use **should** to say that something will probably happen:
- A: Do you think you'll be home late tonight?
- B: I don't think so. I **should be** home at the usual time.

Here, "**I should be** home" means "I will probably be home." You can use **should** to say what will probably happen.

f   You can use **ought to** instead of **should** in the sentences in this unit:
- It's really a good movie. You **ought to go** and see it.
- She's been studying very hard, so she **ought to** pass the exam.

more used in Great Britain

64

UNIT 32   Exercises

32.1 *You are giving advice to a friend. Use* **should** *or* **shouldn't**.

Example: Your friend is always coughing because he smokes too much. Advise him to stop
smoking. *You should stop smoking.* ....

1. Your friend has a bad toothache. Advise her to go to the dentist.   You ....
....
2. Your friend rides his bicycle at night without lights. You think this is dangerous. Advise
him not to do it.   ....
3. Your friend is going to visit Greece. Advise her to learn a few words of Greek before she
goes.   ....

32.2 *This time give your opinion about something. Use* **I think / I don't think** ....

Example: Tom has just been offered a job. You think it would be a good idea for him to
accept it. *I think Tom should accept the job.* ....

1. You think it would be a good idea for all drivers to wear seat belts.
I think ....
2. You don't think it would be a good idea for Jill and Sam to get married.
I...
3. Your friend has a bad cold. Tell him that you think it would be a good idea for him to stay
home tonight.   ....

32.3 *Read the situations and write sentences with* **should (have)** *and* **shouldn't (have)**. *Sometimes
you have to use the present, sometimes the past.*

Examples: The speed limit is 55 miles an hour, but Tom is doing 70.
He shouldn't be driving so fast. ....
When we got to the restaurant there were no empty tables. We hadn't reserved
one. *We should have reserved a table.* ....

1. It's very cold. Mrs. Taylor, who has been sick lately, is standing at the bus stop without a
coat.   She ....
2. We went for a walk. While we were walking we got hungry, but we hadn't brought
anything with us to eat. We said: We ....
3. I went to Paris. Marcel lives in Paris, but I didn't go to see him while I was there. When I
saw him later, he said: You ....
4. The notice says that the store opens every day at 8:30. It is now 9:00, but the store isn't
open.   ....
5. The driver in front of me stopped suddenly without warning, and I drove into the back of
her car. It wasn't my fault.   ....
6. The children normally go to bed at 9:00. It is now 9:30. They are not in bed; they are
watching television. (*two sentences*)   ....
....
7. The accident happened because Tom was driving on the wrong side of the road.
....

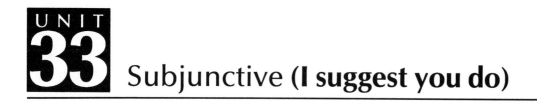

UNIT 33 Subjunctive (**I suggest you do**)

a Study this example:

Mary said to Pete, "Why don't you buy some new clothes?"

Mary suggested (that) Pete **buy** some new clothes.

The subjunctive is always the same as the base form (**I buy**, **he buy**, **she buy**, etc.).

I/he/she/it
we/you/they } **do/buy/be**, etc.

b You can use the subjunctive after these verbs:

suggest — **propose**   **recommend**   **insist**   **demand**

- I **suggest** (that) **you take** a vacation.
- They **insisted** (that) **we have** dinner with them.
- I **insisted** (that) **he have** dinner with me.
- He **demanded** (that) **she apologize** to him.
- The doctor **recommended** (that) **I rest** for a few days.

You can use the subjunctive for the present, past, or future:
- I **insist** (that) you **come** with us.
- They **insisted** (that) I **go** with them.

Note the subjunctive **be** (usually passive):
- I insisted (that) something **be done** about the problem.
- The chairperson proposed (that) the plans **be changed**.

c Other structures are possible after **insist** and **suggest**:
- They **insisted on my having** dinner with them. (see Unit 57a)
- It was a beautiful evening, so I **suggested going** for a walk. (see Unit 51)

You cannot use the *infinitive* after **suggest**:
- She **suggested that he buy** some new clothes. (*not* suggested him to buy)
- What do you **suggest I do**? (*not* suggest me to do)

d **Should** is sometimes used instead of the subjunctive.
- She suggested that he **should buy** some new clothes.
- The doctor recommended that I **should rest** for a few days.

British: I'd prefer you to write

UNIT 33 Exercises

33.1 *Write a sentence that means the same as the first sentence. Begin in the way shown.*

Example: "Why don't you buy some new clothes?" she said to him.
She suggested that *he buy some new clothes.* ....

1. "You really must stay a little longer," she said to me. She insisted that ....
2. "Why don't you visit the museum after lunch?" I said to her.
   I suggested that ....
3. "I think it would be a good idea to see a specialist," the doctor said to me. The doctor
   recommended that ....
4. "You have to pay the rent by Friday at the latest," the landlord said to the tenant.
   The landlord demanded ....
5. "Why don't you go away for a few days?" Jack said to me.
   Jack suggested that ....
6. "Let's have dinner early," Alice said to us.
   Alice proposed that ....

33.2 *Complete these sentences with an appropriate verb.*

Examples: I suggest that you ....*take*............... a vacation.
I insisted that something ....*be*................ done about the problem.

1. Our friends recommended that we .... our vacation in the mountains.
2. You were not invited to the party. I demand that you .... the house
   immediately.
3. The workers at the factory are demanding that their wages .... increased.
4. She doesn't use her car very often, so I suggested that she .... it and
   use the money for something else.
5. You have insulted me! I insist that you ....
6. The local council has proposed that a new shopping center .... built.
7. What do you suggest I .... to the party? A dress?
8. I didn't want her to come to the party, but Jack insisted that she .... invited.

33.3 *Tom is out of shape and his friends made some suggestions:*

ANN *Why don't you give up smoking?*
SANDRA *How about walking to work in the morning?*
Eat more fruit and vegetables BILL
Why don't you try jogging? LINDA

Write sentences beginning "(Ann) suggested . . ." etc.

1. *Ann suggested that he give up smoking.* ....
2. Bill suggested that he ....
3. Sandra suggested ....
4. Linda ....

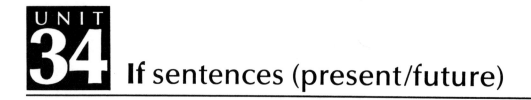

UNIT 34 If sentences (present/future)

a Compare these examples:

> Tom: I think I left my lighter at your house. Have you seen it?
> Ann: No, but I'll look. **If I find** it, I'll give it to you.
>
> In this example there is a real possibility that Ann will find the lighter. So she says: "If I **find . . . I'll . . .**" (see also Unit 9c).
>
> Ann: **If I found** a $100 bill on the street, I would keep it.
>
> This is a different type of situation. Ann is not thinking about a real possibility; she is imagining the situation. So she says: "If I **found . . . I would . . .**" (*not* "If I find . . . I'll . . .").

When you imagine a future happening like this, you use a *past tense* form (**did/came/found,** etc.) after **if.** But the meaning is *not* past:

- What would you do **if** you **won** a million dollars?
- **If** we **didn't go** to their party next week, they would be very angry.
- Ann wouldn't lend me any money **if I asked** her.

b We do not normally use **would** in the **if** part of the sentence:

- I'd be very frightened **if** someone **pointed** a gun at me. (*not* if someone would point)
- **If** we **didn't go** to their party next week, they would be angry. (*not* if we wouldn't go)

Sometimes it is possible to say **if . . . would,** especially when you ask someone to do something in a formal way:

- I would be very grateful **if** you **would** send me your brochure and price list as soon as possible. *(from a formal letter)*

c In the other part of the sentence (not the **if** part) we use **would/wouldn't. Would** is often shortened to **'d,** especially in spoken English:

- If you stopped smoking, you**'d** probably **feel** healthier.
- They **wouldn't come** to the party if you invited them.

You can also use **could** and **might:**

- They **might be** angry if I didn't visit them. (= perhaps they would be)
- If it stopped raining, we **could go** out. (= we would be able to go out)

d Do not use **when** in sentences like the ones in this unit:

- Tom would be angry **if** I didn't visit him. (*not* when I didn't visit)
- What would you do **if** you were bitten by a snake? (*not* when you were)

See also Unit 9c.

For **if** sentences see also Units 35 and 36.

UNIT 34 Exercises

34.1 *Put the verb into the correct form.*

Examples: If I found a $100 bill on the street, I ...*would keep*........ (keep) it.
They'd be very angry if you ....*didn't visit*..... (not/visit) them.

1. If the company offered me the job, I think I ....(take) it.
2. I'm sure Liz will lend you some money. I would be very surprised if she ....
   (refuse).
3. Many people would be out of work if that factory.............................. (close) down.
4. If she sold her car, she .... (not/get) much money for it.
5. They're expecting us. They would be disappointed if we ....
   (not/come).
6. Would George be angry if I .... (take) his bicycle without asking?
7. Ann gave me this ring. She............................... (be) terribly upset if I lost it.
8. If someone.............................. (walk) in here with a gun, I'd be very frightened.
9. What would happen if you............................... (not/go) to work tomorrow?
10. I'm sure she .... (understand) if you explained the situation to her.

34.2 *Make questions.*

Example: Perhaps one day somebody will give you a lot of money.
What would you do if someone gave you a lot of money?..........

1. Perhaps one day a millionaire will ask you to marry him/her.
   What would you do if ....
2. Perhaps one day you will lose your passport in a foreign country.
   What ....
3. Perhaps one day somebody will throw an egg at you.
   What ....
4. Perhaps one day your car will be stolen.
   What ....
5. Perhaps one day somebody will park a car on your foot.

   ....

34.3 *Answer these questions in the way shown.*

Example: Are you going to take the 10:30 train? (we / arrive too early)
No. *If we took the 10:30 train, we would arrive too early.*........

1. Is he going to take the exam? (he / fail it)
   No. If he ...., he ....
2. Are you going to invite Bill to the party? (I / have to invite Linda too)
   No. If I ....
3. Are you going to bed now? (I / not / sleep)
   No. ....
4. Is she going to apply for the job? (she / not / get it)
   No. ....

UNIT 35 — If and **wish** sentences (present)

a   Study this example situation:

> Tom wants to call Sue, but he can't because he doesn't know her telephone number. He says:
>
> **If I knew** her number, **I would call** her.
>
> Tom says "**If I knew** her number . . . ." This tells us that he doesn't know her number. He is imagining the situation. The real situation is that he doesn't know her number.

When you imagine a situation like this, you use a *past tense* form ("I **did** / I **had** / I **knew**," etc.) after **if**. But the meaning is present, not past:
- Tom would travel **if** he **had** more money. (but he doesn't have much money)
- **If I didn't want** to go, I wouldn't. (but I want to go)
- We wouldn't have any money **if** we **didn't work**. (but we work)

b   We also use the past for a present situation after *wish*. We use **wish** to say that we regret something, that something is not as we would like it to be:

I wish I had an umbrella.

I wish I knew Sue's telephone number. (I don't know it.)
Do you ever **wish** you **could** fly? (You can't fly.)
I wish it **didn't rain** so much in this city. (It rains a lot.)
It's crowded here. **I wish** there **weren't** so many people. (There are a lot of people.)
I wish I **didn't have** to work. (I have to work.)

c   In **if** sentences and after **wish** we use **were** instead of **was**:
- If I **were** you, I wouldn't buy that coat. (but I am not you)
- I'd go out if it **weren't** raining. (but it is raining)
- I wish my room **were** larger. (but it isn't very large)

d   Do not use **would** in the **if** part of the sentence or after **wish**:
- If I **were** rich, I would buy a castle. (*not* if I would be rich)
- I wish I **were** taller. (*not* I wish I would be taller.)

But sometimes **I wish . . . would . . .** is possible. See Unit 37.

Could sometimes means "would be able to" and sometimes "was able to":
- She **could** (= would be able to) get a job more easily if she **could** (= was able to) type.

For **if** sentences and **wish** see also Units 34, 36, and 37.

UNIT 35 Exercises

35.1 *Put the verb into the correct form.*

Examples: If *I knew* .... (know) her number, I would call her.
I *wouldn't buy* ...... (not/buy) that coat if I were you.

1. I .... (give) you a cigarette if I had one, but I'm afraid I don't.
2. This soup would taste better if it .... (have) more salt in it.
3. If you .... (not/go) to bed so late every night, you wouldn't be so tired all the time.
4. I wouldn't mind living in England if the weather .... (be) better.
5. I'd help you if I .... (can), but I'm afraid I can't.
6. If I were you, I .... (not/marry) him.
7. We would gladly buy that house if it .... (not/be) so small.

35.2 *Read the situation and write a sentence with* **if**.

Example: We don't visit you very often because you live so far away.
But if *you didn't live so far away, we would visit you more often.*

1. People don't understand him because he doesn't speak very clearly.
   But if he .... , people..............................
2. I'm not going to buy that book because it's too expensive.
   But if that book ....
3. She doesn't go out very often because she can't walk without help.
   But if ....
4. He's fat because he doesn't get any exercise.
   But ....
5. We can't have lunch outside because it's raining.
   ....
6. I can't meet you tomorrow evening because I have to work.
   ....

35.3 *Write sentences with* **I wish . . .**

Example: I don't know many people (and I'm lonely). *I wish I knew more people.*

1. I can't give up smoking (but I'd like to). I wish I ....
2. I don't have any cigarettes (and I need one). I wish ....
3. George isn't here (and I need him). I wish George ....
4. It's cold (and I hate cold weather). I wish ....
5. I live in New York City (and I hate New York City). I ....
6. Tina can't come to the party (she's your best friend). I ....
7. I have to work tomorrow (but I'd like to stay in bed). ....
8. I don't know anything about cars (and my car has just broken down).
   ....
9. I'm not lying on a beautiful sunny beach (and that's a shame).
   ....

UNIT 36 If and **wish** sentences (past)

a Study this example situation:

> Last month Ann was sick. Tom didn't know this, and he didn't go to see her. They met again after Ann got better. Tom said:
>
> **If I had known** that you were sick, **I would have gone** to see you.
>
> The real situation was that Tom didn't know Ann was sick. So he says **If I had known . . .** When you are talking about the past, you use the *past perfect* (**I had done** / **I had been** / **I had known**, etc.) after **if**.

- **If I had seen** you when you passed me in the street, I would have said hello. (but I didn't see you)
- I would have gone out **if I hadn't been** so tired. (but I was too tired)
- **If he had been looking** where he was going, he wouldn't have walked into the wall. (but he wasn't looking)

Do not use **would (have)** in the **if** part of the sentence:

- **If I had seen you**, I would have said hello. (*not* if I would have seen)

Both **would** and **had** can be shortened to **'d**:

- If I**'d** seen (= **had** seen) you, I**'d** have said (= **would** have said) hello.

b Use the *past perfect* (**I had done**) after **wish** when you say that you regret something that happened or didn't happen in the past:

- **I wish I had known** that Ann was sick. I would have gone to see her. (I didn't know that she was sick.)
- I feel sick. **I wish I hadn't eaten** so much. (I ate too much.)
- **Do you wish you had studied** science instead of languages? (You didn't study science.)
- The weather was terrible. **I wish it had been** warmer. (It wasn't warm.)

You cannot use **would have** after **wish**:

- I wish it **had been** warmer. (*not* would have been)

c **Would have (done)** is the past form of **would (do)**:

- If I had gone to the party last night, I **would be** tired now. (I am not tired now – *present*.)
- If I had gone to the party last night, I **would have seen** Ann. (I didn't see Ann – *past*.)

Might have and **could have** are possible instead of **would have**:

- If we'd played better, we **might have won**. (= perhaps we would have won)
- We **could have gone** out if the weather hadn't been so bad. (= we would have been able to go out)

For **if** sentences and **wish** see also Units 34, 35, and 37.

UNIT 36 Exercises

36.1 *Put the verb into the correct form.*

Examples: If I ....*had known*....................(know) that you were sick last week, I'd have
gone to see you.
Tom .*wouldn't have taken*......(not/take) the exam if he had known that it
would be so difficult.

1. Jim got to the bus stop in time. If he ....(miss) the bus, he
   would have been late for his interview.
2. It's good that Ann reminded me about Tom's birthday. I ....
   (forget) if she hadn't reminded me.
3. We might not have stayed at this hotel if Debbie ....
   (not/recommend) it to us.
4. I'd have sent you a postcard while I was on vacation if I ....
   (have) your address.

36.2 *Read the situation and write a sentence with* **if***.*

Example: She didn't eat anything because she wasn't hungry.
If *she had been hungry, she would have eaten something.*..........

1. The accident happened because the driver in front stopped so suddenly.
   If the driver in front ....
2. I didn't wake George because I didn't know he wanted to get up early.
   If I ....
3. I was able to buy the car because Jim lent me the money.
   If ....
4. She wasn't injured in the crash because she was wearing a seat belt.
   If ....
5. You're hungry now because you didn't have breakfast.
   If ....
6. She didn't buy the coat because she didn't have enough money on her.
   If ....

36.3 *Imagine that you are in each situation. Make a sentence with* **I wish** *. . .*

Example: You've eaten too much and now you feel sick.
You say: *I wish I hadn't eaten so much.*...............................

1. You've just painted the door red. Now you decide that it doesn't look very nice.
   You say: I wish I ....
2. You are walking in the country. You would like to take some photographs, but you didn't
   bring your camera. You say: I ....
3. A good friend of yours visited your town, but unfortunately you were away when he
   came. So you didn't see him. You say: ....
4. You've just come back from your vacation. Everything was fine except for the hotel,
   which wasn't very good. You say: ....

For **would** and **would have** in **if** sentences (*conditional*), see Units 34, 35, and 36. For **would** in offers, invitations, etc., see Unit 30. This unit explains some other uses of **would**.

a Sometimes we use **would** after **I wish** . . . . Study this example:

I wish it would stop raining...

It is raining. Tom wants to go out, but not in the rain. He says:

I wish it **would stop** raining.

This means that Tom is complaining about the rain and wants it to stop. We use **I wish** . . . **would** . . . when we want something to happen or somebody to do something. The speaker is complaining about the present situation.

- **I wish** someone **would answer** that telephone. It's been ringing for about five minutes.
- The music next door is very loud. **I wish** they **would turn** it down.

We often use **I wish** . . . **wouldn't** to complain about the way people do things:

- **I wish** you **wouldn't drive** so fast. It makes me nervous.

We use **I wish** . . . **would** when we want something to change or somebody else to do something. So you cannot say "I wish *I* would . . . ."
For more information about **wish**, see Units 35 and 36.

b **Would/wouldn't** is sometimes the past of **will/won't**:

present Tom: **I'll** lend you some money, Ann.
  past Tom said that he **would** lend Ann some money.

present Ann: I promise I **won't** be late.
  past Ann promised that she **wouldn't** be late.

present Tom: Darn it! The car **won't** start.
  past Tom was angry because the car **wouldn't** start.

c You can also use **would** when you look back on the past and remember things that often happened:

- When we were children, we lived by the sea. In summer, if the weather was nice, we **would** all **get up** early and **go** for a swim.
- Whenever Linda was angry, she **would** just **walk** out of the room.

Used to is also possible in these sentences:

- . . . we all **used to get up** early and **go** . . .

See Unit 24 for **used to**.

UNIT 37 Exercises

37.1 *Read the situation and then write a sentence with* **I wish . . . would . . . .**

Example: It's raining. You want to go out, but not in the rain. So you want it to stop raining.
What do you say? *I wish it would stop raining.*...

1. You're waiting for Tim. He's late and you're getting impatient. You want him to come.
   What do you say?   I wish ....
2. A baby is crying and you're trying to sleep. You want the baby to stop crying. What do
   you say?   I ....
3. You're looking for a job – so far without success. You want somebody to give you a job.
   What do you say?   I wish somebody ....
4. Brian has been wearing the same old clothes for years. You think he needs some new
   clothes, and you want him to buy some. What do you say to him?   ....
   ....

37.2 *Use* **I wish . . . wouldn't . . . .**

Example: Tom drives very fast. You don't like this. What do you say to him?
I wish you wouldn't drive so fast....

1. You are telling your friend about the man in the apartment next door. He often plays the
   piano in the middle of the night, and you don't like this. What do you say to your friend?
   I ....
2. A lot of people drop litter in the street. You don't like this. What do you say?
   I wish people ....
3. Jane always leaves the door open. You don't like this. What do you say to her?
   I ....

37.3 *Write a sentence with* **promised**.

Example: I wonder why she's late.   *She promised she wouldn't be late.*...............

1. I wonder why Steve hasn't written to me.   He promised ....
2. I wonder why Ann told Tom what I said.   She promised ....
3. I wonder why they haven't come.   They...

37.4 *These sentences are about things that often happened in the past. Put in* **would** *with one of
these verbs:*   **be**   ~~**walk**~~   **take**   **shake**

Example: Whenever Carol was angry, she ..*would walk*.......... out of the room.

1. We used to live next to a railroad track. Every time a train went past, the whole
   house ....
2. That cafe is nearly always empty now. I remember a few years ago it ....
   crowded every night.
3. When he went out, Jack .... always .... an
   umbrella with him, whether it was raining or not.

UNIT 38 In case

---

a Study this example situation:

Jeff is a soccer referee. He always wears two watches during a game because it is possible that one watch will stop.

He wears two watches **in case one of them stops.**

In case one of them stops = "because it is possible that one of them will stop."

Here are some more examples of **in case**:
- John might call tonight. I don't want to go out **in case he calls.**
  (= because it is possible that he will call)
- I'll draw a map for you **in case you can't find our house.** (= because it is possible that you won't be able to find it)

b Do not use **will** after **in case**. Use a present tense when you are talking about the future:
- I don't want to go out tonight in case Sue **calls.** (*not* "in case she will call")

c **In case** is not the same as **if**. Compare these sentences:
- We'll buy some more food **if** Tom comes. (= Perhaps Tom will come; if he comes, we'll buy some more food; if he doesn't come, we won't buy any more food.)
- We'll buy some more food **in case** Tom comes. (= Perhaps Tom will come; we'll buy some more food now, whether he comes or not; then we'll *already* have the food *if* he comes.)

Compare:
- This letter is for Ann. Can you **give** it to her **if** you see her?
- This letter is for Ann. Can you **take** it with you **in case** you see her?

d You can use **in case** to say why someone did something in the past:
- We bought some more food **in case Tom came.** (= because it was possible that Tom would come)
- I drew a map for her **in case she couldn't find our house.**
- We rang the bell again **in case they hadn't heard it the first time.**

e "In case **of** . . ." is different from **in case. In case of fire** means "if there is a fire":
- **In case of fire**, please leave the building as quickly as possible.
- **In case of emergency**, telephone this number. (= if there is an emergency)

UNIT 38   Exercises

38.1 *Tom is going for a long walk in the country. He has decided to take these things with him: his camera, some chocolate, an umbrella, a towel, a map, and some lemonade. He is taking these things because:*

perhaps he'll get thirsty   perhaps he'll get lost
perhaps he'll want to go swimming   perhaps it will rain
perhaps he'll want to take some pictures   perhaps he'll get hungry

Now write sentences with **in case** *saying why Tom has decided to take these things.*

Example: *He's going to take his camera in case he wants to take some pictures.*

1. He's going to take some chocolate in case ....
2. He's going to take ....
3. ....
4. ....
5. ....

38.2 *Write sentences with* **in case**.

Example: It was possible that John would call. So I didn't go out.
   I didn't go out in case John called. ....

1. It was possible that he would come to Los Angeles one day. So I gave him my address.
   I gave him my address in case ....
2. It was possible that I wouldn't see her again. So I said goodbye.
   I said ....
3. It was possible that her parents were worried about her. So she called them.
   She ....
4. It was possible that I would forget the name of the street. So I wrote it down.
   ....
5. It was possible that they hadn't received my first letter. So I wrote them a second letter.
   ....

38.3 *Put* **in case** *or* **if** *in these sentences.*

Examples: John might call tonight. I don't want to go out *in case* he calls.
   Could you give this book to Bill ... *if* .... you see him?

1. I hope you'll come to Tokyo sometime. .... you come, you must visit us.
2. I've just painted the door. I'll put a "wet paint" sign next to it .... someone doesn't realize the paint is still wet.
3. We have installed a burglar alarm in our house .... somebody tries to break in.
4. The alarm will go off .... somebody tries to break into the house.
5. Write your name and address on your bag .... you lose it.
6. Go to the lost and found office .... you lose your bag.
7. I was advised to arrange for insurance .... I needed medical treatment while I was abroad on vacation.

UNIT 39 Unless, as long as, and provided/providing (that)

a Unless

Study this example situation:

Joe is always listening to music. If you speak to him normally, he can't hear you. If you want him to hear you, you have to shout.

Joe can't hear **unless you shout.**

This means: "Joe *can* hear *only if* you shout." **Unless** means **except if**. We use **unless** to make an exception to something we say.

Here are some more examples of **unless**:

- Don't tell Ann what I said **unless she asks you**. (= except if she asks you)
- I'll come tomorrow **unless I have to work**. (= except if I have to work)
- I wouldn't eat between meals **unless I were extremely hungry**.
  (= except if I were extremely hungry)

We often use **unless** in warnings:

- We'll be late **unless we hurry**. (= except if we hurry)
- **Unless you work harder**, you're not going to pass the exam. (= except if you work harder)
- The thief said he would hit me **unless I told him where the money was**.
  (= except if I told him)

Instead of **unless** it is possible to say **if . . . not**:

- Don't tell Ann what I said **if** she doesn**'t** ask you.
- We'll be late **if** we don**'t** hurry.

b As long as   provided (that)   providing (that)

These expressions mean **but only if**:

- You can use my car **as long as** (*or* **so** long as) **you drive carefully**.
  (= but only if you drive carefully)
- Traveling by car is convenient **provided (that) you have somewhere to park**.
  (= but only if you have somewhere to park)
- **Providing (that) she studies hard**, she should pass the exam. (= but only if she studies hard)

c

When you are talking about the future, do *not* use **will** with **unless, as long as, provided,** or **providing**. Use a *present* tense:

- We'll be late **unless we hurry**. (*not* unless we will hurry)
- **Providing** she **studies** hard . . . (*not* providing she will study)

See Unit 9 for more information about this rule.

UNIT 39   Exercises

39.1 *Read the sentence and then write a new sentence with the same meaning.* Use **unless**.

Example: You have to study more or you won't pass the exam.
You won't pass the exam unless you study more.

1. You should listen carefully or you won't know what to do.
   You won't know what to do ....
2. We have to hurry or we'll miss the train.   We'll ....
3. You have to speak very slowly or he won't be able to understand you.
   He...
4. I have to get a raise or I'll look for another job.
   ....
5. She has to apologize to me or I won't forgive her.
   ....

39.2 *Read the sentence with* **only if** *and then write a new sentence with* **unless**.

Example: Joe can hear only if you shout.   *Joe can't hear unless you shout.*

1. I'm going to the party only if you go too.   I'm not going to the party ....
2. You are allowed into the club only if you are a member.   You're not ....
3. The dog will attack you only if you move.   The dog ....
4. She'll speak to you only if you ask her a question.   She ....

39.3 *Choose the correct word or expression for each sentence.*

Example: You can use my car | ~~unless~~ / as long as | you drive carefully. ("as long as" is correct)

1. I'm playing tennis tomorrow | unless / providing | it rains.

2. We're going to start painting the house tomorrow | unless / provided | it's not raining.

3. You can smoke in here | unless / as long as | you leave a window open to let the smoke out.

4. George doesn't trust anyone. He won't lend you any money | unless / as long as | you promise in writing to pay him back.

5. The children can stay here | unless / providing | they don't make too much noise.

6. I'm going now | unless / provided | you want me to stay.

7. I can't understand why he's late, | unless / as long as | he didn't get our message.

UNIT 40 Passive (1) (be done / have been done)

a *Active* and *passive*   Study this example:

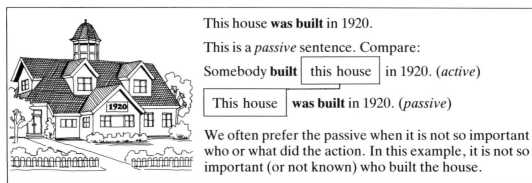

This house **was built** in 1920.

This is a *passive* sentence. Compare:

Somebody **built** | this house | in 1920. (*active*)

| This house | **was built** in 1920. (*passive*)

We often prefer the passive when it is not so important who or what did the action. In this example, it is not so important (or not known) who built the house.

In a passive sentence, if you want to say who did or what caused the action, use **by**:
- This house was built **by my grandfather**. (= my grandfather built it)
- Have you ever been bitten **by a dog**? (= Has a dog ever bitten you?)

b In passive sentences we use the correct form of **be** (**is/are/was/were/has been**, etc.) + the *past participle*:

  (be) done   **(be) cleaned**   **(be) damaged**   **(be) built**   **(be) seen**

For irregular past participles (**done/seen/written**, etc.) see Appendix 2.
For the passive of the present and past tenses see Unit 41.

c We use the base form (. . . **be done, be cleaned, be built,** etc.) after modal verbs (**will, can, must,** etc.) and some other verbs (for example: **have to, be going to, want to**). Compare:

Active: We **can solve** | this problem. |

Passive: | This problem | **can be solved.**

- The new hotel **will be opened** next year.
- George **might be sent** to Venezuela by his company in August.
- The music at the party was very loud and **could be heard** from far away.
- This room **is going to be painted** next week.
- Go away! I **want to be left** alone.

d There is a *past* form after modal verbs: **have been done** / **have been cleaned,** etc.:

Active: Somebody **should have cleaned** | the windows | yesterday.

Passive: | The windows | **should have been cleaned** yesterday.

- My bicycle has disappeared. It **must have been stolen**.
- She **wouldn't have been injured** if she had been wearing a seat belt.
- The weather was terrible. The tennis match **should have been canceled**.

80

UNIT 40   Exercises

Complete these sentences with one of the following verbs (in the correct form):

arrest	wake	knock	check	translate	find	drive
make	spend	~~hear~~	carry			

Example: The music at the party was very loud and could *be heard*.... from far away.

1. A decision will not .... until the next meeting.
2. That building is dangerous. It ought to .... down before it falls down.
3. When you go through Customs, your luggage may .... by a customs officer.
4. I told the hotel receptionist that I wanted to .... up at 6:30.
5. Her new book will probably .... into a number of foreign languages.
6. If you kicked a police officer, you'd ....
7. The police are looking for the missing boy. He can't .... anywhere.
8. Do you think that less money should .... on the military?
9. The injured woman couldn't walk and had to ....
10. I don't mind driving, but I prefer to .... by other people.

40.2 *Complete the sentences. This time use these verbs:*

must	~~should~~	shouldn't	might	would

Example: Did anyone clean the windows?
No. They *should have been cleaned* but they weren't.

1. A: Did anyone invite Ann to the party?
   B: I don't know. She .... – I'm not sure.
2. A: Did anyone see you?
   B: No, but I .... if it hadn't been so dark.
3. A: Has someone fixed this machine?
   B: Well, it's working again so it ....
4. A: Did someone throw those old letters away?
   B: Yes, but it was a mistake. They ....

40.3 *Read the sentence and write another sentence with the same meaning.*

Example: We can solve the problem.   The problem *can be solved.*........................

1. People should send their complaints to the main office.
   Complaints ....
2. They had to postpone the meeting because of illness.
   The meeting ....
3. Somebody might have stolen your car if you had left the keys in it.
   Your car ....
4. A short circuit could have caused the fire.
   The fire ....
5. They are going to hold next year's convention in San Francisco.
   Next year's convention ....
6. They shouldn't have played the soccer match in such bad weather.
   The soccer match ....

UNIT 41 Passive (2) (present and past tenses)

These are the passive forms of the present and past tenses:

Simple present   **am/is/are** + **done/cleaned**, etc.
    Active: Somebody **cleans** | this room | every day.

    Passive: | This room | **is cleaned** every day.

Many accidents **are caused** by dangerous driving.
I'm not often **invited** to parties.
How many people **are injured** in car accidents every day?

Simple past   **was/were** + **done/cleaned**, etc.
    Active: Somebody **cleaned** | this room | yesterday.

    Passive: | This room | **was cleaned** yesterday.

During the night we **were** all **woken** up by a loud explosion.
When **was** that castle **built**?
The house **wasn't damaged** in the storm, but a tree **was blown** down.

Present continuous   **am/is/are being** + **done/cleaned**, etc.
    Active: Somebody **is cleaning** | the room | right now.

    Passive: | The room | **is being cleaned** right now.

Look at those old houses! They **are being knocked** down.
(shop assistant to customer) **Are** you **being helped**, ma'am?

Past continuous   **was/were being** + **done/cleaned**, etc.
    Active: Somebody **was cleaning** | the room | when I arrived.

    Passive: | The room | **was being cleaned** when I arrived.

Suddenly I heard footsteps behind me. We **were being followed**.

Present perfect   **have/has been** + **done/cleaned**, etc.
    Active: The room looks nice. Somebody **has cleaned** | it. |

    Passive: The room looks nice. | It | **has been cleaned**.

Have you heard the news? The President **has been shot**.
Have you ever **been bitten** by a dog?
I'm not going to the party. I **haven't been invited**.

Past perfect   **had been** + **done/cleaned**, etc.
    Active: The room looked much better. Somebody **had cleaned** | it. |

    Passive: The room looked much better. | It | **had been cleaned**.

Jim didn't know about the change of plans. He **hadn't been told**.

UNIT 41   Exercises

41.1 *Read the sentence and then write another sentence with the same meaning. Begin each sentence as shown.*

Examples: Somebody stole my bag in the store.   My bag *was stolen in the store.*
The police have arrested three men.
Three men *have been arrested by the police.*

1. The bill includes service.   Service .... in the bill.
2. People don't use this road very often.   This road ....
3. They canceled all flights because of fog.   All flights ....
4. Somebody accused me of stealing the money.   I ....
5. They are building a new shopping center downtown.
   A new shopping center ....
6. I didn't realize that someone was recording our conversation.
   I didn't realize that our conversation ....
7. They have changed the date of the meeting.   The date of the meeting ....
8. Brian told me that somebody had attacked and robbed him in the street.
   Brian told me that he ....

41.2 *Make a passive sentence from the words in parentheses (. . .).*

Examples: That building looks very old. (when / it / build?) *When was it built?*
A: Is Margaret popular?
B: Yes, (she / like / by everybody) *She is liked by everybody.*

1. This is a very popular television program. (every week it / watch / by millions of people)   Every week it ....
2. What happens to the cars produced in this factory? (most of them / export?)
   ....
3. A: Was there any trouble at the demonstration?
   B: Yes. (about 20 people / arrest)   ....
4. A: There is no longer military service in Britain.
   B: Really? (when / it / abolish?)   ....
5. A: Did anybody call an ambulance to the scene of the accident?
   B: Yes. (but nobody / injure / so it / not / need)   ....
6. A: Last night someone broke into our house.
   B: Oh no! (anything / take?)   ....
7. Mr. Kelly can't use his office right now. (it / redecorate)
   ....
8. Linda didn't have her car yesterday. (it / tune-up / at the garage)
   ....
9. Where's my bicycle? It's gone! (it / steal!)   ....
10. The people next door disappeared six months ago. (they / not / see / since then)
    ....
11. This room looks different. (it / paint / since I was last here?)
    ....
12. A tree was lying across the road. (it / blow / down in the storm)
    ....

Passive (3)

a Some verbs can have two objects. For example, **offer:**
- They didn't offer **Ann the job**. (the two objects are **Ann** and **the job**)

So it is possible to make two different passive sentences:
- **Ann** wasn't offered the job.
- **The job** wasn't offered to Ann.

It is more usual for the passive sentence to begin with the person.
Other verbs like **offer** that can have two objects are:

ask   tell   give   send   show   teach   pay

Here are some examples of passive sentences with these verbs:
- **I was given** two hours to make my decision. (= they gave **me two hours**)
- **The men were paid** $1500 to do the job. (= someone paid **the men $1500**)
- **Have you been shown** the new machine? (= has anyone shown **you the new machine**?)

b **Born:** Remember that **be born** is a *passive* verb and is usually past:
- Where **were you born**? (*not* are you born) ⎫
- **I was born** in Chicago. (*not* I am born) ⎬ *simple past*
- How many babies **are born** in this hospital every day? –*simple present*

c The passive **-ing** form is **being done** / **being cleaned**, etc.:
Active: I don't like people **telling** me what to do.
Passive: I don't like **being told** what to do.
- I remember **being given** a toy drum on my fifth birthday. (= I remember someone giving me ...)
- Hurry up! You know Mr. Miller hates **being kept** waiting. (= he hates people keeping him waiting)
- She climbed over the wall without **being seen**. (= without anyone seeing her)

d Sometimes you can use **get** instead of **be** in the passive:
- There was a fight at the party, but nobody **got** hurt. (= nobody was hurt)
- **Did** Ann **get** fired from her new job? (= was Ann fired from her new job?)

You can use **get** in the passive to say that something happens to someone or something.
Often the action is not planned; it happens by chance:
- The dog **got** run over by a car. (= the dog was run over)

In other types of situation **get** is not usually possible:
- George **is** liked by everyone. (*not* gets liked)

Get is used mainly in informal spoken English. You can use **be** in all situations.

UNIT 42 Exercises

42.1 *Read the sentence and then write a new sentence with the same meaning. Begin in the way shown each time.*

Example: They didn't offer Ann the job.   Ann *wasn't offered the job.*

1. They don't pay Jim very much.   Jim ....
2. They will ask you a lot of questions at the interview.   You ....
   ....
3. Nobody told me that Liz was sick.   I ....
4. His colleagues gave him a present when he retired.   He ....
   ....
5. We will send you your exam results as soon as they are ready.   You ....
   ....
6. They didn't ask me my name.   I ....
7. I think they should have offered Tom the job.   I think Tom ....
   ....

42.2 *When were these famous people born? Choose the right year for each person:*
   1889   1770   1452   ~~1870~~   1564

1. Lenin *was born in 1870.*
2. Shakespeare ....
3. Leonardo da Vinci ....
4. Charlie Chaplin ....
5. Beethoven ....
6. And you? I ....

42.3 *Complete the sentences. Each time use **being** with one of these verbs:*
   ~~keep~~   pay   attack   give   invite   use   ask

Example: Mr. Miller doesn't like *being kept* waiting.

1. He came to the party without ....
2. She won't go out alone after dark. She is afraid of ....
3. I don't like .... stupid questions.
4. Few people are prepared to work without ....
5. Ms. Kelly doesn't like her phone .... by other people.
6. Most people like .... presents.

42.4 *Complete the sentences. Make a passive sentence with **get** and one of these verbs:*
   break   sting   use   damage   ~~hurt~~   steal

Example: There was a fight at the party, but nobody *got hurt.*

1. Ted .... by a bee while he was sitting in the garden.
2. How did that window ....?
3. Did any of these houses .... in the storm last night?
4. These tennis courts don't .... often. Not many people want to play.
5. I used to have a bicycle, but it ....

UNIT 43 It is said that . . . / He is said to . . . , etc., and supposed to

a

Study this example situation:

This is Mary. She is very old, and nobody knows exactly how old she is. But:

It is said that she is 108 years old.

She **is said to be** 108 years old.

Both these sentences mean: "People say that she is 108 years old."

You can also use these structures with:

thought	believed	reported	understood
known	expected	alleged	considered

It is said that Mary eats ten eggs a day.	*or*	**Mary is said to eat** ten eggs a day.
It is believed that the wanted man is living in New York.	*or*	**The wanted man is believed to be living** in New York.
It is expected that the strike will begin tomorrow.	*or*	**The strike is expected to begin** tomorrow.
It is alleged that he stole $100.	*or*	**He is alleged to have stolen** $100.
It was alleged that he stole $100.	*or*	**He was alleged to have stolen** $100.

These structures are often used in news reports:

It is reported that two people were killed in the explosion.	*or*	**Two people are reported to have been killed** in the explosion.

b Supposed to

Sometimes (**be**) **supposed to** means "said to":

- Let's go and see that movie. It's **supposed to be** very good. (= It is said to be very good; people say that it's very good.)
- He **is supposed to have stolen** $100. (= He is said to have stolen $100.)

But sometimes **supposed to** has a different meaning. You can use **supposed to** to say what is planned or arranged (and this is often different from what really happens):

- I'd better hurry. It's nearly 8:00. **I'm supposed to be meeting** Ann at 8:15. (= I arranged to meet Ann; I said I would meet Ann.)
- The train **was supposed to arrive** at 11:30, but it was 40 minutes late. (= The train should have arrived at 11:30, according to the schedule.)
- You **were supposed to clean** the windows. Why didn't you do it?

We use **not supposed to** to say what is not allowed or not advisable:

- You**'re not supposed to park** here. (= You aren't allowed to park here.)
- Mr. Jenkins is much better after his illness, but he's still **not supposed to do** any heavy work.

UNIT 43 Exercises

43.1 *Read the sentence and then write another sentence with the same meaning.*

Examples: It is believed that the wanted man is living in New York.
The wanted man *is believed to be living in New York.*

It is thought that the prisoner escaped by climbing over the wall.
The prisoner *is thought to have escaped by climbing over the wall.*

1. It is said that many people are homeless because of the flood.
   Many people are said ....
2. It is known that the Governor is in favor of the new law.
   The Governor ....
3. It is expected that the President will lose the election.
   The President ....
4. It is believed that the thieves got in through the kitchen window.
   The thieves ....
5. It is alleged that she drove through the town at 90 miles an hour.
   She ....
6. It is reported that two people were seriously injured in the accident.
   Two people ....
7. It is said that three men were arrested after the explosion.
   Three men ....

43.2 *There are a lot of stories about Arthur, but nobody knows whether they are true. Make sentences with* **supposed to.**

Example: People say that Arthur eats spiders. *Arthur is supposed to eat spiders.*

1. People say that Arthur is very rich.   Arthur ....
2. People say that he has 22 children.   He ....
3. People say that he sleeps on a bed of nails. He ....
4. People say that he inherited a lot of money.   He ....
5. People say that he writes poetry.   He ....

43.3 *Now use* **supposed to** *with its other meaning. In each example what happens is not what is supposed to happen. Use* **supposed to** *or* **not supposed to** *with one of these verbs:*

~~clean~~   come   be   ~~smoke~~   call   study   have

Examples: Mary, you're smoking! But you know you *are not supposed to smoke.* in this room.
Why are the windows still dirty? You *were supposed to clean*....them.

1. What are the children doing at home? They .... at school.
2. He .... in the evenings, but he always goes out.
3. Don't put sugar in your tea. You know you ....sugar.
4. Oh no! I .... Ann, but I completely forgot.
5. They arrived very early – at 2:00. They ....until 3:30.

UNIT 44 Have something done

a Study this example situation:

The roof of Bill's house was damaged in a storm, so he arranged for a worker to repair it. Yesterday the worker came and did the job.

Bill **had the roof repaired** yesterday.

This means: Bill didn't repair the roof himself. He arranged for someone else to do it for him.

Compare:
- Bill **repaired** the roof. (= he did it himself)
- Bill **had** the roof **repaired**. (= he arranged for someone else to do it)

Now study these sentences:
- Did Ann design her business cards herself or **did she have them designed**?
- Are you going to repair the car yourself, or **are you going to have it repaired**?

To say that we arrange for someone else to do something for us, we use the structure **have something done**. The word order is important: the *past participle* (**done/repaired**, etc.) comes *after* the object (**the roof**):

	have +	*object* +	*past participle*	
Bill	had	the roof	repaired	yesterday.
Where did you	have	your hair	done?	
We are	having	the house	painted	right now.
Tom has just	had	a telephone	installed	in his house.
How often do you	have	your car	serviced?	
Why don't you	have	that coat	cleaned?	
I want to	have	my picture	taken.	

b "**Get** something done" is possible instead of **have something done** (mainly in informal spoken English):
- I think you should **get your hair cut**. (= have your hair cut)

c **Have something done** sometimes has a different meaning. For example:
- He **had all his money stolen** while he was on vacation.

This doesn't mean that he arranged for somebody to steal his money! "He **had all his money stolen**" means only: "All his money was stolen."

With this meaning, we use **have something done** to say that something (often something not nice) happened to someone: George **had his nose broken** in a fight. (= his nose was broken)

UNIT 44 Exercises

44.1 *Answer the questions in the way shown.*

Example: "Did Liz make that dress herself?"   "No, *she had it made.*................"

1. "Did you cut your hair yourself?"   "No, I ...."
2. "Did they paint the house themselves?"   "No, they ...."
3. "Did Jim cut down that tree himself?"   "No, ..."
4. "Did Sue repair the car herself?"   "No, ..."

44.2 *This time complete the sentences. Use the words in parentheses (. . .).*

Examples: We *are having the house painted* (the house / paint) at the moment.
 Did you have your hair cut.... (you / your hair / cut) last week?

1. Your hair is too long. I think you should .... (it / cut).
2. How often .... (you / your car / tune up)?
3. The engine in Tom's car couldn't be repaired, so he had to ....
   (a new engine / put in).
4. .... (you / your newspaper / deliver) or do you buy it
   yourself at the store?
5. A: What are those workers doing in your garden?
   B: Oh, I .... (a swimming pool / build).
6. A: Can I see the pictures you took on your vacation?
   B: I'm afraid not. I .... (not / the film / develop) yet.
7. Is it true that many years ago he .... (his portrait /
   paint) by a famous artist?

44.3 *Now read each situation and then write a sentence with **have something done**.*

Example: Jill's coat was dirty, so she took it to the cleaners. Now it is clean. What has Jill
 done?   *She has had her coat cleaned.*...

1. Tom thinks his eyesight is getting worse, so he's going to the eye doctor. What is Tom
   going to do there?   He is ....
2. Sue is at the beauty parlor at the moment. A hairdresser is cutting her hair. What is Sue
   doing?   ....
3. Ann's watch was broken, so she took it to a jeweler. Now it's working again. What has
   Ann done?   ....

44.4 *Now use **have something done** with its second meaning (see section c).*

Example: George's nose was broken in a fight. What happened to George?
 He had his nose broken in a fight....

1. John's wallet was stolen from his pocket. What happened to John?   He ....
2. Fred's hat was blown off by the wind. What happened to Fred?   ....
3. Carol's passport was taken from her at the police station. What happened to Carol?

   ....

Direct speech: I said to Ann, "I'll be late"
I said, "I'll be late"
Indirect : I told Ann that I would be late
I said that I would be late

UNIT 45

Reported speech (1)

no commas

a   Study this example situation:

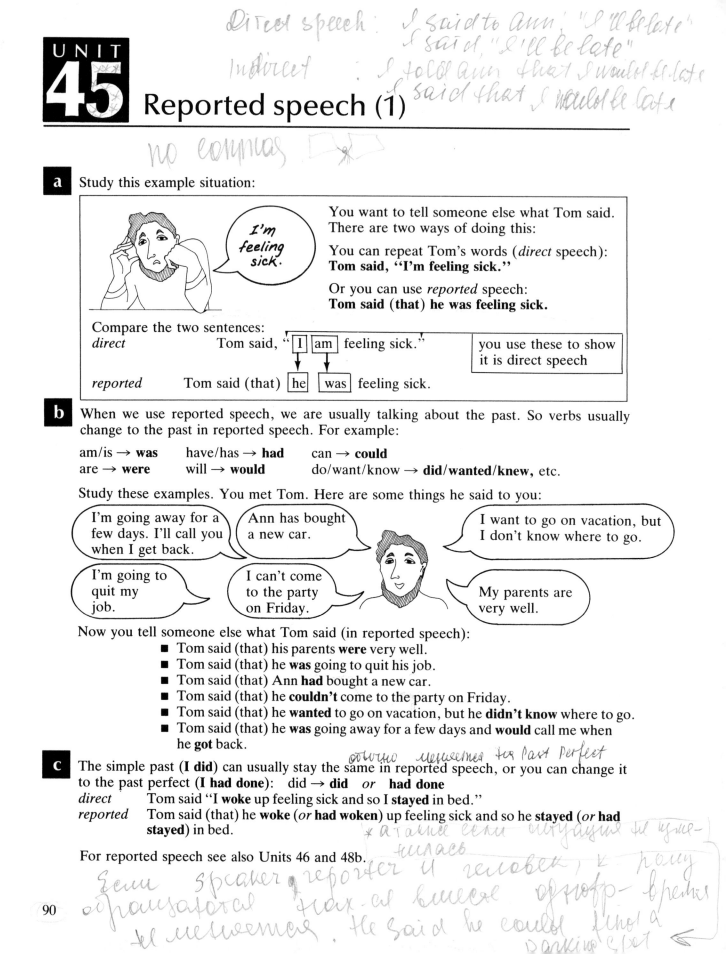

> *I'm feeling sick.*

You want to tell someone else what Tom said.
There are two ways of doing this:

You can repeat Tom's words (*direct* speech):
Tom said, "I'm feeling sick."

Or you can use *reported* speech:
Tom said (that) he was feeling sick.

Compare the two sentences:
direct   Tom said, " I am feeling sick." | you use these to show it is direct speech |

reported   Tom said (that) he was feeling sick.

b

When we use reported speech, we are usually talking about the past. So verbs usually change to the past in reported speech. For example:

am/is → **was**   have/has → **had**   can → **could**
are → **were**   will → **would**   do/want/know → **did/wanted/knew,** etc.

Study these examples. You met Tom. Here are some things he said to you:

> I'm going away for a few days. I'll call you when I get back.

> Ann has bought a new car.

> I want to go on vacation, but I don't know where to go.

> I'm going to quit my job.

> I can't come to the party on Friday.

> My parents are very well.

Now you tell someone else what Tom said (in reported speech):

- Tom said (that) his parents **were** very well.
- Tom said (that) he **was** going to quit his job.
- Tom said (that) Ann **had** bought a new car.
- Tom said (that) he **couldn't** come to the party on Friday.
- Tom said (that) he **wanted** to go on vacation, but he **didn't know** where to go.
- Tom said (that) he **was** going away for a few days and **would** call me when he **got** back.

c

The simple past (**I did**) can usually stay the same in reported speech, or you can change it to the past perfect (**I had done**):   did → **did**   *or*   **had done**
direct   Tom said "I **woke** up feeling sick and so I **stayed** in bed."
reported   Tom said (that) he **woke** (*or* **had woken**) up feeling sick and so he **stayed** (*or* **had stayed**) in bed.

For reported speech see also Units 46 and 48b.

90

Direct → Reported: this → that
these → those
here → there
now → then
at that time
yet → already, then
today → that day
must → must
tomorrow – the next day

UNIT 45 Exercises

45.1 *Yesterday you ran into a friend of yours, Helen. Helen told you a lot of things. Here are some of the things she said to you:*

> 1. I'm thinking of going to live in France.

> 2. My father is in the hospital.

> 3. Sue and Jim are getting married next month.

> 4. I haven't seen Bill for a while.

> 5. I've been playing tennis a lot lately.

> 6. Barbara has had a baby.

> 7. I don't know what Fred is doing.

> 8. I hardly ever go out (these) days.

> 9. I work 14 hours a day.

> 10. I'll tell Jim I saw you.

> 11. You can come and stay with me if you (are) ever in Toronto.

> 12. Tom had an accident last week, but he wasn't injured.

> 13. I saw Jack at a party a few months ago, and he seemed fine.

Later that day you tell another friend what Helen said. Use reported speech.

1. *Helen said that she was thinking of going to live in France.*
2. Helen said that *he father was*
3. ....
4. ....
5. ....
6. ....
7. *She didn't know what Fred was doing*
8. ....
9. ....
10. *She would tell Jim she saw me*
11. ....
12. ....
13. ....

45.2 *In this exercise someone says something to you that is the opposite of what they said before. You have to answer* **I thought you said . . .**

Example: "That restaurant is expensive." *"I thought you said it wasn't expensive."*

1. "Ann is coming to the party." "I thought you said she ...."
2. "Bill passed his exam." "I thought you said ...."
3. "Ann likes Bill." "I thought ...."
4. "I've got many friends." "I thought you said you ...... *you hadn't got many* ...." friends
5. "Jack and Karen are going to get married." " ...."
6. "Tom works very hard." " ...."
7. "I want to be rich and famous." " ...."
8. "I'll be here next week." " ...."
9. "I can afford a vacation this year." " ...."

last night → previous night
next week → following week, week after
still → at that time, then (+exceptions)

UNIT 46 Reported speech (2)

a It is not always necessary to change the verb when you use reported speech. If you are reporting something and you feel that it is still true, you do not need to change the tense of the verb:

direct   Tom said, "New York **is** bigger than London."
reported Tom said (that) New York **is** (*or* **was**) bigger than London.
direct   Ann said, "I **want** to go to Turkey next year."
reported Ann said (that) she **wants** (*or* **wanted**) to go to Turkey next year.

Notice that it is also correct to change the verb into the *past*.
But you *must* use a past tense when there is a difference between what was said and what is really true. Study this example situation:

> You met Ann. She said, "**Jim is sick.**" *(direct speech)*
> Later that day you see Jim playing tennis and looking fine. You say:
> "I'm surprised to see you playing tennis, Jim. Ann said that you **were** sick."
> (*not* that you are sick, because he isn't sick)

Must, might, could, would, should, and **ought** stay the same in reported speech. **May** in direct speech normally changes to **might** in reported speech.

b **Say** and **tell**
If you say *who* you are talking to, use **tell**:
    ■ Tom **told me** (that) he didn't like Brian. (*not* Tom said me . . .)
Otherwise use **say**:
    ■ Tom **said** (that) he didn't like Brian. (*not* Tom told (that) he . . .)
Also: you can't say "Tom told about his trip to Mexico." You have to say:
    ■ Tom told **us** (*or* **me/them/Ann**, etc.) about his trip to Mexico.
If you don't say who he told, you have to say:
    ■ Tom **talked** (*or* **spoke**) about his trip to Mexico. (*but not* said about)

c We also use the *infinitive* (**to do/to stay**, etc.) in reported speech, especially with **tell** and **ask** (for orders and requests):

direct   "**Stay** in bed for a few days," the doctor said to me.
reported The doctor **told me to stay** in bed for a few days.
direct   "**Don't shout**," I said to Jim.
reported **I told Jim not to shout**.
direct   "Please **don't tell** anyone what happened," Ann said to me.
reported Ann **asked me not to tell** anyone what (had) happened.
direct   "**Can you open** the door for me, Tom?" Ann asked.
reported Ann **asked Tom to open** the door for her.

Said is also possible with the infinitive:
    ■ The doctor **said to stay** in bed for a few days. (*but not* said me)

UNIT 46   Exercises

46.1 *Write what you would say in these situations.*

Example: Ann says, "I'm tired." Five minutes later she says, "Let's play tennis." What do you say? *You said you were tired.*...

1. Your friend says, "I'm hungry," so you go to a restaurant. When you get there he says, "I don't want to eat." What do you say?   "You said ...."
2. Tom tells you, "Ann has gone away." Later that day you meet her. What do you say? "Tom told ...."
3. George said, "I don't smoke." A few days later you see him smoking a cigarette. What do you say to him?   "You said ...."
4. You arranged to meet Jack. He said, "I won't be late." At last he arrives – 20 minutes late. What do you say?   "You ...."
5. Sue said, "I can't come to the party tonight." That night you see her at the party. What do you say to her?   " ...."
6. Ann says, "I'm working tomorrow evening." Later that day she says, "Let's go out tomorrow evening." What do you say?   " ...."

46.2 *Now complete these sentences with **said, told,** or **talked.***

Example: Tom ...*said*........ that he didn't like Brian.

1. Jack .... me that he was enjoying his new job.
2. Amy .... it was a nice restaurant, but I didn't like it very much.
3. The doctor .... that I would have to rest for at least a week.
4. Mrs. Taylor .... us she wouldn't be able to come to the next meeting.
5. Ann .... Tom that she was going away.
6. George couldn't help me. He .... to ask Jack.
7. At the meeting the director .... about the problems facing the company.
8. Jill .... us all about her trip to Japan.

46.3 *Now read each sentence and write a new sentence with the same meaning.*

Examples: "Listen carefully," he said to us. He told *us to listen carefully.*...............
"Don't wait for me if I'm late," Ann said.
Ann said *not to wait for her if she was late.*...............................

1. "Eat more fruit and vegetables," the doctor said.
   The doctor said ....
2. "Read the instructions before you use the machine," he said to me.
   He told ....
3. "Shut the door but don't lock it," she said to us.
   She told ....
4. "Can you speak more slowly? I can't understand," he said to me.
   He asked .... because ....
5. "Don't come before 6:00," I said to her.
   I told ....

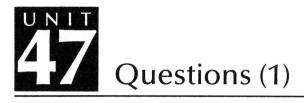

UNIT 47 Questions (1)

a We usually make questions by changing the word order: we put the *auxiliary verb (AV)* before the *subject (S)*: S + AV   AV + S

it	is	→	is	it?	**Is it** raining?
you	can	→	can	you?	When **can you** come and see us?
Tom	has	→	has	Tom?	Where **has Tom** gone?

We make questions with the verb **be** in the same way:

they were   → were they?   **Were they** surprised?

b In *simple present* questions use **do/does**:

- **Do you like** music? (*not* like you)   ■ **Do you have** a light?
- Where **does Jack live**? (*not* where lives Jack)

In *simple past* questions use **did**:

- When **did they get** married? (*not* when got they)
- Why **did Ann sell** her car? (*not* why sold Ann)
- **Did you have** a good time?

But be careful with **who/what/which** questions. If **who/what/which** is the *subject* of the sentence, do not use **do/does/did**. Compare:

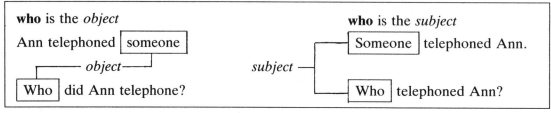

In these examples **who/what/which** is the *subject*:

- **Who wants** something to eat? (*not* who does want)
- **Who invented** the steam engine? (*not* who did invent)
- **What happened** to you last night? (*not* what did happen)
- **Which switch operates** this machine? (*not* which switch does operate)

c We use negative questions especially:

To show surprise:

- **Didn't you hear** the bell? I rang it four times.

In exclamations:

- **Doesn't that dress** look nice! (= that dress looks nice)

When we expect the listener to agree with us:

- "**Haven't we met** somewhere before?" "Yes, I think we have."

Notice the meaning of **yes** and **no** in answers to negative questions:

- **Didn't Dave pass** his exams? ┌─**Yes.** (= Yes, he passed them.)
                                   └─**No.** (= No, he didn't pass them.)

Note the word order in negative questions with **Why . . . ?**:

- **Why didn't you lock** the door? (*not* why you didn't lock)
- **Why don't we go** out to eat? (*not* why we don't go)
- **Why can't you help** me? (*not* why you can't help me)
- **Why wasn't Mary invited** to the party? (*not* why Mary wasn't)

94

UNIT 47   Exercises

47.1   *Ask questions about Ed and Liz.*

Example: (Ed and Liz / be / married?) *Are Ed and Liz married?* "Yes, they are."

1. (where / Ed and Liz live?) .... "In Detroit."
2. (how long / they / be / married?) .... "15 years."
3. (what / Liz do for a living?) .... "She's a math teacher."
4. (she / like being a teacher?) .... "Yes, she does."
5. (what / Ed do for a living?) .... "He's a police officer."
6. (he / enjoy his job?) .... "Yes, very much."
7. (he / arrest anyone yesterday?) .... "No."
8. (they / have / a car?) .... "Yes."
9. (when / they / buy it?) .... "A year ago."
10. (they / go / on vacation next summer?) .... "Yes."
11. (where / they / go?) .... "To Florida."

47.2   *This time make questions with* **who** *or* **what**.

Examples: "Somebody hit me."   "Who *hit you* ....?"
   "I hit somebody."   "Who *did you hit* ....?"

1. "Something happened."   "What ....?"
2. "Someone lives in that house."   "Who ....?"
3. "Somebody gave me this key."   "Who ....?"
4. "Henry gave me something."   "What ....?"
5. "Tom meets someone every day."   "Who ....?"
6. "I fell over something."   "What ....?"
7. "Something fell on the floor."   "What ....?"
8. "This word means something."   "What ....?"

47.3   *Make negative questions. Each time you are surprised.*

Example: "We won't see Ann this evening." "Oh! (she / not / come to the party tonight?)"
   Isn't she coming to the party tonight? ....

1. "I hope we don't meet Brian tonight."   "Why? (you / not / like him?)"   ....
2. "I'll have to borrow some money."   "Why? (you / not / have / any?)"   ....
3. "Don't go and see that movie."   "Why? (it / not / be / good?)"   ....

47.4   *Make negative questions with "Why . . . ?"*

Examples: (I didn't lock the door.) *Why didn't you lock the door?* ....
   (Mary wasn't invited to the party.) *Why wasn't Mary invited to the party?*

1. (I don't like George.)   ....you ....?
2. (Jim wasn't at work today.)   Why ....?
3. (I'm not ready yet.)   Why ....?
4. (Sue doesn't eat fruit.)   ....?
5. (Maria can't come to the meeting.)   ....?

95

UNIT 48 Questions (2) (Do you know where...?/He asked me where...)

a When we ask people for information, we sometimes begin our question with **Do you know...?** or **Could you tell me...?**. If you begin a question in this way, the word order is different from the word order in a simple question:

> Compare: Where has Tom gone? *(simple question)*
>
> **Do you know** where **Tom has** gone?

When the question (**Where has Tom gone?**) is part of a bigger sentence (**Do you know...**), it loses the normal question word order. Compare:

- When **will Ann arrive**?   Do you have any idea when **Ann will arrive**?
- What time **is it**?   Could you tell me what time **it is**?
- Why **are you laughing**?   Tell us why **you are laughing**.

Be careful with **do/does/did** questions:

- When **does the movie begin**?   Do you know when **the movie begins**?
- Why **did Ann leave** early?   I wonder why **Ann left** early.

Use **if** or **whether** when there is no other question word:

- Did he see you?   Do you know **if** (or **whether**) he saw you?

b The same changes in word order happen in *reported* questions:

direct   The police officer said to us, "Where | **are you going** | ?"

reported   The police officer asked us where | **we were going** | .

direct   Tom said, "What time | **do the banks close** | ?"

reported   Tom wanted to know what time | **the banks closed** | .

In reported questions the verb usually changes to the past (**were, closed**). For more information about this see Unit 45.

Now study these examples. Here are some questions you were asked at a job interview:

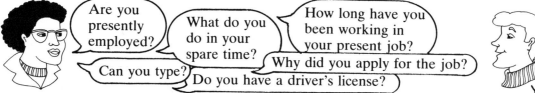

Are you presently employed?

What do you do in your spare time?

How long have you been working in your present job?

Can you type?

Why did you apply for the job?

Do you have a driver's license?

You

Now you tell a friend (in reported speech) what the interviewer asked you:

- She asked (me) if **I was** presently employed.
- She asked whether (*or* if) **I had** a driver's license.
- She wanted to know whether (*or* if) **I could** type.
- She wanted to know how long **I had been** working in my present job.
- She asked (me) what **I did** in my spare time.
- She asked (me) why **I had applied** for the job. (*or* why **I applied**)

UNIT 48 Exercises

48.1 *Make a new sentence from these questions.*

Example: Where has Tom gone? Do you know *where Tom has gone.* ....?

1. Where is the post office? Could you tell me ....?
2. What does this word mean? Do you know ....?
3. What time is it? I wonder ....
4. Where did you park your car? Can't you remember ....?
5. Is Ann coming to the meeting? I don't know ....
6. Where does Jack live? Do you have any idea ....?
7. What time did he leave? Do you know ....?
8. Where can I change some money? Could you tell me ....?
9. What qualifications do I need? I want to know ....
10. Why didn't Mary come to the party? I don't know ....
11. How much does it cost to park here? Do you know ....?

48.2 *You are making a phone call. You want to speak to Sue, but she isn't there. Someone else answers the phone. You want to know three things: (1)* **Where has she gone?** *(2)* **When will she be back?** *and (3)* **Did she go out alone?** *Complete the conversation:*

1. "Do you know ....?" "Sorry. I have no idea."
2. "Never mind. I don't suppose you know .... " "No, I'm afraid I don't."
3. "One more thing. Do you happen to know ....?" "I'm afraid I didn't see her go out."

48.3 *You have been away for a while and have just come back to your hometown. You meet Jerry, a friend of yours. He asks you lots of questions:*

1. How are you?
2. How long have you been back?
3. What are you doing now?
4. Where are you living?
5. Are you glad to be back?
6. Are you going away again?
7. Why did you come back?
8. Do you still smoke?
9. Can you come to dinner on Friday?

Now you tell another friend what Jerry asked you. Use reported speech.

1. *He asked me how I was.* ....
2. He asked me ....
3. He asked ....
4. He ....
5. ....
6. ....
7. ....
8. ....
9. ....

97

UNIT 49 Auxiliary verbs in short answers/ questions, etc.: **So/Neither am I**, etc.

a

| **Can** you swim? | I **have** lost my key. | He **might** not come. |

In these sentences **can, have,** and **might** are *auxiliary* (= helping) verbs.
We often use auxiliary verbs when we don't want to repeat something:
- "Are you working tomorrow?" "Yes, I **am**." (= I am working tomorrow)
- He could lend us the money, but he **won't**. (= he won't lend us the money)

Use **do/does/did** for simple present and past short answers:
- "Does he smoke?" "He **did**, but he **doesn't** anymore."

b We use auxiliary verbs in short questions:
- "It rained every day during our vacation." "**Did** it?"
- "Ann isn't feeling very well today." "Oh, **isn't** she?"
- "I've just seen Tom." "Oh, **have** you? How is he?"

These short questions (**Did it?, isn't she?, have you?**) are not real questions. We use them to show polite interest in what someone has said, and they help to keep the conversation going.

Sometimes we use short questions to show surprise:
- "Jim and Sue are getting married." "**Are they?** Really?"

c We also use auxiliary verbs with **so** and **neither**:
- "I'm feeling tired." "**So am I.**" (= I am feeling tired too)
- "I never read newspapers." "**Neither do I.**" (= I never read them either)

Note the word order after **so** and **neither** (*verb* before *subject*):
- I passed the exam and **so did Tom**. (*not* so Tom did)

Nor can be used instead of **neither**:
- "I can't remember her name." "**Nor** can I. / **Neither** can I."

Not . . . either can be used instead of **neither** and **nor**:
- "I don't have any money." "**Neither** do I." *or* "I don't **either**."

d **I think so / hope so,** etc.
We use **so** in this way after a number of verbs, especially **think, hope, guess, suppose,** and **I'm afraid**:
- "Is she Canadian?" "**I think so.**"
- "Will Eric come?" "**I guess so.**"
- "Has Ann been invited to the party?" "**I suppose so.**"

The negative form depends on the verb:

I think so	– **I don't think so**
I hope so / I'm afraid so	– **I hope not/I'm afraid not**
I guess	– **I guess not**
I suppose so	– **I don't suppose so** *or* **I suppose not**

- "Is she Italian?" "**I don't think so.**"
- "Is it going to rain?" "**I hope not.** (*not* I don't hope so)
- "Are you going to drive in this snowstorm?" "**I guess not.**"

UNIT 49 Exercises

49.1 *You are talking to someone. Answer him or her in the way shown.*

Examples: I'm hungry.   *Are you? I'm not.*
I'm not tired.   *Aren't you? I am.*

1. I like Brian.   ....
2. I can't ride a horse.   ....
3. I have plenty of friends.   ....
4. I didn't enjoy the movie very much.   ....
5. I'd get married if I were Tom.   ....
6. I don't like living in the city.   ....
7. I'm not going to have anything to eat.   ....
8. I've never been to Korea.   ....
9. I thought the exam was easy.   ....

49.2 *You are talking to a friend. You both have the same ideas, taste, etc. Use* **So . . .** *or* **Neither . . .** *each time.*

Examples: I'm feeling tired.   *So am I.*   I don't like eggs.   *Neither do I.*

1. I need a vacation.   ....
2. I don't like milk.   ....
3. I couldn't get up this morning.   ....
   ....
4. I'd love a cup of tea.   ....
5. I've never been to Africa.   ....

6. I was sick yesterday.   ....
7. I should smoke less.   ....
8. I spent the whole evening watching
   television.   ....
9. I didn't know that Ann was in the
   hospital.   ....

49.3 *You are B in each conversation. Read the information in parentheses (. . .), then answer with* **I think so, I hope not,** *etc.*

Example: (You hate rain.)   A: Is it going to rain?   B: (hope)   *I hope not.*

1. (You need more money quickly.)
   A: Do you think you'll get a raise soon?   B: (hope)   ....
2. (You think Tom will probably get the job he applied for.)
   A: Do you think Tom will get the job?   B: (guess)   ....
3. (You're not sure whether Jill is married – probably not.)
   A: Is Jill married?   B: (think)   ....
4. (You don't have any money.)
   A: Can you lend me some money?   B: (afraid)   ....
5. (Your friend's sister has been badly injured in an accident.)
   A: Is she badly injured?   B: (afraid)   ....
6. (Ann normally works every day, Monday to Friday – tomorrow is Wednesday.)
   A: Is Ann working tomorrow?   B: (guess)   ....
7. (You're in a hurry to catch your train – it's important that you don't miss it.)
   A: Do you think we're going to miss the train?   B: (hope)   ....
8. (You're not sure, but the concert probably begins at 7:30.)
   A: Does the concert begin at 7:30?   B: (think)   ....

UNIT 50 Tag questions (are you? doesn't he?, etc.)

a

| You're not working late, **are you?**   It was a good film, **wasn't it?** |

Are you? and **wasn't it?** are *tag questions* (= mini-questions that we put on the end of a sentence). In tag questions we use the auxiliary verb (see Unit 49). For the present and past use **do/does/did:**   They came by car, **didn't they?**

b

Normally we use a positive tag question with a negative sentence:

| *negative sentence* + *positive tag* |
| Tom **won't** be late,   **will he?** |
| They **don't** like us,   **do they?** |
| That **isn't** George over there,   **is it?** |

And normally we use a negative tag question with a positive sentence:

| *positive sentence* +   *negative tag* |
| Ann **will** be here soon,   **won't she?** |
| Tom **should** pass his exam,   **shouldn't he?** |
| They **were** very angry,   **weren't they?** |

Notice the meaning of **yes** and **no** in answers to tag questions:

- You're not going to work today, are you? $\begin{cases} \textbf{Yes.} \ (= \text{I am going}) \\ \textbf{No.} \ \ (= \text{I'm not going}) \end{cases}$

c

The meaning of a tag question depends on how you say it. If the voice goes *down*, you aren't really asking a question; you are only asking the other person to agree with you:
- "Tom doesn't look very well today, does he?"   "No, he looks awful."
- She's very attractive. She has beautiful eyes, doesn't she?

But if the voice goes *up*, it is a real question:
- "You haven't seen Ann today, have you?"   "No, I'm afraid I haven't."
  (= Have you seen Ann today?)

We often use a *negative sentence + positive tag* to ask for things or information, or to ask someone to do something. The voice goes up at the end of the tag in sentences like these:
- "You wouldn't have a cigarette, would you?"   "Yes, here you are."
- "You couldn't do me a favor, could you?"   "It depends what it is."
- "You don't know where Ann is, do you?"   "Sorry, I have no idea."

d

After **Let's** . . . the tag question is **shall we?:**
- **Let's** go out for a walk, **shall we?**

After the imperative (**do/don't do** something) the tag is **will you?:**
- **Open** the door, **will you?**

Notice that we say **aren't I?** (= am I not):
- I'm late, **aren't I?**

UNIT 50 Exercises

50.1 *Put a tag question on the end of each sentence.*

Examples: Tom won't be late, *will he* ... ?   They were very angry, *weren't they* . ?

1. Ann's on vacation, ...?
2. You weren't listening, ...?
3. Sue doesn't like onions, ...?
4. Jack applied for the job, ...?
5. You have a camera, ...?
6. You can type, ...?
7. He won't mind if I leave early, ...?
8. Tom could help you, ...?
9. There are a lot of people here, ...?
10. Let's have dinner, ...?
11. This isn't very interesting, ...?
12. I'm too fat, ...?
13. You wouldn't tell anyone, ...?
14. I shouldn't have gotten angry, ...?
15. They had to go home, ...?
16. He'd never seen you before, ...?

50.2 *Read the situation and then write a sentence with a tag question. In each example you are asking your listener to agree with you.*

Example: You are with a friend outside a restaurant. You are looking at the prices. It's very expensive. What do you say?   *It's very expensive, isn't it ?* ....

1. You look out of the window. It's a beautiful day. What do you say to your friend?   It's
   ....
2. You've just come out of a movie theater with your friend. You both really enjoyed the movie. You thought it was great. What do you say?   The movie ....
3. Bob's hair is much shorter. Clearly he has had his hair cut. What do you say to him?
   You ....
4. You are shopping. You are trying on a jacket. You look in the mirror: it doesn't look very good. What do you say to your friend?   It ....
5. You are talking about Bill. You know that Bill works very hard. Everyone knows this. What do you say about Bill?   Bill ....

50.3 *In these situations you are asking people for information, asking people to do things, etc. Make sentences like those in section c.*

Example: You want a cigarette. Perhaps Tom has one. Ask him.
   Tom, you don't have a cigarette, do you ? ....

1. Jack is just going out. You want him to get some stamps. Ask him.
   Jack, you couldn't ....
2. You're looking for Ann. Perhaps Alan knows where she is. Ask him.
   Alan, you ....
3. You need some paper. Perhaps Tom has some. Ask him.
   Tom, ...
4. Ann has a car, and you don't want to walk home. You want her to give you a lift. Ask her.   Ann, ...
5. You're looking for your purse. Perhaps Liz has seen it. Ask her.
   ....

101

Verb + ing

a

stop	enjoy	dislike	admit	consider	miss
finish	mind	imagine	deny	involve	postpone
delay	suggest	regret	avoid	practice	risk

If these verbs are followed by another verb, the structure is usually *verb* + **-ing**:

- **Stop** talk**ing!**
- I'll do the shopping when I've **finished** clean**ing** the apartment.
- I don't **miss** work**ing** late every night.
- Have you ever **considered** go**ing** to live in another country?
- I can't **imagine** George rid**ing** a motorcycle.
- When I'm on vacation, I **enjoy not** hav**ing** to get up early.

The following expressions also take **-ing**:

give up (= stop)	**keep** *or* **keep on** (= do something
go on (= continue)	continuously or repeatedly)
put off (= postpone)	

- Are you going to **give up** smok**ing?**
- He **kept (on)** interrupt**ing** me while I was speaking.

Note the *passive* form (**being done** / **being seen** / **being told**, etc.):

- I don't mind **being told** what to do.

You cannot normally use the *infinitive* (**to do** / **to dance**, etc.) after these verbs and expressions:

- I **enjoy** danc**ing.** (*not* to dance)
- Would you **mind** clos**ing** the door? (*not* to close)
- Jill **suggested** go**ing** to the movies. (*not* to go)

b When you are talking about finished actions, you can also say **having done** / **having stolen**, etc. But it is not necessary to use this form. You can also use the simple **-ing** form for finished actions:

- He admitted **stealing** (*or* **having stolen**) the money.
- They now regret **getting** (*or* **having gotten**) married.

c With some of the verbs in this unit (especially **admit, deny, regret,** and **suggest**) you can also use a **that . . .** structure:

- He **denied that** he had stolen the money. (*or* **denied** stealing)
- Jill **suggested that** we go to the movies. (*or* **suggested** going)

For **suggest** see also Unit 33.

For verbs + **-ing** see also Units 54 and 55.

UNIT 51 Exercises

51.1 *Complete the sentences with these verbs:*

try	steal	meet	look	write	make	be run
wash	~~play~~	eat	splash	go	drive	take

Example: Do you miss ..*playing*..... tennis every afternoon?

1. Could you please stop .... so much noise?
2. I don't enjoy .... letters.
3. Does your job involve .... a lot of people?
4. I considered .... the job, but in the end I decided against it.
5. If you use the shower, try and avoid .... water on the floor.
6. Jack gave up .... to be an actor and decided to become a teacher.
7. Have you finished .... your hair yet?
8. The phone rang while Ann was having dinner. She didn't answer it; she just went on
....
9. She admitted .... the car but denied .... it dangerously.
10. Why do you keep on .... at me like that?
11. They had to postpone .... away because their son was sick.
12. If you cross the street without looking, you risk .... over by a car.

51.2 *Read each sentence and write a second sentence with the same meaning. Begin your sentence in the way shown.*

Examples: Do you have to travel in your job? Does your job involve **traveling**........ ?
He is sorry now that he didn't study harder when he was in college.
He now regrets *not studying harder when he was in college.*......

1. Maybe I'll go out this evening. I wouldn't mind ....
2. Are you sorry you didn't take the job? Do you regret ....?
3. Why don't you go away tomorrow instead of today?
Why don't you put off .... until .... ?
4. It's not a good idea to travel during the rush hour.
It's better to avoid ....
5. Could you turn the radio down, please? Would you mind ....?
6. The driver of the car said it was true that he didn't have a license.
The driver of the car admitted ....
7. Sue said, "Let's have fish for dinner." Sue suggested ....

51.3 *Now make your own sentences. Complete each sentence using -ing.*

Example: I really enjoy ...*going for long walks in the country.*...................

1. On weekends I enjoy ....
2. I dislike ....
3. I often regret ....
4. Learning English involves ....
5. I think people should stop ....

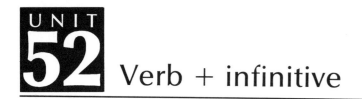

UNIT 52 Verb + infinitive

a

agree	offer	decide	appear	forget	need
refuse	attempt	plan	seem	learn (how)	mean
promise	manage	arrange	pretend	dare	intend
threaten	fail	hope	afford	tend	

If these verbs are followed by another verb, the structure is usually *verb + infinitive:*
- It was late, so we **decided to take** a taxi home.
- I like George, but I think he **tends to talk** too much.
- How old were you when you **learned to drive**? (*or* learned how to drive)
- They **agreed to lend** me some money when I told them the position I was in.
- He's lazy. He **needs to work** harder.
- I'm sorry. I **didn't mean to hurt** you.

Note these examples with the *negative* **not to . . .** :
- We **decided not to go** out because of the weather.
- She **pretended not to see** me as she passed me on the street.

With other important verbs you cannot use the infinitive. For example **think** and **suggest**:
- Are you **thinking of buying** a car? (*not* thinking to buy)
- Jill **suggested going** to the movies (*not* suggested to go)

b There is a *continuous* infinitive (**to be doing**) and a *perfect* infinitive (**to have done**). We use these especially after **seem, appear,** and **pretend**:
- I **pretended to be reading**. (= I pretended that I was reading)
- You **seem to have lost** weight. (= it seems that you have lost weight)
- He **appears to be doing** a good job. (= it appears that he is doing a good job)

c **Dare**: You can say **dare to do** or **dare do** (without **to**):
- I wouldn't **dare to ask** him. *or* I wouldn't **dare ask** him.

d After the following verbs you can use a question word (**what/where/how**, etc.) + infinitive:

ask   decide   know   remember   forget   explain   understand

We **asked**	how	to get	to the station.
Have you **decided**	where	to go	for your vacation?
Tom **explained** (to me)	how	to change	the tire on the car.
I don't **know**	whether	to go	to the party or not.

Also: **show/tell/ask** someone **what/how/where** to do something:
- Can someone **show me how to change** the film in this camera?
- Ask Jack. He'll **tell you what to do**.

For verbs + infinitive see also Units 53–55.

UNIT 52   Exercises

52.1   *Complete each sentence with an appropriate verb.*

Example: Don't forget ..*to mail*........ the letter I gave you.

1. Tom refused ...*to lend*..... me any money.
2. Jill has decided not ....*to drive*...... a car.
3. The thief got into the house because I forgot ......*to close*... the window.
4. There was a lot of traffic but we managed ....*to get*........ to the airport in time.
5. One day I'd like to learn .....*to pilot*...... an airplane.
6. I shouted to him. He pretended not ......*hear*.......... me, but I'm sure he did.
7. Why hasn't Sue arrived yet? She promised not ....*to be*.......... late.
8. Our neighbor threatened .....*to call*..... the police if we didn't stop making noise.
9. Ann offered .... care of our children while we were out.
10. The teacher was very strict. Nobody dared .... during his class.
11. I don't need .... to the meeting, do I?
12. Oh no! I meant ......*to buy*... some eggs, but I forgot.

52.2   *This time make sentences with* **seem** *and* **appear.**

Examples: Is he waiting for someone?   He appears *to be waiting for someone.*
             Has she lost weight?   She seems *to have lost weight.*

1. Is Tom worried about something?   He seems ...*to be worried*...............
2. Does Ann like Jack?   She appears ...*to like*...............
3. Is that man looking for something? He appears ...*to be looking*...............
4. Has that car broken down?   It seems ...*to have broken down*...............
5. Have they gone out?   They appear ...*to have gone out*...............

52.3   *Now use the structure in section d. Complete each sentence using* **what** *or* **how** *with one of the following verbs:*   do   say   ~~get~~   use   ride   cook

Example: Do you know *how to get*... to John's house?

1. Have you decided *what* *to cook* for dinner this evening?
2. Can you show me .... the washing machine?
3. Do you know .... if there's a fire in the building?
4. You'll never forget .... a bicycle once you've learned.
5. I was really astonished. I didn't know ....

52.4   *Now make your own sentences. Complete each sentence with the infinitive.*

Example: This evening I plan *to go to the theater.*...................

1. Not many people can afford ...*to buy a new car*...
2. I would like to learn ...*how to fly that airplane*...
3. One day I hope ...*to be able to afford to buy a new home*...
4. I wouldn't dare ...*to think of doing this*...
5. Sometimes I tend ...*to exaggerate*...
6. I intend ...*to stay at your place on Sunday*...

105

Verb + object + infinitive

a

want	ask	expect	help	would like	would prefer

There are two possible structures after these verbs:

verb + infinitive	*verb + object + infinitive*
I **asked to see** the manager.	I **asked Tom to help** me.
We **expected to be** late.	We **expected him to be** late.
He **would like to come.**	He **would like me to come.**

After **help** you can use the verb with or without **to**:
- Can somebody **help me (to) move** this table?

Be especially careful with **want**. Do not say "want that . . .":
- Everyone **wanted him to win** the race. (*not* wanted that he won)
- Do you **want me to come** early? (*not* want that I come)

b

tell	remind	force	enable	persuade
order	warn	invite	teach (how)	get (= persuade)

These verbs have the structure *verb + object + infinitive*:
- **Remind me to call** Ann tomorrow.
- He **warned me not to touch** anything.
- Who **taught you (how) to drive**?
- I **got Jack to fix** my car.

Here is an example in the *passive*:
- **I was warned not to touch** anything.

You cannot use **suggest** with the infinitive (see also Unit 33c):
- Tom **suggested that I buy** a car. (*not* Tom suggested me to buy)

c

advise	encourage	allow	permit

There are two possible structures after these verbs. Compare:

verb + -ing (without an object)	*verb + object + infinitive*
I wouldn't **advise staying** at that hotel.	I wouldn't **advise you to stay** at that hotel.
They don't **allow smoking** in this building. (= Smoking is not allowed in this building.)	They don't **allow you to smoke** in this building. (= You are not **allowed to smoke** in this building.)

d **Make** and **let**

These verbs have the structure *verb + base form* (**do, read**, etc.):
- Hot weather **makes me feel** uncomfortable. (= causes me to feel)
- I only did it because they **made me do it**. (= forced me to do it)
- She wouldn't **let me read** the letter. (= allow me to read)

Do not use **to** after **make** and **let**:
- They **made me do** it. (*not* they made me to do it)
- Tom **let** me **drive** his car yesterday. (*not* Tom let me to drive)

But in the *passive* **make** is followed by **to** (**to do**):
- I only did it because **I was made to do** it.

UNIT 53 Exercises

53.1 *Read each sentence and write a second sentence from the words given.*

Example: Jill didn't have any money.
she / want / Ann / lend her some   *She wanted Ann to lend her some...*

1. Tom's parents were disappointed when he decided to leave home.
   they / want / Tom / stay with them   ....
2. Please don't tell anyone that I'm leaving my job.
   I / not / want / anyone / know   ....
3. There's a football game next Saturday between Army and Navy.
   you / want / Navy / win?   ....
4. Unfortunately someone had told Sue that I was going to visit her.
   I / want / it / be a surprise   ....

53.2 *Read the sentence and then write a second sentence with the same meaning. Each time begin in the way shown.*

Examples: "Don't touch anything," the man said to me.
The man told *me not to touch anything.*..
My father said I could use his car.   My father allowed *me to use his car.*....

1. "Don't forget to mail the letter," Jack said to me.
   Jack reminded   ....
2. She told me that it would be best if I told the police about the accident.
   She advised   ....
3. I told you that you shouldn't tell him anything.   I warned   ....
4. I was surprised that it rained.   I didn't expect   ....
5. "Would you like to have dinner with me?" Tom said to Ann.
   Tom invited   ....
6. At first I didn't want to play tennis, but Jane persuaded me.
   Jane persuaded   ....
7. The sudden noise caused me to jump.   The sudden noise made   ....
8. If you have a car, you are able to travel around more easily.
   Having a car enables   ....
9. She wouldn't allow me to read the letter.   She wouldn't let   ....

53.3 *Put the verb in the right form: -ing (doing), base form (do), or infinitive (to do).*

Example: Mr. Thomas doesn't allow *smoking*........(smoke) in his office.

1. Mr. Thomas doesn't let anyone ....*smoke*......... (smoke) in his office.
2. I don't know Jack, but I'd like ....*to meet*...... (meet) him.
3. Where would you advise me ......*to go*...... (go) for my vacation?
4. I don't advise ....*eating*...... (eat) in that restaurant. The food's awful.
5. The film was very sad. It made me ......*cry*......... (cry).
6. Linda's parents have always encouraged her ....*to study*.... (study) hard.
7. We were kept at the police station for an hour and then allowed ....*to*............ (go).
8. Everybody helped ......*to clean*....(clean) up after the party.

UNIT 54 Infinitive or -ing? (1) – like, would like, etc.

a

like	hate	can't bear
love	can't stand	

After these verbs and expressions you can use **-ing** or the *infinitive*.

- I **like** gett**ing** up early.   *or*   I **like to get** up early.
- I **love** meet**ing** people.   *or*   I **love to meet** people.
- I **hate** wash**ing** dishes.   *or*   I **hate to wash** dishes.
- She **can't stand** be**ing** alone.   *or*   She **can't stand to be** alone.
- He **can't bear** liv**ing** in the city.   *or*   He **can't bear to live** in the city.

b

dislike	enjoy	mind

After these verbs you can use **-ing**, but not the infinitive:

- I **enjoy** be**ing** alone. (*not* enjoy to be)
- Why do you **dislike living** here? (*not* dislike to live)
- Tom doesn't **mind** work**ing** at night. (*not* mind to work)

c **Would like** is followed by the *infinitive:*

- I **would like to be** rich.
- **Would you like to come** to a party?

Notice the difference in meaning between **I like** and **I would like. I would like** is a polite way of saying **I want**. Compare:

- I **like** play**ing** tennis.   *or*   I **like to play** tennis. (= enjoy it in general)
- I **would like to play** tennis today. (= I want to play)

See also Unit 30.

We also use the *infinitive* after **would love/hate/prefer**:

- **Would** you **prefer to have** dinner now or later?
- **I'd love to be able** to travel around the world.

d You can also say "I would like **to have done** something" (= I regret that I didn't or couldn't do something):

- It's too bad we didn't visit Tom. I **would like to have seen** him again.
- We**'d like to have taken** a vacation, but we didn't have enough money.

The same structure is possible after **would love/hate/prefer**:

- Poor Jim! I **would hate to have been** in his position.
- **I'd love to have gone** to the party, but it was impossible.
- We went to a restaurant but I didn't enjoy it. **I'd prefer to have eaten** at home.

UNIT 54   Exercises

54.1 *Answer these questions using the verbs given.*

Examples: Why don't you ever fly? (hate) *I hate flying.. or.. I hate to fly.*
Why does Tom go to the movies so often? (like) *He likes going to the movies.*
or He likes to go to the movies.

1. Why do you always wear a hat? (like)   I .... *like to* ....
2. Why does Ann watch television so often? (enjoy)   She .... *enjoys watching* ....
3. Why don't you ever stay up late? (not/like) ....
4. Why does Jack take so many pictures? (like) ....
5. Why don't you work in the evenings? (hate) ....

54.2 *Put the verb into the correct form: -ing or infinitive. Sometimes either form is possible.*

Examples: I enjoy .... *being* .... (be) alone.
Would you like .... *to come* ..... (come) to a party?

1. Do you mind .... *travelling* .... (travel) such a long distance to work every day?
2. Beth loves .. *to cooking* .. (cook), but she hates .... *to ~ up* .... (clean) up.
3. I don't like that house. I would hate .... *living to live* (live) there.
4. Do you like .. *to ~ ing* ...... (drive)?
5. When I have to catch a plane, I'm always worried about missing it. So I like ....
   (get) to the airport in plenty of time.
6. I very much enjoy .. *listening* ...... (listen) to classical music.
7. I would love .... *to come* .... (come) to your wedding, but it just isn't possible.
8. Sometime I'd like .... *to* .... (learn) to play the guitar.

54.3 *Make your own sentences. Say whether you like or don't like the things in parentheses*
(. . .). *Choose one of these verbs for each of your sentences:*

(don't) like   **love**   **hate**   **enjoy**   **don't mind**

Example: (reading) *I like reading very much.*..

1. (playing cards)   I ....
2. (learning languages) ....
3. (visiting museums) ....
4. (lying on the beach in the sun) ....
5. (shopping) ....

54.4 *Now write sentences like those in section c.*

Example: It's too bad I couldn't go to the wedding. (like)
I would like to have gone to the wedding...

1. It's too bad I didn't meet Ann. (love)   I would love ....
2. I'm glad I didn't lose my watch. (hate)   I ....
3. I'm glad I wasn't alone. (not/like) ....
4. It's too bad I couldn't go by train. (prefer) ....
5. It's too bad I didn't see the movie. (like) ....

UNIT 55

Infinitive or -ing? (2) – begin, start, continue, remember, try

a

| begin | start | continue |

These verbs can usually be followed by **-ing** or the *infinitive*. So you can say:

- The baby **began crying**. *or* The baby **began to cry**.
- It has **started raining**. *or* It has **started to rain**.
- He **continued working** after his illness. *or* He **continued to work** after his illness.

b

Remember to do and **remember doing**

You **remember to do** something *before* you do it. **Remember to do something** is the opposite of "forget to do something":

- I **remembered to lock** the door before I left, but I forgot to shut the windows. (= I remembered to lock the door, and then I locked it)
- Please **remember to mail** the letter. (= don't forget to mail it)

You **remember doing** something *after* you do it. **I remember doing something** = I did something, and now I remember it:

- I clearly **remember locking** the door before I left. (= I locked it, and now I clearly remember this)
- He could **remember driving** along the road just before the accident happened, but he couldn't remember the accident itself.

c

Try to do and **try doing**

Try to do = attempt to do, make an effort to do:

- I was very tired. I **tried to keep** my eyes open, but I couldn't.
- Please **try to be** quiet when you come home. Everyone will be asleep.

Try doing

Try also means "do something as an experiment or test":

- **Try** some of this tea – maybe you'll like it. (= drink some of it to see if you like it)
- We **tried** every hotel in town, but they were all full. (= we went to every hotel to see if they had a room)

If **try** (with this meaning) is followed by a verb, we say **try -ing**:

- "I can't find anywhere to live." "Why don't you **try putting** an ad in the newspaper?" (= do this to see if it helps you to find a place to live)
- I've got a terrible headache. I **tried taking** an aspirin, but it didn't help. (= I took an aspirin to see if it would stop my headache)

UNIT 55 Exercises

55.1 *Here is some information about Tom when he was a child.*

1. He was in the hospital when he was four.
2. He went to Los Angeles when he was eight.
3. He fell into the lake.
4. He cried on his first day of school.
5. He said he wanted to be a doctor.
6. He was bitten by a dog.

He can still remember 1, 2, and 4. But he can't remember 3, 5, and 6. Make sentences beginning **He can remember . . .** *or* **He can't remember . . . .**

1. *He can remember being in the hospital.*   4. ....
2. ....   5. ....
3. ....   6. ....

55.2 *Your friend has some problems, and you have to be helpful. For each problem write a question with* **try.**

Example: I can't find a place to live. (put an ad in the newspaper)
Have you tried putting an ad in the newspaper ?

1. My electric shaver is not working. (change the batteries)
   Have you tried ....
2. I can't contact Fred. He's not at home. (phone him at work)
   Have you ....
3. I'm having trouble sleeping at night. (take sleeping pills)
   Have ....
4. The television picture isn't very good. (move the antenna)
   ....

55.3 *Put the verb into the correct form:* **-ing** *or the infinitive. (Sometimes either form is possible.)*

Examples: Please remember ....*to mail*......... (mail) this letter.
Look! It's started *to snow or snowing*.. (snow).

1. A: You lent me some money a few months ago.
   B: Did I? That's strange. I don't remember .... (lend) you any money.
2. We tried ....(put) the fire out, but we were unsuccessful. We had to call the fire department.
3. When you see Liz, remember .... (give) her my regards, will you?
4. Someone must have taken my bag. I clearly remember .... (leave) it by the window and now it's gone.
5. When she saw what had happened, she began .... (laugh) loudly.
6. Sue needed some money. She tried .... (ask) Gerry, but he couldn't help her.
7. He tried .... (reach) the shelf, but he wasn't tall enough.
8. "Did you remember ....(call) Ann?" "Oh no, I completely forgot."
9. I asked them to be quiet, but they continued .... (make) a lot of noise.

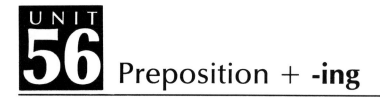

UNIT 56 Preposition + -ing

a If a verb comes after a preposition (**in/at/with/about**, etc.), the verb ends in **-ing**. Study these examples:

Are you interested	**in**	work**ing**	for us?
I'm not very good	**at**	learn**ing**	languages.
I'm fed up	**with**	study**ing.**	
The children are excited	**about**	go**ing**	on vacation.
What are the advantages	**of**	hav**ing**	a car?
This knife is only	**for**	cutt**ing**	bread.
John went to work	**in spite of**	feel**ing**	sick. (See Unit 104.)
I bought a new bicycle	**instead of**	go**ing**	away on vacation.

b You can use **-ing** with **before** and **after**:
- **Before** go**ing** out I called Ann.

You can also say: "**Before I went** out I . . . "
- What did you do **after** leav**ing** school?

You can also say: " . . . **after you left** school?"

c You can use **by -ing** to say *how* something happened:
- They got into the house **by** break**ing** a kitchen window and climbing in.
- You can improve your English **by** do**ing** a lot of reading.

d You can use **-ing** after **without**:
- Jim left **without** finish**ing** his dinner.
- She ran five miles **without** stopp**ing**.
- He climbed through the window **without** anybody see**ing** him. (*or* . . . **without** being seen.)
- She needs to work **without** people disturb**ing** her. (*or* . . . **without** be**ing** disturbed.)
- It's nice to go on vacation **without** hav**ing** to worry about money.

e **To** is a part of the *infinitive*. For example:
- They decided **to go** out.   ■ I want **to play** tennis.

But **to** is also a *preposition*. For example:
- Tom went **to** Hawaii.   ■ I prefer cities **to** the country.
- He gave the book **to** Mary.   ■ I'm looking forward **to** the weekend.

If a preposition is followed by a verb, the verb ends in **-ing** (see section **a**). So, if **to** is a preposition and it is followed by a verb, you must say **to -ing**. For example:
- I prefer bicycling **to** driv**ing**. (*not* to drive)
- I'm looking forward **to** see**ing** Sue again. (*not* to see)

For **be/get used to -ing** see Unit 59.

112

UNIT 56   Exercises

56.1 *Read the sentence and then write a second sentence with the same meaning. Each time begin in the way shown.*

Example: I called Ann, and then I went out.   After *I called Ann, I went out.*

1. Liz went to bed, but first she had a hot drink.
   Before ....
2. The plane took off, and soon afterward it crashed.
   Soon after ....
3. We didn't eat at home. We went to a restaurant instead.
   Instead of ....
4. You put people's lives in danger if you drive dangerously.
   You put people's lives in danger by ....
5. He hurt his leg, but he managed to win the race.
   In spite of ....
6. Bill is a very good cook.   Bill is very good at ....
7. I don't intend to lend her any money.   I have no intention of ....
8. George exercised more, and lost 10 pounds.
   By ....
9. She was angry with me because I was late.   She was angry with me for ....
10. Jane thinks that doing nothing is better than working.
    Jane prefers doing nothing to ....

56.2 *Read each situation and then write a sentence with* **without -ing**.

Examples: She ran five miles. She didn't stop. *She ran five miles without stopping.*
He left the room. Nobody saw him. *He left the room without anyone seeing him.*

1. He translated the article. He didn't use a dictionary.
   He translated the article without ....
2. Look right and left before you cross the street.
   Don't cross ....
3. She got married. Nobody knew about it.   She ....

56.3 *This time read each situation and write a sentence with* **look forward to**.

Examples: You are going on vacation next week. How do you feel about this?
I'm looking forward to going on vacation.
She is taking an exam next week. She's not very happy about it. How does she feel about it? *She is not looking forward to taking the exam.*

1. A good friend is coming to visit you soon, so you will see him/her again. How do you feel about this?   I'm ....
2. You are going to the dentist. You don't like visits to the dentist. How do you feel about it? ....
3. Carol is a student. She hates school, and she is graduating next summer. How does she feel about this?   She ....

UNIT 57 Verb + preposition + -ing

a Many verbs have the structure *verb (V) + preposition (P) + object*. For example, **talk about**:

- We **talked about the problem.** (**the problem** is the *object*)

If the object is another verb, it ends in **-ing**:

- We talked about go**ing** to Japan. (*V + P +* **-ing**)

Here are some more verbs that have the structure *V + P +* **-ing**:

succeed in	Has Tom succeeded	**in**	find**ing** a job yet?
feel like*	I don't feel	**like**	go**ing** out tonight.
think about/of	Are you thinking	**of/about**	buy**ing** a house?
dream of	I've always dreamed	**of**	be**ing** rich.
approve/disapprove of	She doesn't approve	**of**	smok**ing.**
look forward to	I'm looking forward	**to**	meet**ing** her.
insist on	She insisted	**on**	buy**ing** me a cup of coffee.
decide against	We decided	**against**	mov**ing** to California.
apologize for	He apologized	**for**	keep**ing** me waiting.

***I feel like doing** = I'd like to do, I'm in the mood to do.

We say "apologize **to** someone for something":

- He apologized **to me** for keeping me waiting. (*not* he apologized me)

With some of these verbs you can also use the structure *verb + preposition + someone + -ing*. For example:

- We are all looking forward to **Peter** (*or* **Peter's**) com**ing** home.
- She doesn't approve of **her son** (*or* **son's**) stay**ing** out late at night.
- They insisted on **me** (*or* **my**) stay**ing** with them. (See also Unit 33c.)

b These verbs have the structure *verb + object + preposition + -ing*:

accuse	They accused	me	**of**	tell**ing** lies.
suspect	Did they suspect	the man	**of**	be**ing** a spy?
congratulate	I congratulated	Ann	**on**	pass**ing** the exam.
prevent	What prevented	him	**from**	com**ing** to the wedding?
stop	We stopped	everyone	**from**	leav**ing** the building.
thank	I thanked	her	**for**	be**ing** so helpful.
forgive	Please forgive	me	**for**	not writ**ing** to you.
warn	They warned	us	**against**	buy**ing** the car.

Some of these verbs are often used in the passive:

- **I was accused of** tell**ing** lies.
- **Was the man suspected of** be**ing** a spy?
- **We were warned against** buy**ing** it.

114

UNIT 57 Exercises

57.1 *Write the correct preposition and put the verb into the correct form. Use the verb in parentheses (. . .) at the end of each sentence.*

Example: Jack insisted ..*on going*.......... out by himself. (go)

1. After a long time we eventually succeeded ....*in*.................... an apartment. (find)
2. I've been thinking ...*of* ..*about*...... for a new job. (look)
3. His parents didn't approve .....*of*............... his ....*staying*...... out so late. (stay)
4. I wonder what prevented him .... to the party. (come)
5. I'm getting hungry. I'm looking forward .... dinner. (have)
6. I don't feel ....today. (study)
7. Forgive me .... you, but I must ask you a question. (interrupt)
8. The arrested man was suspected .... into a house. (break)
9. Have you ever thought .... married? (get)
10. I've always dreamed .... on a small island in the Pacific. (live)
11. The cold water didn't stop her .... for a swim. (go)
12. Have you ever been accused .... a crime? (commit)
13. She apologized .... so rude to me. (be)
14. We have decided .*against*........... a new car because we can't afford one. (buy)

57.2 *Change direct speech into reported speech. Begin each of your sentences in the way shown.*

Example: "It was nice of you to help me. Thanks very much." (George said to you)
George thanked *me for helping him.*..................................

1. "I'll drive you to the airport. I insist." (Tom said to Ann)
Tom insisted ....
2. "I hear you passed your exams. Congratulations!" (Jim said to you)
Jim congratulated ...*me on passing my exams*
3. "It was nice of you to visit me. Thank you." (Mrs. Richmond said to Sue)
Mrs. Richmond thanked ....*Sue for visiting him*
4. "Don't stay at the hotel near the airport." (I said to Jack)
I warned .....*Jack against staying*
5. "I'm sorry I didn't call you earlier." (Margaret said to you)
Margaret apologized .*to me for*.... not ....*calling me earlier*
6. "You didn't pay attention to what I said." (The teacher said to the boy)
The teacher accused .....*the boy of not paying attention*

57.3 *Now write some sentences about yourself. Use* **-ing.**

Example: Today I don't feel like ..*going out.*...................................

1. This evening I feel like ....
2. I'm looking forward to ....
3. I'm thinking of ....
4. I would never dream of ....

UNIT 58 Expressions + -ing

When these expressions are followed by a verb, the verb ends in **-ing**:

It's no use . . .
- **It's no use worrying** about it. There's nothing you can do.
- **It's no use trying** to persuade me. You won't succeed.

There's no point in . . .
- **There's no point in buying** a car if you don't want to drive it.
- **There was no point in waiting,** so we went.

It's (not) worth . . .
- My house is only a short walk from here. **It's not worth taking** a taxi.
- It was so late when we got home, **it wasn't worth going** to bed.

You can say: "a book is **worth reading** / a movie is **worth seeing**, etc.:
- Do you think **this book is worth reading**?
- You should go and see that movie. **It's** really **worth seeing**.

(Have) difficulty/trouble . . .
- I had **difficulty finding** a place to live. (*not* to find)
- Did you have any **trouble getting** a visa?
- People often have great **difficulty reading** my writing.

Remember that we say "difficulty" (*not* difficulties) and "trouble" (*not* troubles):
- I'm sure you'll have no **difficulty/trouble** passing the exam.

You can also say "(have) difficulty **in** -ing":
- He's shy. He has difficulty **in** talking to people he doesn't know well.

A waste of money/time . . .
- It's **a waste of time reading** that book. It's trash.
- It's **a waste of money buying** things you don't need.

Spend/waste (time) . . .
- **I spent hours trying** to repair the clock.
- **I waste a lot of time daydreaming.**

Go -ing

We use **go -ing** for a number of activities (especially sports):

go shopping	**go swimming**	**go skiing**	**go fishing**
go climbing	**go sailing**	**go riding**	**go sightseeing**

- How often do you **go swimming**?
- I'm **going skiing** next year.
- I have to **go shopping** this morning.
- I've never **been sailing.**

For "I've **been** / I've **gone**" see Unit 13d.

116

UNIT 58 Exercises

58.1 Join two sentences to make one sentence.

Examples: Don't worry about it. It's no use. *It's no use worrying about it.*
Don't get a taxi. It's not worth it. *It's not worth getting a taxi.*

1. Don't try to escape. It's no use. It's no use ....
2. Don't smoke. It's a waste of money. It's a waste ....
3. Don't ask Tom to help you. It's no use. It's no use ....
4. Don't hurry. It's not worth it. It's not worth ....
5. Don't study if you're feeling tired. There's no point.
   There's no point ....
6. Don't read newspapers. It's a waste of time. It's a ....
7. Don't get angry. It's not worth it. It's not ....
8. Don't work if you don't need the money. There's no point.
   There's no ....

58.2 Make sentences with **worth**.

Examples: I'd read this book if I were you. This book *is worth reading.*
I wouldn't read this book if I were you. This book *isn't worth reading.*

1. I'd visit the museum if I were you. The museum ....
2. I wouldn't repair those shoes if I were you. Those shoes ....
3. I wouldn't keep these old clothes if I were you. These old clothes ....
4. I'd consider the plan if I were you. The plan ....

58.3 Read these sentences and each time write a new sentence using **difficulty** or **trouble**.

Example: I found a place to live but it was difficult.
I had difficulty finding a place to live. or I had trouble finding a place to live.

1. Tom finds it difficult to meet people. Tom has ....
2. She found a job. This wasn't difficult. She had no ....
3. It won't be difficult to get a ticket for the concert.
   You won't have any ....
4. I find it difficult to understand him when he speaks quickly.
   I have ....

58.4 Complete these sentences with one of the following expressions. Put the verb into the correct form.   **go skiing   go shopping   go swimming   ~~go sailing~~   go riding**

1. Barry lives by the water and he has a boat, so he often *goes sailing.*
2. There's plenty of snow in the mountains, so we'll be able to ....
3. It was a very hot day, so we .... in the river.
4. Margaret likes horses. She often ....
5. The stores are closed now. It's too late to ....

UNIT 59 Be/get used to something (I'm used to . . .)

a Study this example situation:

WELCOME KEEP LEFT
TENIR A VOTRE GAUCHE
LINKS FAHREN

Jane is American, but she has lived in Britain for three years. When she first drove a car in Britain, she found it very difficult because she had to drive on the left instead of on the right. Driving on the left was strange and difficult for her because:

She **wasn't used to it.**
She **wasn't used to driving** on the left.

After a lot of practice, driving on the left became less strange:
- She **got used to driving** on the left.

Now after three years, driving on the left is no problem for her:
- She **is used to driving** on the left.

I'm used to something = it is not new or strange for me:
- Frank lives alone. He doesn't mind this because he has lived alone for 15 years. So he **is used to it.** He **is used to living** alone.
- My new shoes felt a bit strange at first because I **wasn't used to them.**
- Our new apartment is on a very busy street. I suppose we'll **get used to the noise,** but at the moment we find it very annoying.
- Fred has a new job. He has to get up much earlier – at 6:30. He finds this difficult right now because he **isn't used to getting** up so early.

b Notice that we say "She **is used to** driving on the left." (*not* she is used to drive). **To** in be/get used to is a *preposition*, not a part of the infinitive (see also Unit 56e). So we say:
- Frank is used **to living** alone. (*not* is used to live)
- Jane had to get used **to driving** on the left. (*not* get used to drive)

c Do not confuse **I am used to doing** (be/get used to) with **I used to do.** They are different in structure and in meaning.

I am used to (doing) something = something isn't strange for me:
- I am used **to the weather** in this country.
- I am used **to driving** on the left because I've lived in Britain a long time.

I used to do something means only that I did something regularly in the *past* (see Unit 24). You can't use this structure for the *present*. The structure is "I **used** to do" (*not* I **am** used to do):
- Nowadays I usually stay in bed until late. But when I had a job, **I used to get** up early.

UNIT 59   Exercises

59.1 *Read these situations and write three sentences with* **used to,** *as in the example.*

Example: Jane is American. She went to Britain and found driving on the left difficult.
   a) At first she *wasn't used to driving on the left.*
   b) But soon she *got used to driving on the left.*
   c) Now she has no problems. She *is used to driving on the left.*

1. Juan came to the United States from Spain. In Spain he always had dinner late in the evening. But in the United States dinner was at 6:00. Juan found this strange at first.
   a) At first he wasn't ....
   b) But after some time he got ....
   c) Now he finds it normal. He ....
2. Diana is a nurse. She started working nights two years ago. At first she found it strange and didn't like it.
   a) At first she ....
   b) But after a while ....
   c) Now she doesn't mind it at all. ....

59.2 *Read these situations and write a sentence with* **be/get used to.**

Example: Frank lives alone. He doesn't mind this. He has always lived alone.
         (he/ used / live / alone)   *He is used to living alone.*

1. Ron sleeps on the floor. He doesn't mind this. He has always slept on the floor.
   (he / used / sleep / on the floor)   He ....
2. Sue moved from a big house to a much smaller one. What did she have to get used to?
   (she had / used / live / in a smaller house)   She had ....
3. Jack once went to the Middle East. It was too hot for him.
   (he / not / used / the heat)   ....
4. Bill doesn't have any money. He doesn't find this unusual because he has never had any money. (he / used / have / no money)   ....
5. Amy is going to live in your country. What will she have to get used to? *(Write your own answer!)*   She'll have to ....

59.3 *Put the verb into the correct form,* **-ing** *or infinitive (***I am used to doing** *or* **I used to do***). If necessary, study Unit 24 first.*

Examples: Jane had to get used to ....*driving*......... on the left.   (drive)
         Bill used to .... in good shape. Now he's in terrible shape.   (be)

1. When I was a child, I used to .... swimming every day.   (go)
2. It took me a long time to get used to .... contact lenses.   (wear)
3. There used to .... a cafe on this corner, but it was torn down.   (be)
4. I'm the boss. I'm not used to .... told what to do.   (be)
5. You'll have to get used to .... less if you want to lose weight.   (eat)
6. I used to .... Ann, but now she gets on my nerves.   (like)
7. Ron got tired very quickly. He wasn't used to .... so fast.   (run)
8. Tom used to .... to a lot of parties when he was a student.   (go)

UNIT 60 Infinitive of purpose – "I went out to mail a letter." So that . . .

a We use the *infinitive* (**to do**) to talk about the purpose of doing something (= why someone does something):

- I went out **to mail** a letter. (= because I wanted to mail a letter)
- She called me **to invite** me to a party.
- We shouted **to warn** everyone of the danger.

We also use the *infinitive* to talk about the purpose of something, or why someone has/wants/needs something:

- This wall is **to keep** people out of the garden.
- The President has two bodyguards **to protect** him.
- I need a bottle opener **to open** this bottle.

You can also use **in order to** (**do** something):

- We shouted **in order to warn** everyone of the danger.

Do *not* use **for** in these sentences:

- I'm going to Mexico **to learn** Spanish. (*not* for learning / for to learn)

b We also use the *infinitive* to say what can be done or must be done with something:

- It's usually difficult to find **a place to park** downtown. (= a place where you can park)
- Do you have a lot of **work to do** this evening? (= work that you must do)
- Would you like **something to eat?**
- There were no **chairs to sit on**, so we all had to sit on the floor.
- She is lonely. She has **nobody to talk to.**

We also say **time/opportunity/chance/money/energy to do something**:

- They gave me some **money to buy** some food. (*not* for buying)
- Did you have **time to answer** all the questions on the exam?
- These days I don't get **much chance to watch** television. I'm too busy.
- Do you have **much opportunity to speak** English? (= much chance to speak)

c Sometimes you have to use **so that** (*not the infinitive*) to talk about the purpose of doing something. We use **so that**:

i) when the purpose is *negative* (**so that . . . won't/wouldn't . . .**):

- I hurried **so that I wouldn't** be late. (= because I didn't want to be late)
- Leave early **so that** you **won't** (or **don't**) miss the bus.

ii) with **can** and **could** (**so that . . . can/could . . .**):

- He's learning English **so that** he **can** study in the United States.
- We moved to London **so that** we **could** visit our friends more often.

iii) when one person does something so that *another* person does something else:

- I gave him my address **so that he** could contact me.
- **He** wore glasses and a false beard **so that nobody** would recognize him.

120

UNIT 60 Exercises

60.1 *Use the words in parentheses (. . .) to answer these questions.*

Example: Why did you go out? (buy some bread) *I went out to buy some bread.*

1. Why do you have to go to the bank? (change some money)
   I have to go ....
2. Why did she knock on your door? (wake me up)   She ....
3. Why are you saving money? (go to Europe)   I ....
4. Why is Ron going into the hospital? (have an operation)

   ....
5. Why are you wearing two sweaters? (keep warm)   ....
6. Why did you go to the police station? (report that my car had been stolen)

   ....

60.2 *Complete these sentences with an appropriate verb.*

Examples: The President has a bodyguard ..*to protect*.. him.
             There were no chairs .....*to sit*........ on, so we all had to sit on the floor.

1. We are having a party .... Ann's birthday.
2. I didn't have enough time .... the newspaper today.
3. We have no furniture – not even a bed .... in.
4. I think I need some new clothes ....
5. Tom didn't have enough energy......................... the mountain.
6. There will be a meeting next week .... the problem.
7. I need a box .... these books in.
8. It's a shame we don't have any pictures .... on the wall.
9. I wish I had enough money .... a new car.
10. We're always busy at work. We don't get much chance......................... to each other.
11. I'd like to have the opportunity.........................to Europe.

60.3 *Write sentences with* **so that***.*

Examples: I hurried. I didn't want to be late. *I hurried so that I wouldn't be late.*
             I'll give you my number. I want you to be able to call me.
             I'll give you my number so that you can (or will be able to) call me.

1. We wore warm clothes. We didn't want to get cold.
   We wore ....
2. I spoke very slowly. I wanted the man to understand what I said.
   I ....
3. I whispered. I didn't want anyone to hear our conversation.
   .... no one ....
4. Please arrive early. We want to be able to start the meeting on time.
   Please arrive ....
5. She locked the door. She didn't want to be disturbed.

   ....
6. I slowed down. I wanted the car behind me to be able to pass me.

   ....

UNIT 61 Prefer and would rather

a Prefer to do and prefer doing

You can use "prefer **to do**" or "prefer **doing**" to say what you prefer in general.

- I don't like cities. **I prefer to live** (or **I prefer living**) in the country.

Study the difference in structure:

	I prefer	**(doing)**	something	**to (doing)**	something else
but:	I prefer	**to do**	something	**rather than (do)**	something else

- I **prefer** tea **to** coffee.
- Tom **prefers driving to traveling** by train.
- *but:* Tom **prefers to drive rather than travel** by train.
- I **prefer to live** in the country **rather than** (**live**) in a city.

Use **would prefer** to say what someone wants (to do) in a particular situation. You can say **would prefer to (do)** or **would prefer (do)ing**:

- "**Would** you **prefer** tea or coffee?" "Coffee, please."
- "Should we go by train?" "Well, **I'd prefer to go** by car." *or*
  "Well, **I'd prefer going** by car."

b

Would rather (do) = would prefer to do. After **would rather** we use the base form. Compare:

Should we go by train?	{ Well, **I'd prefer to go** by car.
	Well, **I'd rather go** by car. (*not* to go)

- "**Would** you **rather have** tea or coffee?" "Coffee, please."
- I'm tired. **I'd rather not go** out this evening, if you don't mind.
- "Do you want to go out this evening?" "**I'd rather not.**"

Note the structure:

I'd rather do something **than (do)** something else

- **I'd rather stay** at home **than go** to the movies.

c Would rather someone did something

When you want someone else to do something, you can say **I'd rather you did . . . /I'd rather he did . . .**, etc. We use the *past* in this structure, but the meaning is present or future, not past. Compare:

I'd rather **cook** dinner now.
I'd rather **you cooked** dinner now. (*not* I'd rather you cook)

- "Shall I stay here?" "Well, **I'd rather you came** with us."
- **I'd rather you didn't tell** anyone what I said.
- "Do you mind if I smoke?" "**I'd rather you didn't.**"

UNIT 61   Exercises

61.1 *Make sentences using "**I prefer** (something) **to** (something else)."*

Example: (driving / traveling by train)   *I prefer driving to traveling by train.*

1. (San Francisco / Los Angeles)   I prefer San Francisco ....
2. (calling people / writing letters)   I prefer ....
3. (going to the movies / watching movies on TV)
   I ....

*Now rewrite sentences 2 and 3 using the structure "**I prefer to do** (something) . . . ."*
Example: *I prefer to drive rather than travel by train.*..

4. (2) I prefer to call   ....
5. (3) I   ....

61.2 *Answer these questions using **I'd rather** . . . . Use the words in parentheses (. . .) for your answers.*

Example: Would you like to walk? (go by car)   *I'd rather go by car.*........................

1. Would you like to play tennis? (go for a swim)   I'd ....
2. Do you want to watch television? (read a book)   I ....
3. Shall we leave now? (wait for a few minutes)   ....
4. Would you like to go to a restaurant? (eat at home)   ....
5. Should we decide now? (think about it for a while)   ....

*Now make sentences using **I'd rather . . . than . . .** (see section b).*

Example: (walk / go by car)   I'd rather *walk than go by car.*..................................

6. (go for a swim / play tennis)   I'd rather...
7. (read a book / watch television)   I ....
8. (wait for a few minutes / leave now)   ....
9. (eat at home / go to a restaurant)   ....
10. (think about it for a while / decide now)   ....

61.3 *Use "**I'd rather you** (did something)." You are talking to a friend. You say you'll do something, but really you want your friend to do it.*

Example: I'll cook the dinner if you really want me to, but   *I'd rather you cooked it.*

1. I'll call Tom if you really want me to, but I'd rather   ....
2. I'll do the dishes if you really want me to, but   ....
3. I'll go to the bank if you really want me to, but   ....
4. I'll tell Ann what happened if you really want me to, but   ....

UNIT 62
Had better do something
It's time someone did something

a Had better do something

The meaning of **had better (I'd better)** is similar to **should. "I'd better do** something" = I should do something or it is advisable for me to do something; if I don't do this, something bad might happen:

- I have to meet Tom in ten minutes. **I'd better go** now or I'll be late.
- "Should I take an umbrella?" "Yes, you**'d better**. It might rain."
- We've almost run out of gas. We**'d better stop** at the next gas station to fill up.

The negative form is **had better not ('d better not)**:

- You don't look very well. You**'d better not go** to work today.
- "Are you going out tonight?" "**I'd better not**. I've got a lot of work to do."

The form is always "**had** better" (usually **'d better** in spoken English). We say **had** but the meaning is present or future, not past:

- **I'd better go** to the bank **this afternoon**.

Remember that **had better** is followed by the base form (*not* **to . . .**):

- It might rain. We**'d better take** an umbrella. (*not* better to take)

b It's time . . .

You can say "**it's time** (for someone) **to do** something":

- It's time **to go** home.
- It's time **for us to go** home.

There is another structure: **It's time someone did something:**

- It's nearly midnight. **It's time we went** home.

We use the *past* (**went**) after **It's time someone . . .** , but the meaning is present or future, not past:

- Why are you still in bed? **It's time you got** up. (*not* time you get up)

We use the structure **It's time someone did something** especially when we are complaining or criticizing, or when we think someone should have already done something:

- **It's time the children were** in bed. It's long past their bedtime.
- You've been wearing the same clothes for ages. **Isn't it time you bought** some new ones?
- I think **it's time the government did** something about pollution.

We also say $\left\{ \begin{array}{l} \text{"It's \textbf{high} time}\\ \text{"It's \textbf{about} time} \end{array} \right\}$ someone **did** something."

This makes the complaint or criticism stronger:

- You're very selfish. **It's high time you realized** that you're not the most important person in the world.
- **It's about time Jack did** some studying for his exams.

UNIT 62   Exercises

62.1 *Read each situation and write a sentence with* **had better.**

Examples: You're going out for a walk with Tom. You think you should take an umbrella
because it might rain. What do you say to Tom? *We'd better take an umbrella.*
Tom doesn't look very well. You don't think he should go to work today. What
do you say to Tom?   *You'd better not go to work today.*

1. Mary suddenly begins to feel sick. You think she should sit down. What do you say to
   her? ....
2. You and Tom are going to the theater. You've just missed the bus. You think you should
   take a taxi. What do you say to Tom?   We ....
3. Ann wants to play the piano late at night. You know that she'll wake up the people next
   door. What do you say to Ann?   ....
4. You and Sue are going to a restaurant for a meal. You think you should make a
   reservation because the restaurant might be crowded. What do you say to Sue?

   ....
5. Joe has just cut himself. You think he should put a Band-Aid on the cut. What do you say
   to him?   ....
6. You are going to take your car on your vacation. You think you should have the oil
   changed before you go. What do you say (to yourself)?   ....
7. You are by a river. It's a hot day and your friend suggests going for a swim. You don't
   think you should because the river looks dirty. What do you say?

   ....

62.2 *Write sentences with* **It's time someone did something**.

Examples: You think the children should be in bed. It's already 11:00.
   It's time the children were in bed. (or went to bed.)
   You think something should be done about the traffic problem downtown.
   It's (about) time something was done about the traffic problem downtown.

1. You think you should take a vacation because you haven't taken one in a very long time.
   It's time I   ....
2. You think Tom should write to his parents. He hasn't written to them for ages.
   It's time   ....
3. This room should be redecorated. It looks awful.
   It's ....
4. You're waiting for Ann. She is late. She should be here by now.

   ....
5. You're sitting on a plane waiting for it to take off. It's already five minutes late.

   ....
6. You feel very strongly that the government should stop spending money on weapons and
   should concentrate on raising the standard of living.

   ....
7. You think you should start getting dinner ready. It's nearly dinnertime already.

   ....
8. You haven't been to the dentist in almost a year. You should go every six months.

   ....

UNIT 63 See someone do and see someone doing

a Study this example situation:

Tom got into his car and drove away. You saw this. You can say:
- I **saw** Tom **get** into his car and **drive** away.

In this structure we use the *base form* (**get, drive**, etc.):

Someone **did** something.
I saw this. → I saw someone **do** something.

Remember that we use the *base form* (*not* **to**):
- I saw her **go** out. (*not* to go out)

b Now study this example situation:

Yesterday you saw Ann. She was waiting for a bus. You can say:
- I **saw** Ann **waiting** for a bus.

In this structure we use **-ing** (**waiting**):

Someone **was doing** something.
I saw this. → I saw someone **doing** something.

c Now study the difference in meaning between the two structures:

"I saw him **do** something" = he did something (*simple past*) and I saw this. I saw the complete action from beginning to end:
- He **fell** to the ground. I saw this. → I **saw** him **fall** to the ground.
- The accident **happened**. We saw this. → We **saw** the accident **happen**.

"I saw her **doing** something" = she was doing something (*past continuous*) and I saw this. I saw her when she was in the middle of doing something. This does not mean that I saw the complete action:
- **She was walking** along the street. I saw this when I drove past in my car. → I **saw** her **walking** along the street.

The difference is not always important. Sometimes you can use either form:
- I've never seen Tom **dance**.   *or*   I've never seen Tom **dancing**.

d We use these structures especially with **see** and **hear**, and also with **watch, listen to, feel**, and **notice**:
- I didn't **hear** you **come** in.
- He suddenly **felt** someone **touch** him on the shoulder.
- Did you **notice** anyone **go** out?
- I could **hear** it **raining**.
- The missing girls **were** last **seen playing** near the river.
- **Listen to** the birds **singing**!

After **smell** and **find** you can use the **-ing** structure only:
- Can you **smell** something **burning**?
- She **found** him **reading** her letters.

UNIT 63   Exercises

63.1   *Answer these questions, beginning in the way shown.*

Examples: "Does Tom ever dance?"   "I've never seen *him dance (or dancing)* "
"How do you know I came in late?"   "I heard *you come in late* "

1. "Does Liz ever smoke?"   "I've never seen ..... *her smoke* "
2. "How do you know the man took the money?"   "I saw ..... *him take the money* "
3. "Did Jack lock the door?"   "Yes, I heard ..... *him lock the door* "
4. "Did the bell ring?"   "I'm not sure. I didn't hear ..... *the bell ring* "
5. "How do you know Ann can play the piano?"   "I've heard ..... *her play the* "
6. "Did Bill trip over the dog?"   "Yes, I saw ..... *him trip over* "
7. "Did the girl fall into the river?"   "I didn't see ..... *her fall* "

63.2   *In each of these situations you and a friend saw, heard, or smelled something. This is what you said at the time:*

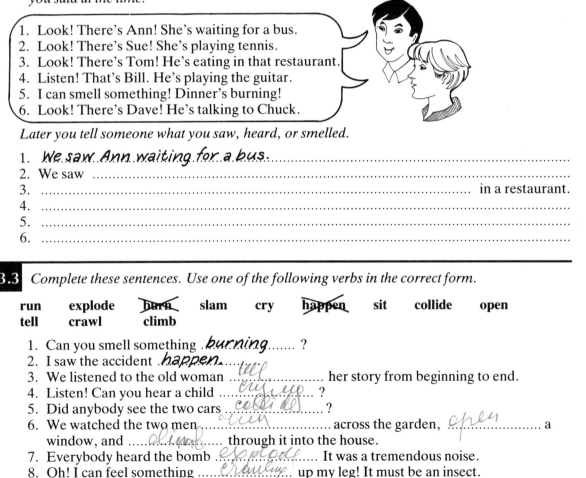

1. Look! There's Ann! She's waiting for a bus.
2. Look! There's Sue! She's playing tennis.
3. Look! There's Tom! He's eating in that restaurant.
4. Listen! That's Bill. He's playing the guitar.
5. I can smell something! Dinner's burning!
6. Look! There's Dave! He's talking to Chuck.

Later you tell someone what you saw, heard, or smelled.

1. *We saw Ann waiting for a bus.*
2. We saw ....
3. .... in a restaurant.
4. ....
5. ....
6. ....

63.3   *Complete these sentences. Use one of the following verbs in the correct form.*

run   explode   ~~burn~~   slam   cry   ~~happen~~   sit   collide   open
tell   crawl   climb

1. Can you smell something . *burning* ... ?
2. I saw the accident . *happen* .
3. We listened to the old woman ..... *tell* ..... her story from beginning to end.
4. Listen! Can you hear a child ..... *crying* ... ?
5. Did anybody see the two cars ..... *collide* ... ?
6. We watched the two men ..... *run* ..... across the garden, ... *open* ..... a window, and ..... *climb* ..... through it into the house.
7. Everybody heard the bomb ..... *explode* ..... It was a tremendous noise.
8. Oh! I can feel something ..... *crawling* ... up my leg! It must be an insect.
9. I heard someone ..... *slam* ..... the door in the middle of the night. It woke me up.
10. We couldn't find Tom at first. Finally we found him ..... *sitting* ... in the garden.

127

UNIT 64 -ing clauses – "**Feeling tired**, I went to bed early."

a A *clause* is a part of a sentence. Some sentences have two clauses:
- **Feeling tired**, I went to bed early.

In this sentence, "I went to bed early" is the *main clause*.
Feeling tired is the **-ing** *clause*.

b When two things happen at the same time, you can use **-ing** for one of the verbs. The main clause usually comes first:
- She was sitting in an armchair **reading** a book. (= she was sitting, and she was reading)
- I ran out of the house **shouting**. (= I was shouting when I ran out of the house)

We also use **-ing** when one action happens during another. Use **-ing** for the longer action. The longer action is the second part of the sentence.
- Jim hurt his arm **playing** tennis. (= while he was playing)
- I cut myself **shaving**. (= while I was shaving)

You can also use **-ing** after **while** or **when**:
- Jim hurt his arm **while playing** tennis. (= while he was playing)
- Be careful **when crossing** the street. (= when you are crossing)

c When one action happens before another action, you can use **having** (**done**) for the first action:
- **Having found** a hotel, they looked for somewhere to have dinner.
- **Having finished** our work, we went home.

You could also say **After -ing**:
- **After finishing** our work, we went home.

If the second action happens immediately after the first, you can use the simple **-ing** form (**doing** instead of **having done**):
- **Taking** a key out of his pocket, he opened the door.

These structures are used mainly in written English.

d You can also use an **-ing** clause to explain something or to say why someone did something. The **-ing** clause usually comes first:
- **Feeling** tired, I went to bed early. (= because I felt tired)
- **Being** unemployed, she doesn't have much money. (= because she is unemployed)
- **Not having** a car, she finds it difficult to get around. (= because she doesn't have a car)
- **Having** already **seen** the film twice, I didn't want to go to the movies. (= because I had already seen it twice)

These structures are used more in written than in spoken English.

UNIT 64 Exercises

64.1 *From each pair of sentences make one sentence using an* **-ing** *clause.*

Example: She was sitting in an armchair. She was reading a book.
She was sitting in an armchair reading a book.

1. Jill was lying on the bed. She was crying.   Jill was ....
2. I got home. I was feeling very tired.   I got ....
3. The old man was walking along the street. He was talking to himself.
   The old man ....

In these sentences one thing happens during another.

Example: Jim was playing tennis. He hurt his arm.   ....

4. Ann was watching television. She fell asleep.   Ann ....
5. The man slipped. He was getting off the bus.   The man ....
6. The girl was crossing the street. She was run over.
   The girl ....
7. The fire fighter was overcome by smoke. He was trying to put out the fire.
   The fire fighter ....

64.2 *This time make sentences beginning* **Having . . . .**

Example: We finished our work. We went home. *Having finished our work, we went home.*

1. We bought our tickets. Then we went into the theater.
   ....
2. They had dinner. Then they continued on their trip.
   ....
3. Sue did all her shopping. Then she went for a cup of coffee.
   ....

64.3 *Now make sentences beginning* **-ing** *or* **Not -ing** *(as in section d).*

Example: I felt tired. So I went to bed early. *Feeling tired, I went to bed early.*

1. I thought they might be hungry. So I offered them something to eat.
   Thinking ....
2. She is a foreigner. So she needs a visa to stay in this country.
   ....
3. I didn't know his address. So I couldn't contact him.
   Not ....
4. The man wasn't able to understand English. So he didn't know what I said.
   ....
5. She has traveled a lot. So she knows a lot about other countries.
   Having ....
6. We had spent nearly all our money. So we couldn't afford to stay in a hotel.
   ....

UNIT 65 Uncountable nouns (gold, music, advice, etc.)

Nouns can be *countable* or *uncountable*. For *countable* nouns see Unit 66.

a *Uncountable* nouns are, for example: **gold   music   blood   excitement**

Uncountable nouns are things we cannot count. They have no plural. You cannot say "musics," "bloods," or "excitements."

b Before uncountable nouns you can say **the/some/any/much/this/his**, etc.:
  the music   **some** gold   **much** excitement   **his** blood

But you cannot use **a/an** before an uncountable noun. So you cannot say "a music," "an excitement," or "a blood."

You can also use uncountable nouns alone, with no article (see Unit 70):
  ■ This ring is made of **gold**.   ■ **Blood** is red.

c Many nouns can be used as countable or as uncountable nouns. Usually there is a difference in meaning. For example:

paper   I bought **a paper.** (= a newspaper – *countable*)
       I bought **some paper.** (= material for writing on – *uncountable*)
hair   There's **a hair** in my soup! (= one single hair – *countable*)
       She has beautiful **hair.** (= hair on her head – *uncountable*)
experience   We had **many** interesting **experiences** on our vacation. (= things that
          happened to us – *countable*)
       You need **experience** for this job. (= knowledge of something because
          you have done it before – *uncountable*)

d Some nouns are usually uncountable in English but often countable in other languages. Here are the most important of these:

advice	bread	information	permission	traffic	weather
baggage	chaos	luggage	progress	travel	work
behavior	furniture	news	scenery	trouble	

These nouns are *uncountable*, so (i) you cannot use **a/an** before them; and (ii) they cannot be plural: ■ Tom gave me **some** good **advice.** (*not* some good advices)
         ■ Where are you going to put all your **furniture**? (*not* furnitures)
         ■ We don't have **much luggage** to carry. (*not* many luggages)
         ■ I'm afraid I have **some** bad **news.** (*not* a bad news)
Remember that **news** is not plural:
         ■ The news **is** very depressing today. (*not* The news are . . .)
Do not use **travel** to mean **trip/journey**:
         ■ We had **a good trip.** (*not* a good travel)
Note these pairs of countable (C) and uncountable (UNC) nouns:
         ■ I'm looking for **a job**. (C)   *but* I'm looking for **work.** (UNC)
         ■ What **a** beautiful **view**! (C)   *but* What beautiful **scenery**! (UNC)

UNIT 65   Exercises

65.1 *Which of the underlined parts of these sentences is right?*

Example: Sue was very helpful. She gave me some good advice/~~advices~~. ("advice" is right)

1. Margaret has very long black hair / hairs.
2. We had a very good weather / very good weather when we were on vacation.
3. Can I help you with your luggage / luggages?
4. I want something to read. I'm going to buy a / some paper.
5. I want to write some letters. I need a / some writing paper.
6. It's very difficult to find a work / job at the moment.
7. Bad news don't / doesn't make people happy.
8. Our travel / trip from Paris to Frankfurt by train was very interesting.
9. The apartment is empty. We don't have any furnitures / furniture yet.
10. When the fire alarm rang, there was a complete chaos / complete chaos.
11. Can I talk to you? I need an / some advice.
12. Do you have any experience / experiences in sales?

65.2 *Complete these sentences using these words:*

**progress   advice   hair   work   experience   ~~air~~   information   paper
permission**

Example: The room was very crowded. We had to open the windows for *(some) air.*

1. I don't think Ann will get the job. She hasn't got ....
2. They'll tell you all you want to know. They'll give you plenty of ....
3. You'll recognize Alan easily. He's got green ....
4. Carla's English has improved. She has made ....
5. I want to write down your address. Do you have .... ?
6. If you want to leave early, you have to ask for ....
7. George is unemployed at the moment. He is looking for ....
8. I didn't know what to do. So I asked Jack for ....

65.3 *Write what you would say in these situations. Each time begin in the way shown and use one of the words in section d of this unit.*

Example: Your friends have just arrived at the station. You can't see any suitcases or bags.
You say: Do you have *any luggage* ....?

1. You go into the tourist office. You want to know about places to see in the town. You
   say: I'd like ....
2. The weather is beautiful. You say: What ....!
3. You are a student. You want your teacher to advise you about which exams to take. You
   say: Can you give me ....?
4. You want to watch the news on television, but you don't know what time it is on. You ask
   your friend: What time ....?
5. You are standing at the top of a mountain. You can see a very long way. It is beautiful.
   You say: What ....!

UNIT 66 Countable nouns with **a/an** and **some**

Nouns can be *countable* or *uncountable*. For *uncountable* nouns see Unit 65.

a Countable nouns are, for example:

    dog   **umbrella**   **job**   **suggestion**   **girl**

Countable nouns are things we can count. We can make them plural:

    two dogs   **six** jobs   **some** girls   **many** suggestions

b Before singular countable nouns you can use **a/an**:

- That's **a** good suggestion.   ■ Do you need **an** umbrella?

You cannot use singular countable nouns alone (without **a/the/my**, etc.):

- I'm looking for **a** job. (*not* I'm looking for job)
- Be careful of **the** dog. (*not* Be careful of dog)
- I've got **a** headache.   ■ Would you like **a** cigarette?

For **a/an** and **the** see Unit 67.

c We often use **a/an** + noun when we say what something/someone is, or what something/someone is like:

- A dog is **an animal**.
- This is **a** really beautiful **house**.
- What **a** nice **dress!**
- Sue is **a** very nice **person**.
- Jack has **a** big **nose**.

Remember to use **a/an** for jobs:

- Tom's mother is **a doctor**. (*not* Tom's mother is doctor)
- I wouldn't like to be **an English teacher**.

In sentences like these, we use plural countable nouns alone (*not* with *some*):

- Tom's parents are **very nice people.**
  (*not* some very nice people)
- Ann has **blue eyes.**
- What **awful shoes!**
- Dogs are **animals.**
- Are most of your friends **students**?

d We also use **some** with plural countable nouns. **Some** = **a number of** / **a few of** (but we don't know or say exactly how many):

- I've seen **some** good **movies** lately.
- **Some friends** of mine are coming to stay for the weekend.

Do not use **some** when you are talking about things in general:

- I love **bananas**. (*not* some bananas)

Sometimes you can use **some** or leave it out:

- There are (**some**) eggs in the refrigerator if you're hungry.

For **some** and **any** see Unit 80.

e You have to use **some** when you mean *some, but not all / not many*, etc.

- **Some children** learn very quickly. (but not all children)
- **Some police officers** in Britain carry guns, but most of them don't.

For plural countable nouns see also Unit 70.

UNIT 66   Exercises

66.1   *What are these things? Try and find out if you don't know.*

Example: an ant? *It's an insect.*.........   ants? bees? *They are insects.*...........

1. an onion?   It's ....
2. a pigeon?   It ....
3. a dandelion?   ....
4. a skyscraper?   ....

5. Earth? Mars? Venus? Jupiter?   They
   ....
6. the Rhine? the Nile? the Mississippi?
   ....

And who were these people?
Example: Beethoven? *He was a composer.*   Beethoven? Bach? *They were composers.*

7. Picasso?   He was ....
8. Shakespeare?   He ....
9. Einstein?   ....
10. Marilyn Monroe?   ....

11. Kennedy? Johnson? Nixon?   They
    ....
12. Elvis Presley? John Lennon?   ....
    ....

66.2   *Read about someone's job and then write what his or her job is.*

Example: Ron flies airplanes.   *He's a pilot.*...

1. Sue types letters and answers the phone in an office.   She is ....
2. Tim plans people's vacations for them.   He ....
3. Carol takes care of patients in a hospital.   She ....
4. Mary teaches math.   ....
5. Martha directs movies.   ....
6. John translates what people are saying from one language into another, so that they can understand each other.   ....

66.3   *Put in* **a/an** *or* **some***, or leave a space (without a word).*

Examples: I've seen *some*.... good movies recently.   Do you have .....*a*........headache?
   Are most of your friends ...———..... students?

1. Do you have ....camera?
2. Would you like to be .... actor?
3. Bill has .... big feet.
4. Do you collect .... stamps?
5. Tom always gives Ann ....
   flowers on her birthday.
6. Those are .... really nice
   slacks. Where did you get them?
7. What .... beautiful garden!
8. What .... nice children!
9. .... birds, for example the
   penguin, cannot fly.
10. Jack has .... very long legs,
    so he's ....fast runner.

11. You need .... visa to visit ....
    foreign countries, but not all of them.
12. I'm going shopping. I'm going to get
    .... new clothes.
13. Jane is ....teacher. Her
    parents were ....teachers too.
14. When we got downtown, ...
    stores were still open, but most of
    them were already closed.
15. Do you enjoy going to ....
    concerts?
16. When I was .... child, I used to
    be very shy.

133

A/an and the

a Study this example:

For lunch I had a sandwich and an apple. The sandwich wasn't very good.

> The speaker says "**a** sandwich / **an** apple" because this is the first time he talks about them.

> The speaker says "**the** sandwich" because the listener now knows which sandwich he means – the sandwich he had for lunch.

Here are some more examples:

- There was **a** man talking to **a** woman outside my house. **The** man looked American, and I think **the** woman was Indian.
- When we were on vacation, we stayed at **a** hotel. In the evenings, sometimes we had dinner at **the** hotel and sometimes in **a** restaurant.
- I saw **a** movie last night. **The** movie was about **a** soldier and **a** beautiful woman. **The** soldier was in love with **the** woman, but **the** woman was in love with **a** teacher. So **the** soldier shot **the** teacher and married **the** woman.

b We use **a/an** when the listener doesn't know which thing we mean. We use **the** when it is clear which thing we mean:

- Tom sat down on a chair. (we don't know which chair)
  Tom sat down on **the** chair **nearest the door**. (we know which chair)
- Ann is looking for **a** job. (not a particular job)
  Did Ann get **the** job **she applied for?** (a particular job)
- Do you have **a** car? (not a particular car)
  I cleaned **the** car yesterday. (a particular car, my car)

c We use **the** when it is clear in the situation which thing or person we mean. For example, in a room we talk about "**the** light / **the** floor / **the** ceiling / **the** door / **the** carpet," etc. Study these examples:

- Can you turn off **the** light, please? (= the light in this room)
- Where is **the** bathroom, please? (= the bathroom in this building/house)
- I enjoyed the movie. Who was **the** director? (= the director of the movie)
- I took a taxi to **the** station. (= the station of that town)
- We got to **the** airport just in time for our flight.

Also: **the** police / **the** fire department / **the** army.

We also say **the bank, the post office**:

- I have to go to **the** bank to change some money, and then I'm going to **the** post office to buy some stamps. (The speaker is usually thinking of a particular bank or post office.)

We also say **the doctor, the dentist, the hospital**:

- John wasn't feeling very well. He went to **the** doctor. (= his doctor)
- Two people were taken to **the** hospital after the accident.

For **the** see also Units 68–73.

UNIT 67   Exercises

67.1   *Put in* **a/an** *or* **the**.

Example: There was ...*a*...... man and ...*a*...... woman in the room. *The*.... man was
American, and ..*the*.... woman looked Indian.

1. This morning I bought ....*a*...... newspaper and ....*a*...... magazine. ...*The*....newspaper is
   in my bag, but I don't know where ...*the*...... magazine is.
2. My parents have ...*a*........cat and ....*a*...... dog. ....*the*....dog never bites ...*the*.... cat, but
   ....*the*... cat often scratches .....*the*... dog.
3. I saw .....*an*.... accident this morning. ......*a*... car crashed into ....*a*..... wall. ...*The*....
   driver of ....*the*.... car was not hurt, but ..*the*..... car was badly damaged.
4. When you turn onto Pine Tree Drive, you will see three houses: .....*a*....red one, ..*a*.....
   blue one, and ...*a*...... white one. I live in .....*the*....white one.
5. We live in .....*an*.... old house in ...*the*..... middle of town. There is .....*a*.... garden behind
   ...*the*..... house. ....*The*.... roof of ...*the*....house is in bad condition.

67.2   *Put in* **a/an** *or* **the**.

Examples: I'm looking for ....*a*....... job.   Did Ann get .*the*..... job she applied for?

1. Would you like ....*an*.....apple?
2. Could you close ....*the*....door, please?
3. We live in .....*a*....small apartment near ...*the*..... center of town.
4. Have you finished with ....*the*..... book I lent you last week?
5. We went out for .....*a*.... meal last night. ...*the*..... restaurant we went to was excellent.
6. Did...*the*.... police find ...*the*..... person who stole your bicycle?
7. This is a nice house. Does it have ...*a*.... garden?
8. It was warm and sunny, so we decided to sit in ...*the*..... garden.
9. This morning I had ....*a*..... soft-boiled egg and toast for breakfast.   *? uncountable*
10. ....*The*...President of the United States is elected every four years.   *toasts*
11. As I was walking along the street, I saw ......*a*... $20 bill on ...*the*... sidewalk.
12. I went into the store and asked to speak to ...*the*..... manager.
13. "Do you have ...*a*..... car?"   "No, I've never had .....*a*..... car in my life."
14. There's no need to buy a paper. ...*The*.... newspaper carrier brings it every morning.

67.3   *Complete these sentences using* **the** + *noun*.

Example: It was getting dark in the room, so I turned on .*the light*..............................

1. There were no chairs, so we all had to sit on ...*the floor*..................
2. As soon as I saw the fire, I called ....*the fire department*.............
3. We didn't have any stamps, so we had to go to .....*the post office*.............
4. I had a toothache, so I made an appointment with ...*the dentist*................
5. Ann had to catch a train, so I took her to ....*to the station*.............
6. When we found that someone had broken into our house, we called ....*the police*.........
7. Bill wasn't feeling well, so he went to .....*the doctor*................
8. We didn't have any money, so we had to go to ...*the bank*...................
9. The plane was delayed, so we had to wait at .... for three hours.
10. Jill had a car accident. She'll be in ....*in the hospital*..... for at least two weeks.

135

UNIT
68 The (1)

For the difference between **the** and **a/an** see Unit 67.

a We say **the ...** when there is only one of something:
- What is **the** longest river in the world? (There is only one longest river in the world.)
- We went to **the** most expensive restaurant in town.
- **The** only television program she watches is the news.
- Paris is **the** capital of France. *Paris is a capital*
- Everybody left at **the** end of the meeting.
- **The** earth goes around **the** sun. (also: **the** moon / **the** world / **the** universe)

b We say: **the sea**   **the sky**   **the ground**   **the city** / **the country**
- Would you rather live in **the city** or in **the country**?
- Don't sit on **the ground!** It's wet.
- We looked up at all the stars in **the sky**.

We say **go to sea** / **be at sea** (without **the**) when the meaning is **go/be on a voyage**:
- Ken is a seaman. He spends most of his life **at sea**.

but: I would love to live near **the** sea. (*not* near sea)

We say **space** (*not* the space) when we mean space in the universe:
- There are millions of stars **in space**. (*not* in the space)

but: He tried to park his car, but **the** space wasn't big enough.

c **Movies**   **theater**   **radio**   **television**
We say **the movies** / **the theater**:
- We went to **the movies** last night.
- Do you often go to **the theater**?

I'm going to a theatre
I like the theatre

Note that when we say **the** theater, we do not necessarily mean one particular theater.

We usually say **the radio**:
- We often listen to **the radio**.   ■ I heard the news on **the radio**.

But we usually say **television** (without **the**):
- We often watch **television**.   ■ I watched the news on **television**.

but: Can you turn off **the** television, please? (= the television set)

d *Meals:* We do not normally use **the** with the names of meals:
- What time is **lunch?**
- We had **dinner** in a restaurant.
- What did you have for **breakfast?**
- Ann invited me to (*or* for) **dinner**.

But we say **a meal**:
- We had **a meal** in a restaurant.

We also say **a** when there is an adjective before **lunch/breakfast**, etc.
- Thank you. That was **a very nice** lunch. (*not* that was very nice lunch)

For more information about **the** see Units 67 and 69–73.

UNIT 68 Exercises

68.1 *Answer these questions in the way shown.*

Example: "Was it a good movie?" "Yes, it was ..*the best movie*.. I've ever seen."

1. "Is it a big hotel?" "Yes, it is .... in the city."
2. "Is he a rich man?" "Yes, he is .... I've ever met."
3. "Was it a bad accident?" "Yes, it was .... I've ever seen."
4. "Is it a cheap restaurant?" "Well, it is .... you will find."
5. "It's hot today, isn't it?" "Yes, it is .... day of the year."

68.2 *Put in **a/an** or **the**. Sometimes you don't need either word – you leave it blank. (If necessary see Unit 67 for **a/an** and **the**).*

Examples: We went to ..*the*..... most expensive restaurant in town.
Do you want to watch ....—.... television this evening?
Last night we went out for .....*a*....... meal in ....*a*........ restaurant.

1. I wrote my name at ....*the*... top of the page.
2. .... moon goes around .... earth every 27 days.
3. The Soviet Union was ...*the*....... first country to send a man into .... space. ?
4. Did you see the movie on .... television or in ....*a*..... movie theater?
5. After .... lunch, we went for a walk by ...*the*..... sea.
6. I'm not very hungry. I had ....*a*...... big breakfast.
7. John was .....*the*... only person I talked to at the party.
8. Liz lives in .....*a*..... small village in ...*the*..... country.
9. Peru is ......*a*.... country in South America. ...*the*.... capital is Lima.
10. I never listen to ....*the*....radio. In fact, I don't have ....*a*.... radio.
11. It was .....*a*......beautiful day. ...*The*.... sun shone brightly in ....*the*.. sky.
12. I've invited Tom to .... dinner next Wednesday.
13. What is ....*the*...... highest mountain in ...*the*....... world?
14. We don't go to .... theater very much these days. In fact, in .... town where we live there isn't .... theater.
15. It was a long voyage. We were at .... sea for four weeks.
16. I prefer swimming in .... sea to swimming in pools.
17. Can you turn .... television down, please? It's a little loud.

68.3 *Here are some things Tom did yesterday. Write a sentence for each.*

Morning:	8:00 breakfast	8:30–9:00 radio	9:30 walk/country
Afternoon:	1:00 lunch	2:30 movies	
Evening:	6:30 dinner	8:00–10:00 television	

1. *At 8:00 he had breakfast* ....
2. From 8:30 until 9:00 he listened ....
3. At 9:30 he went for a walk in ....
4. At 1:00 he ....
5. At 2:30 ....
6. At 6:30 ....
7. From ....

UNIT 69 The (2)

a

Study these sentences:

- **The rose** is my favorite flower.
- **The giraffe** is the tallest of all animals.

In these examples **the . . .** doesn't mean one particular thing. **The rose** = roses in general, **the giraffe** = giraffes in general. We use **the** + *a singular countable noun* in this way to talk about a type of plant, animal, etc. Note that you can also use a plural noun without **the**:

- **Roses** are my favorite flowers. (*but not* The roses . . . – see Unit 70)

We also use **the** + *a singular countable noun* when we talk about a type of machine, an invention, etc. For example:

- When was **the telephone** invented?
- **The bicycle** is an excellent means of transportation.

We also use **the** for musical instruments:

- Can you play **the guitar?** (*not* Can you play guitar?)
- **The piano** is my favorite instrument.

b

The + *adjective*

We use **the** with some adjectives (without a noun). The meaning is always plural. For example, **the rich** = rich people in general:

- Do you think **the rich** should pay more taxes?

We use **the** especially with these adjectives:

the rich	the old	the blind	the sick	the disabled	the injured
the poor	the young	the deaf	the dead	the unemployed	the homeless

- That man over there is collecting money for **the homeless**.
- Why doesn't the government do more to help **the unemployed?**

These expressions are always plural. You cannot say "a blind" or "an unemployed." You have to say "**a blind man**," "**an** unemployed **woman**," etc.

c

The + *nationality words*

You can use **the** with some nationality adjectives when you mean "the people of that country." For example:

- **The French** are famous for their food. (= the French people)
- **The English** are known for being polite. (= the English people)

You can use **the** in this way with these nationality words:

the British	the Welsh	the Spanish	the Dutch
the English	the Irish	the French	the Swiss

You can also use **the** with nationality words ending in **-ese** (**the Japanese** / **the Chinese**, etc.). With other nationalities you have to use a plural noun ending in **-s**:

(the) Russians   (the) Italians   (the) Arabs   (the) Germans   (the) Turks

For **the** see also Units 67, 68, and 70–73.

UNIT 69 Exercises

69.1 *Answer these questions about yourself and your favorite things. Use a dictionary if you don't know the English words you need.*

Example: What is your favorite flower? .the rose...

1. What is your favorite tree? ...... *the birch* ......
2. Which bird do you like most? ......
3. What is your favorite car? ......
4. What is your favorite musical instrument? ......

69.2 *Make sentences from the words in parentheses (. . .).*

Example: (Mary / play / piano very well) *Mary plays the piano very well.*......

1. (Jack / play / guitar very badly)   Jack plays ......
2. (Jill / play / violin in an orchestra) ......
3. (I'd like / learn / play / piano) ......
4. (you / play / guitar?) ......

69.3 *Complete these sentences about animals. Choose one of the words in parentheses. Use a dictionary if you don't know these words.*

Example: .The giraffe...... is the tallest of all animals.   (elephant/lion/giraffe)

1. ...... is the fastest of all animals.   (tiger/cheetah/elephant)
2. ...... is a mammal, but it lives in the sea.   (octopus/elephant/whale)
3. ...... is the largest living bird.   (eagle/sparrow/ostrich)

69.4 *Complete these sentences using* **the** *with these adjectives:*

rich   sick   ~~blind~~   poor   injured   unemployed   dead

Example: Braille is a system of reading and writing by touch for *the blind.*......

1. Many people were killed in the plane crash. The bodies of ...... were taken away. ...... were taken to the hospital.
2. Do you know the story of Robin Hood? It is said that he robbed ...... and gave the money to ....
3. For people with jobs, life is easier than it is for ....
4. Linda has been a nurse all her life. She has spent her life caring for ......

69.5 *What do you call the people from these places?*

Examples: England? *.the English*...... Russia? *.the Russians*......

1. Britain? ......
2. Ireland? ......
3. Greece? ......
4. Korea? ......
5. Spain? ......
6. France? ......
7. Japan? ......
8. Germany? ......
9. China? ......
10. Canada? ......
11. Switzerland? ......
12. America (the U.S.)? ......
13. the Netherlands? ......
14. and your country? ......

139

UNIT 70

Plural and uncountable nouns with and without **the (flowers/the flowers)**

a We don't use **the** before a noun when we mean something *in general*:

- I love **flowers**. (*not* the flowers)
  (**flowers** = flowers *in general*, not a particular group of flowers)
- I'm afraid of **dogs**.
- **Doctors** are paid more than **teachers.**
- **Crime** is a problem in most big cities. (*not* the crime)
- **Life** has changed a lot since I was young. (*not* the life)
- I prefer **classical music** to **pop music**. (*not* the classical/pop music)
- Do you like **Chinese food / American television**? (*not* the . . .)
- My favorite subject at school was **history/physics/English**.
- I like **soccer/athletics/skiing/chess**.
- Do you collect **stamps**?

We say **most people / most dogs**, etc. (*not* the most . . .):

- **Most people** like George. (*not* the most people – see also Unit 78)

b We say **the . . .** when we mean *something in particular*:

- I like your garden. **The flowers** are beautiful. (*not* Flowers are . . .)
  (**the flowers** = the flowers in your garden, not flowers in general)
- **Children** learn a lot from playing. (= children in general)
- *but:* We took **the children** to the zoo. (= a particular group of children, perhaps the speaker's own children)

- **Salt** is used to flavor food.
- *but:* Can you pass **the salt**, please? (= the salt on the table)

- I often listen to **music**.
- *but:* The movie wasn't very good, but I liked **the music**. (= the music in the movie)

- All **cars** have wheels.
- *but:* All **the students** in the class like their teacher.

- Are **American people** friendly? (= American people in general)
- *but:* Are **the American people you know** friendly? (= only the American people you know, not American people in general)

c The difference between "something in general" and "something in particular" is not always very clear. Study these sentences:

- I like working with **people**. (= people in general)
- I like working with **people who are lively**. (not all people, but **people who are lively** is still a general idea)
- *but:* I like **the people I work with**. (= a particular group of people)

- Do you like **coffee**? (= coffee in general)
- Do you like **strong black coffee?** (not all coffee, but **strong black coffee** is still a general idea)
- *but:* Did you like **the coffee** we had after dinner? (= particular coffee)

UNIT 70 Exercises

70.1 *Write whether you like or dislike something. Begin your sentences with:*

I like . . .   **I don't like . . .**   **I love . . .**   **I hate . . .**   **I don't mind . . .**
I'm (not) interested in . . .   **I have no opinion about . . .**

Example: (hot weather) *I don't like hot weather.* ....

1. (soccer) ....
2. (small children) ....
3. (cats) ....
4. (modern art) ....
5. (horror movies) ....

70.2 *What do you think about these things? Write a sentence about each one. Begin with:*

In my opinion . . .   **I think . . .**   **I don't think . . .**   **I don't agree with . . .**
I'm against . . .   **I'm in favor of . . .**

Example: (divorce) *I think divorce is sometimes necessary.* ....

1. (violence) ....
2. (smoking) ....
3. (exams) ....
4. (capital punishment) ....
5. (nuclear power) ....

70.3 *Choose the correct form, with or without* **the.**

Examples: I'm afraid of dogs / ~~the dogs~~.   Can you pass ~~salt~~ / the salt, please?

1. Apples / ~~The apples~~ are good for you.
2. Look at ~~apples~~ / the apples on that tree! They're very large.
3. Women / ~~The women~~ are sometimes better teachers than men / the men.
4. In Britain coffee / ~~the coffee~~ is more expensive than tea / ~~the tea~~.
5. We had a very nice meal in that restaurant. Service / The service was good too.
6. Most people / ~~The most~~ people still believe that marriage / ~~the marriage~~ and family life / ~~the family life~~ are the basis of our society.
7. They got married but marriage / ~~the marriage~~ wasn't successful.
8. I know someone who wrote a book about ~~life~~ / the life of Gandhi.
9. Life / ~~The life~~ would be very difficult without electricity / ~~the electricity~~.
10. Skiing / ~~the skiing~~ is my favorite sport, but I also like swimming / ~~the swimming~~.
11. ~~Second World War~~ / The Second World War ended in 1945.
12. Do you know people / ~~the people~~ who live next door?
13. Are you interested in art / ~~the art~~ or architecture / ~~the architecture~~?
14. ~~All books~~ / All the books on the top shelf belong to me.
15. Don't stay in that hotel. Beds / ~~The beds~~ are very uncomfortable.
16. Two of the biggest problems facing our society are crime / ~~the crime~~ and unemployment / ~~the unemployment~~.
17. I hate violence / ~~the violence~~.

School / the school, prison / the prison, etc.

university?

a | School   college   prison/jail   church

Compare these examples:

The children are going **to school**.	Mrs. Kelly went **to the school** to meet her son's teachers.

We say:

- a child goes **to school** (as a student)
- a student goes **to college** (to study)
- a criminal goes **to prison** *or* **to jail** (as a prisoner)
- someone goes **to church** (for a religious service)

We do *not* use **the** when we are thinking of the idea of these places and what they are used for:

- Mr. Kelly goes **to church** every Sunday. (*not* to **the** church)
- After I finish **high school**, I want to go **to college**.
- Ken's brother was sent **to prison** for robbing a bank.

We say: "be **in** *or* **at** school/college" (but "be **in high school**") and "be **in** prison/jail":

- What did you learn **at** (*or* **in**) **school** today?
- Ken's brother is **in jail**. (*or* **in prison**)

Now study these examples with **the**:

- Mrs. Kelly went to **the school** to meet her son's teachers. (she went there as a visitor, not as a pupil)
- Ken went to **the prison** to visit his brother. (as a visitor, not as a prisoner; he went to the jail where his brother was)
- The workers went to **the church** to repair the roof. (they didn't go to a religious service)

b | bed   work   home

We say:

"go **to bed** / be **in bed**" (*not* the bed):

- It's time to go **to bed** now.   ■ Is Tom still **in bed**?

"go **to work** / be **at work** / start **work** / finish **work**," etc. (*not* the work):

- Why isn't Ann **at work** today?   ■ What time do you **finish work**?

"**go home** / **come home** / **get home** / **arrive home**" (*no preposition*):

- Come on! Let's **go home**.   ■ What time did you **get home**?

"be **(at) home** / stay **(at) home**":

- Will you be **(at) home** tomorrow?   ■ We stayed **(at) home**.

UNIT 71   Exercises

71.1   *Complete these sentences using the words in this unit.*

Example: Fred robbed a bank but was caught by the police. He was sent *to jail.*

1. I was very tired and it was very late, so I went *to bed*
2. Tom doesn't often go out in the evenings. He usually stays *at home*
3. Jill isn't a religious person. She never goes *to church*
4. In the U.S., children over the age of five have to go *to school*
5. Children sometimes get into trouble if they are late for
6. There is a lot of traffic in the morning when everybody is going *to work*
7. Fred was arrested by the police and spent the night
8. When Sue finishes high school, she wants to study economics *in college*
9. Bill never gets up before 9:00. It's 8:30 now, so he is still *in bed*

71.2   *Write short answers to these questions.*

Example: If you wanted to meet your children's teachers, where would you go?
To the school.

1. A friend of yours is in prison. Where would you go to visit your friend?
2. Where are criminals sent?
3. Where do children go during the day?
4. A friend of yours is at church. If you wanted to meet your friend immediately after the service, where would you go?
5. Where can you go if you want to study after finishing high school? *to college*

71.3   *Choose the correct form, with or without* **the**.

Example: Ken's brother is in prison / ~~the prison~~ for robbery. ("prison" is correct)

1. Some children hate school / the school.
2. What time do your children finish school / the school?
3. Every term parents are invited to school / the school to meet the teachers.
4. After leaving high school / the high school, Jane worked as a nurse in a hospital.
5. All over the world, people are in prison / the prison because of their political beliefs.
6. The other day the fire department had to go to prison / the prison to put out a fire.
7. On the way to Boston we passed through a small village with an old church. We stopped to visit church / the church. It was a beautiful building.
8. John's mother is a regular churchgoer. She goes to church / the church every Sunday. John himself doesn't go to church / the church.
9. After work / the work, Ann usually goes home / to home.
10. Tom left college / the college without taking his exams.
11. I like to read in bed / the bed before going to sleep.
12. What time do you have to start work / the work tomorrow morning?
13. "Did they catch the thief?"   "Yes, I'm sure he's in jail / the jail by now."

UNIT 72 Geographical names with and without **the**

a *Continents:* We do not say **the** with the names of continents:
Africa (*not* the Africa)   Asia   Europe   South America

b *Countries and states:* We do not usually say **the** with the names of countries and states:
France (*not* the France)   Japan   Germany   Nigeria   Texas

But we say **the** with names that include words like "republic," "kingdom," "states":

the Dominican **Republic**   the **Republic** of Ireland   the United **States** (of
the People's **Republic**   the United **Kingdom**   America)
 of China   the United Arab **Emirates**
We also use **the** with *plural* names:
the Netherlands   the Philippines

c *Cities:* We do not use **the** with the names of cities/towns/villages:
Cairo (*not* the Cairo)   New York   Madrid   Tokyo
Exception: **The** Hague (in the Netherlands)

d *Islands:* Island groups usually have *plural* names with **the:**
the Bahamas   the Canaries/the Canary Islands   the British Isles   the Virgin Islands
Individual islands usually have singular names without **the:**
Corfu   Sicily   Bermuda   Easter Island

e *Regions:* We say:
the Middle East   the Far East
the north of France   the south of Spain   the west of Canada
(*but:* **northern** France / **southern** Spain / **western** Canada – without **the**)

f *Mountains:* Mountain ranges usually have *plural* names with **the:**
the Rocky Mountains / the Rockies   the Andes   the Alps
But individual mountains usually have names without **the:**
(Mount) Everest   (Mount) Fuji   (Mount) Etna

g *Lakes:* Lakes usually have names without **the:**
Lake Superior   Lake Victoria

h Names of *oceans/seas/rivers/canals* have **the:**
the Atlantic (Ocean)   the Indian Ocean   the Mediterranean (Sea)   the Red Sea
the (English) Channel   the Nile   the Amazon   the Mississippi
the Rhine   the Suez Canal   the Panama Canal
Note: On maps **the** is not usually included in the name.

Place names with **of** usually have **the:**
the Bay of Naples   the United States of America
the Sea of Japan   the Gulf of Mexico

UNIT 72 Exercises

72.1 *Read these sentences carefully. Some are correct, but some need* **the** *(perhaps more than once). Correct the sentences where necessary.*

Examples: Everest was first climbed in 1953.   *R.I.G.H.T.....*
Milan is in north of Italy.   *W.R.O.N.G. - the north of Italy*

1. Last year we visited Canada and *the* United States.   ....
2. Africa is much larger than Europe.   ....
3. *The* South of England is warmer than *the* north.   ....
4. We went to Spain for our vacation and swam in *the* Mediterranean.   ....
5. Tom has visited most countries in western Europe.   ....
6. There are many different languages spoken in *the* Far East.   ....
7. Next year we are going skiing in *the* Swiss Alps.   ....
8. Malta has been a republic since 1974.   ....
9. *The* Nile is *the* longest river in Africa.   ....
10. *The* United Kingdom consists of Great Britain and Northern Ireland.   ....

72.2 *Here are some geography questions. Choose the right answer. Sometimes you need* **the**, *sometimes not. Try and find out the answers if you don't know them.*

Example: What is the longest river in the world? (Amazon / Rhine / Nile)   *the Amazon.*

1. Where is Bolivia? (Africa / South America / North America)   *in South America*
2. Where is Ethiopia? (Asia / South America / Africa)   *in Africa*
3. Of which country is Manila the capital? (Indonesia / Philippines / Japan)   *the Philippines*
4. Of which country is Stockholm the capital?
   (Norway / Denmark / Sweden)   ....
5. Which country lies between Mexico and Canada?
   (Venezuela / El Salvador / United States)   ....
6. Which is the largest country in the world?
   (United States / China / Russia)   ....
7. Which is the largest continent? (Africa / South America / Asia)   ....
8. What is the name of the mountain range in the west of North America?
   (Rocky Mountains / Andes / Alps)   ....
9. What is the name of the ocean between America and Asia?
   (Atlantic / Pacific / Indian Ocean)   ....
10. What is the name of the ocean between Africa and Australia?
    (Atlantic / Pacific / Indian Ocean)   ....
11. What is the name of the sea between England and France?
    (Mediterranean Sea / English Channel / French Sea)   *the English Channel*
12. What is the name of the sea between Africa and Europe?
    (Black Sea / Red Sea / Mediterranean Sea)   ....
13. What is the name of the sea between Britain and Norway?
    (Norwegian Sea / English Channel / North Sea)   ....
14. Which river flows through Vienna, Budapest, and Belgrade?
    (Rhine / Danube / Volga)   *the Danube*
15. What joins the Atlantic and Pacific oceans?
    (Suez Canal / Panama Canal)   ....

145

UNIT 73 Names of streets, buildings, etc. with and without **the**

a We do not normally use **the** with names of streets, roads, avenues, boulevards, squares, etc.:

Bloor Street	Fifth Avenue	Piccadilly Circus
Wilshire Boulevard	Broadway	Red Square

b Many names (for example, of airports or universities) are two or three words:
   Kennedy Airport   Boston University
The first word is usually the name of a person ("Kennedy") or a place ("Boston"). We do not usually say **the** with names like these:

Pearson International Airport	Buckingham Palace
Penn Station	Hyde Park

But we say "**the** White House," "**the** Royal Palace" because "white" and "royal" are not names. This is only a general rule. There are exceptions. See section (c) for hotels, etc., and section (e) for names with **of**.

c We usually say **the** before the names of these places:

hotels	**the** Hilton Hotel, **the** Sheraton (Hotel)
restaurants	**the** Bombay Restaurant, **the** Stage Delicatessen
theaters	**the** Shubert (Theater), **the** National Theater
movie theaters	**the** RKO Plaza, **the** Quad
museums/galleries	**the** Metropolitan Museum, **the** National Gallery, **the** Louvre
buildings/monuments	**the** Empire State Building, **the** Washington Monument

But banks do not usually take **the**:
   First Interstate Bank   Citibank   Lloyds Bank

d Many stores and restaurants are named after the people who started them. These names end in **s** or **'s**. We do not use **the** with these names:
   ■ "Where did you buy that hat?" "At Macy's." (*not* the Macy's)
   ■ We're going to have lunch at Mama Leone's. (*not* the Mama Leone's)

Churches are sometimes named after saints (St. = Saint):
   St. John's Church   St. Patrick's Cathedral

e We say **the** before the names of places, buildings, etc., with **of**:

the Tower **of** London	**the** Museum **of** Modern Art
the Great Wall **of** China	**the** University **of** Southern California

UNIT 73   Exercises

73.1   *Use the map to answer the questions in the way shown. Write the name of the place and the street it is on. On maps we don't normally use* **the**; *in your sentences, use* **the** *if necessary.*

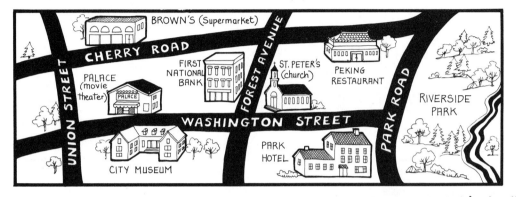

Example: "Is there a movie theater near here?"   "Yes, *the Palace on Washington.*"

1. "Is there a supermarket near here?"   "Yes, ... on ....?
2. "Is there a hotel near here?"   "Yes, ... on ....?
3. "Is there a bank near here?"   "Yes, ...on ....?
4. "Is there a restaurant near here?"   "Yes, ... on ....?
5. "Is there a church near here?"   "Yes, ...?
6. "Is there a museum near here?"   "Yes, ...?
7. "Is there a park near here?"   "Yes, ... at the end of ....?

73.2   *Choose the correct form, with or without* **the**.

Example: When we were in Washington, D.C., we visited ~~National Gallery~~ / the National Gallery.

1. The President lives in ~~White House~~ / the White House.
2. One of the nicest buildings in Washington is ~~Supreme Court Building~~ / the Supreme Court Building, which is very close to ~~Capitol Building~~ / the Capitol Building.
3. Frank is a student at Georgetown University / ~~the Georgetown University~~.
4. If you want to buy some new clothes, the store I would recommend is Jack's / ~~the Jack's~~.
5. We flew from Washington to O'Hare Airport / ~~the O'Hare Airport~~ in Chicago.
6. ~~Smithsonian~~ / The Smithsonian is an important museum in Washington.
7. A favorite restaurant is Luigi's / ~~the Luigi's~~.
8. Have you ever visited ~~Lincoln Memorial~~ / the Lincoln Memorial?
9. "Which hotel are you staying at?" "At ~~Sheraton~~ / the Sheraton."
10. Did you see the movie at ~~Quad~~ / the Quad (movie theater)?
11. In my opinion, the best stores in Toronto are on Yonge Street / ~~the Yonge Street~~.
12. Yesterday I opened a checking account at Barclay's Bank / ~~the Barclay's Bank~~.

Singular or plural?

a We use some nouns only in the *plural*. For example:

slacks/pants jeans shorts pajamas scissors glasses

You can also use **a pair of...** with these words:
- I need **some** new slacks. *or* I need **a new pair of** slacks.

b We do not often use the plural of **person** ("persons"). Instead we use **people**:
- He is **a** nice **person**.   They are nice **people**. (*not* nice persons)

c These nouns end in **-s** but they are not usually plural:

mathematics   physics   economics   athletics   gymnastics   news
- **Gymnastics is** my favorite sport.
- What time **is the news** on television? (See also Unit 65d.)

These words end in **-s** and can be singular *or* plural:

means	**a means** of transportation	**many means** of transportation
series	**a** television **series**	**two** television **series**
species	**a species** of bird	**200 species** of bird

d We always use a plural verb with **the police**:
- **The police have** arrested Tom.
- **Are** the police paid well?

e Sometimes we use a plural noun with a singular verb. We do this when we talk about a sum of money, a period of time, a distance, etc.:
- **Five thousand dollars** (= it) was stolen in the robbery. (*not* were stolen)
- **Three years** (= it) is a long time to be without a job. (*not* are)

f We say "**a** vacation of three **weeks**" but "**a** three-**week** vacation":
- I have **a** three-**week** vacation in July. (*not* a three-weeks vacation)

Here, **three-week** is used as an adjective before "vacation." When we use "three-weeks" as an adjective, it loses the **s**. So we say:

a ten-dollar bill (**not** dollars)   two 14-**year**-old girls
a four-week English course   **a six-hour** journey

You can also say "I have three weeks' vacation." See Unit 75d.

UNIT 74   Exercises

74.1   *Complete the sentences with words from sections a, b, and c. Sometimes you need **a** or **some**.*

Examples: She can't see very well. She needs *glasses*.
This plant is *a* very rare *species*.

1. Soccer players don't wear long pants when they play. They wear ...*shorts*........... .
2. The bicycle is ...*a means*.... of transportation.
3. The bicycle and the car are ......*means*........ of transportation.
4. I want to cut this piece of material. I need ...*a pair of scissors*....
5. Ann is going to write ...*a series*..... of articles for her local newspaper.
6. There are a lot of American television ......*series*........on television throughout the world.
7. While we were out walking, we saw 25 different ......*species*.....of bird.
8. We need at least four ...*people*........... to play this game.

74.2   *Choose the correct form, singular or plural. Sometimes either singular or plural is possible.*

Example: Gymnastics is / ~~are~~ my favorite sport. ("is" is correct)

1. The pants you bought for me ~~doesn't~~ / don't fit me.
2. Physics was / were my best subject at school.
3. Fortunately the news wasn't / weren't as bad as we had expected.
4. The police wants / want to interview Fred about a robbery.
5. Three days isn't / aren't long enough for a good vacation.
6. "Have you seen my sunglasses?"   "Yes, it's / they're on the table."
7. Does / Do the police know about the stolen money?
8. Can I borrow your scissors? Mine isn't / aren't sharp enough.
9. I'm going to take a taxi. Six miles is / are too far for me to walk.

74.3   *Use the structure in section e.*

Examples: Our vacation lasted three weeks.   It was *a three-week vacation.*...........
The girls were 14 years old.   They were. *14-year-old girls.*........................

1. The woman was 27.   She was a...
2. The flight lasted three hours.   It was a ....
3. The strike lasted four days.   It was a ....
4. The book has 200 pages.   It is a...
5. The boys were ten years old.   They were ....
6. The television series has ten parts.   It is..
7. The bottle holds two liters.   It is...
8. Each of the tickets cost ten dollars.   They were ....
9. The building has ten stories (= *floors*).   It is ....
10. This bag of potatoes weighs five pounds.   It is ....
11. We walked for five miles.   It was...

149

75 ...'s (apostrophe s) and ...of...

a We normally use **'s** when the first noun is a person or an animal:
the **manager's** office (*not* the office of the manager)
Mr. Evans's daughter   the **horse's** tail   a **police officer's** hat
Otherwise (with things) we normally use **...of...**
the door **of the room** (*not* the room's door)
the beginning **of the story** (*not* the story's beginning)
Sometimes you can use **'s** when the first noun is a thing. For example, you can say:
the book's title *or* **the title of the book**
But it is safer and more usual to use **...of...** (but see also section **b**).

b You can usually use **'s** when the first noun is an organization (= a group of people). So
you can say:
the government's decision   *or*   the decision **of the government**
the company's success   *or*   the success **of the company**
It is also possible to use **'s** with places. So you can say:
the city's new theater   **the world's** population
France's system of government   **Italy's** largest city

c After a singular noun we use **'s**. After a plural noun (which ends in **-s**) we use only an
apostrophe (**'**):
my sister**'s** room (*one* sister)   Mr. Carter**'s** house
my sisters**'** room (*more than one* sister)   the Carters**'** house (*Mr. and Mrs. Carter*)
If a plural noun does not end in **-s**, we use **'s**:
a children**'s** book

Note that you can use **'s** after more than one noun:
Jack and Jill's wedding   **Mr. and Mrs. Carter's** house

But we would not use **'s** in a sentence like this:
■ I met the wife **of the man who lent us the money**. ("the man who lent us the
money" is too long to be followed by **'s**)
Note that you can use **'s** without a following noun:
■ Tom's apartment is much larger than **Ann's**. (= Ann's apartment)

d You can also use **'s** with time words (**tomorrow**, etc.):
■ **Tomorrow's** meeting has been canceled.
■ Do you still have **last Saturday's** newspaper?
You can also say: **yesterday's ... today's ... this evening's ... next week's ...
Monday's ...** etc.

We also use **'s** (or only an apostrophe (**'**) with plurals) with periods of time:
■ I have **a week's** vacation.
■ I have **three weeks'** vacation.
■ I need **eight hours'** sleep a night.
■ My house is very near here – only about **five minutes'** walk.
Compare this structure with "**a three-week** vacation" (Unit 74e).

UNIT 75 Exercises

75.1 *Join two nouns. Sometimes you have to use an apostrophe ('), with or without* **s**. *Sometimes you have to use* **. . . of . . . .**

Examples: the door / the room *the door of the room* the mother / Ann *Ann's mother*

1. the camera / Tom................................
2. the eyes / the cat ....
3. the top / the page ....
4. the daughter / Charles........................
5. the newspaper / today.........................
6. the toys / the children ....
7. the name / your wife ....
8. the name / this street...........................
9. the name / the man I saw you with yesterday ....
10. the new manager / the company...
11. the result / the football game ....
12. the car / Mike's parents ....
13. the birthday / my father...
14. the new principal / the school...
15. the garden / our neighbors..
16. the ground floor / the building ....
17. the children / Don and Mary..
18. the economic policy / the government ....
19. the husband / the woman talking to Tom..
20. the house / my aunt and uncle..

75.2 *Read each sentence and write a new sentence using* **'s** *with the underlined words.*

Example: The meeting <u>tomorrow</u> has been canceled. *Tomorrow's meeting has been canceled.*

1. The storm <u>last week</u> caused a lot of damage.
   Last *week's storm*
2. The only movie theater in <u>the town</u> has been closed down.
   The t ....
3. Exports from <u>Canada</u> to the United States have fallen recently.
   C ....
4. There will be a big crowd at the football game <u>this evening</u>.
   There will be a big crowd at this ....
5. Tourism is the main industry in <u>the region</u>.
   The r ....

75.3 *Use the information given to complete the sentences.*

Example: If I leave my house at 9:00 and drive to Houston, I arrive at about 12:00.
   So it's about ..*three hours'* drive to Houston from my house.

1. I'm going on vacation on the 12th. I have to be back at work on the 26th.
   So I have .... vacation.
2. I went to sleep at 3:00 this morning and woke up an hour later at 4:00.
   So I only had .... sleep.
3. If I leave my house at 8:50 and walk to work, I get to work at 9:00.
   So it's only .... walk from my house to work.

UNIT 76 Reflexive pronouns (myself / yourself, etc.), by myself

a The *reflexive pronouns* are:

singular:	myself	yourself (*one person*)	himself/herself/itself/
plural:	ourse**lves**	yourse**lves** (*more than one person*)	themse**lves**

We use a reflexive pronoun when the subject and object are the same:

Tom   cut   himself   while he was shaving. (*not* Tom cut him)
- **The old lady** sat in a corner talking to **herself**.
- Don't get angry. Control **yourself**! (*said to one person*)
- If **you** want more to eat, help **yourselves**. (*said to more than one person*)
- The party was great. **We** enjoyed **ourselves** very much.

But we do not use "myself," etc., after **bring/take something with . . .** :
- I went out and **took** an umbrella **with me**. (*not* with myself)

b We do not use "myself," etc., after **feel/relax/concentrate**:
- **I feel great** after going for a swim. (*not* I feel myself great)
- Why don't you try and **concentrate**?
- It's good to **relax**.

We do not normally use "myself," etc., after **wash/dress/shave**:
- I got up, **shaved, washed,** and **dressed**. (*not* shaved myself, etc.)

But we say: **I dried myself**.

Note how we use **meet**:
- What time shall we **meet**? (*not* meet ourselves / meet us)

c Study the difference between **-selves** and **each other**:
- Tom and Ann stood in front of the mirror and looked at **themselves**.
  (= *Tom and Ann* looked at *Tom and Ann*)
- *but:* **Tom** looked at **Ann** and **Ann** looked at **Tom**. They looked at **each other**.

You can use **one another** instead of **each other**:
- Sue and Ann don't like **each other** (*or* **one another**).

d We also use **myself**, etc., in another way. For example:
- "Who fixed your bicycle for you?" "Nobody. **I fixed it myself**."

I fixed it myself = *I* fixed it, not anybody else. We use **myself** here to emphasize **I**. Here are some more examples:
- I'm not going to do it for you. **You** can do it **yourself**.
- **Let's** paint the house **ourselves**. It will be much cheaper.
- **The movie itself** wasn't very good, but I liked the music.
- I don't think Tom will get the job. **Tom himself** doesn't think he'll get it. (*or* **Tom** doesn't think he'll get it **himself**.)

e **By myself/yourself**, etc. = **alone**. We say:
- I like living **by myself**.
- Did you go on vacation **by yourself**?
- Jack was sitting **by himself** in a corner of the cafe.

UNIT 76 Exercises

76.1 *Complete these sentences using* **myself/yourself**, *etc., with these verbs:*

kick   teach   ~~cut~~   lock   take care of   burn   talk to   blame

Example: Tom ..*cut himself*............ while he was shaving this morning.

1. Be careful! That pan is very hot. Don't ....
2. They couldn't get back into the house. They had .... out.
3. It isn't her fault. She really shouldn't ....
4. What a stupid fool I am! I could ....!
5. I'm trying to .... Spanish but I'm not making much progress.
6. He spends most of his time alone, so it's not surprising that he ....
7. Don't worry about us. We can ....

76.2 *Complete these sentences with these verbs. This time, use* **myself**, *etc., only where necessary:*

dry   concentrate   feel   enjoy   relax   wash   ~~shave~~   meet

Example: Tom is growing a beard because he doesn't like .*shaving*...........................
1. I really ....good today – much better than yesterday.
2. She climbed out of the pool, picked up a towel, and ....
3. I tried to study but I just couldn't ....
4. Jack and I first .... at a party five years ago.
5. You're always rushing around. Why don't you .... more?
6. It was a great vacation. We really .... very much.
7. I overslept this morning. I didn't have time to .... or have breakfast.

76.3 *Write* **-selves** *or* **each other**.

Examples: Tom and Ann stood in front of the mirror and looked at .*themselves*.......... .
How long have Tom and Ann known .*each other*.......... ?

1. At Christmas friends often give .... presents.
2. Did the children enjoy .... when they were on vacation?
3. They had an argument last week. They are still not speaking to ....
4. Some people are very selfish. They only think of................................... .
5. Sue and I don't see .... very often these days.

76.4 *Answer these questions using* **myself/yourself**, *etc., or* **by myself/yourself**, *etc.*

Examples: "Who repaired the bicycle for you?"   "Nobody. I *repaired it myself.*......"
I like living .*by myself.*...............................

1. "Who cut your hair for you?"   "Nobody. I cut ...."
2. "Who did you go to the movies with?"   "No one. I went ...."
3. "Who told you Linda was getting married?"   "Linda ...."
4. "Does Mr. Thomas have a secretary to type his letters?"   "No, he ...."
5. "Does she like working with other people?"   "Not really. She prefers to work..............."
6. "Do you want me to mail that letter for you?"   "No, I'll..............................."
7. "Can you clean the windows for me?"   "Why don't you ....?"

UNIT 77

"A friend of **mine**," "**my own** house"

a | **A friend of mine / a friend of Tom's**

We say "a friend **of mine/yours/his/hers/ours/theirs**." (*not* a friend of me/you/him, etc.):

- A friend **of mine** is coming to stay with me next week. (*not* a friend of me)
- We went on vacation with some friends **of ours**. (*not* some friends of us)
- Tom had an argument with a neighbor **of his**.
- It was a good suggestion **of yours** to go swimming this afternoon.

We also say "a friend **of Tom's**," "a friend **of my brother's**," etc.:

- That man over there is a friend **of my brother's**.
- It was a good idea **of Tom's** to go swimming.

b | **My own... / your own...**, etc.

You cannot say "an own..." ("an own house," "an own car," etc.)

You must use **my/your/his/her/its/our/their** before **own**:

    my own house   **your own** car   **her own** room

My own... = something that is only mine, not shared or borrowed:

- The Browns live in an apartment, but they'd like to have **their own house**. (*not* an own house)
- I don't want to share with anyone. I want **my own room**.
- Unfortunately the apartment doesn't have **its own entrance**.
- It's **my own fault** that I don't have any money. I spend it too quickly.
- Why do you want to borrow my car? Why can't you use **your own** (car)?

You can also use **...own...** to say that you do something yourself instead of somebody else doing it for you. For example:

- Do you grow **your own vegetables?** (= do you grow them yourself in your garden instead of buying them?)
- Ann always cuts **her own hair**. (= she cuts it herself; she doesn't go to the hairdresser)

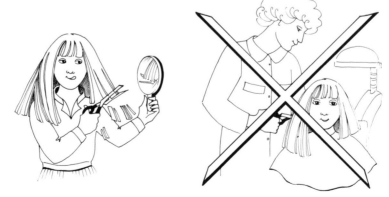

UNIT 77 Exercises

77.1 *Write new sentences using the structure in section a (**a friend of mine**, etc.).*

Example: I am writing to <u>one of my friends</u>. *I'm writing to a friend of mine.*

1. We met <u>one of your relatives</u>. We met a..
2. Henry borrowed <u>one of my books</u>. Henry..
3. Tom invited <u>some of his friends</u> to his apartment. Tom ....
4. We had dinner with <u>one of our neighbors</u>. ....
5. Ann is in love with <u>one of her colleagues</u>. ....
6. They went on vacation with <u>two of their friends</u>. ....
7. I just saw <u>one of your teachers</u>. ....
8. We're spending the weekend with <u>one of our friends</u>. ....
9. We met <u>one of Jane's friends</u>. We met ....

77.2 *Make sentences from the words in parentheses (. . .). Each time use **my own** / **your own**, etc.*

Example: I don't want to share a room. (want / have / room) *I want to have my own room.*

1. I don't watch television with the rest of the family. (have / television / in my bedroom) I have .... in my bedroom.
2. Jack and Bill are fed up with working for other people. (want / start / business)
   They ....
3. Henry is extremely rich. (have / private jet) He ....
4. The Isle of Man is an island off the coast of Britain. It is not completely independent but it (have / parliament and laws) ....
5. At the moment we're living in an apartment, but we're saving our money. (want / buy / house) We ....
6. You can give her advice, but she won't listen. (have / ideas) She ....
7. He's worked for the company for 10 years, but ....
   (not / have / office) He shares one with a colleague.

77.3 *Now complete these sentences using **my own** / **your own**, etc.*

Examples: Why do you want to borrow my car? Why can't you use *your own car?*
            Ann never goes to the hairdresser. She cuts *her own hair.*

1. Don't blame me. It's not my fault. It's ....
2. He's always smoking my cigarettes. Why doesn't he buy ....?
3. Why do you want my pen? Can't you use ....?
4. I don't often buy clothes. I usually make..
5. Nobody cooks Don's meals for him. He has to cook...
6. She doesn't buy ready-made cigarettes. She rolls ....
7. She doesn't need to borrow money from me. She has...

155

All / all of,   no / none of,
most / most of, etc.

few — a few?

a

| all | no/none | some | any | much/many | most | little/few | each | half |

You can use these words (except **none** and **half**) with a noun:
- **All cars** have wheels.
- I have **no money**.
- **Some people** are very unfriendly.
- Did you put **any salt** in the soup?
- Hurry! We have very **little time**.
- Study **each sentence** carefully.

Be careful with **most**:
- **Most tourists** do not visit this part of the town. (*not* most of tourists, *not* the most tourists)
- George is much richer than **most people**.

b

You can also use these words (except **no**) alone, without a noun:
- "I need some money. Do you have **any?**"   "Yes, but not **much**."
- "How many cigarettes do you have?"   "**None**."
- Most people like Tom, but **some** don't.

We usually say **each one** instead of **each** alone:
- There were three boxes on the table. **Each one** was a different color.

For **all** see Unit 83a.

c

You can also use these words (except **no**) with **of** . . . . So you can say **some of the people, all of these cars, none of my money**, etc.

When you use these words with **of**, you need **the/this/that/these/those/my/your/his**, etc. You cannot say "some of people," "all of cars." You must say: "some of **the** people," "all of **these** cars," etc.:
- **Some of the** people at the party were very friendly.
- **Most of my** friends live in Montreal.
- **None of this** money is mine.
- **Each of the** rooms in the hotel has its own bathroom.
- I haven't read **many of these** books.

With **all** and **half** we usually leave out **of**:
all my friends (= all **of** my friends)
half the money (= half **of** the money) (*not* the half)

d

After **all of / none of**, etc., you can also use **it/us/you/them**:
- "How many of these people do you know?" "**None of them**."
- Do **any of you** want to come to a party tonight?
- "Do you like this music?" "**Some of it**. Not **all of it**."

You must say "all **of**" and "half **of**" before **it/us/you/them**:
all of us (*not* "all us")   **half of them** (*not* "half them")

For **no** and **none** see Unit 81b.

For more information about the words in this unit see Units 79–83.

UNIT 78 Exercises

78.1 *Read each situation and then make a sentence from the words in parentheses (. . .).*

Example: I need someone who can speak Spanish. (any / your friends / speak Spanish?)
Do any of your friends speak Spanish?

1. We went out and it started to rain. We all got wet because (none / us / have / an umbrella)
   none...
2. When they got married, they kept it a complete secret. (they / not / tell / any / their friends)   They ....
3. I don't want all this lemonade. (you / want / some / it?)   Do.....................................
4. This is a very old town. (many / the buildings / over 800 years old)
   ....
5. Jim won a lot of money last year. (he / spend / half / it on a new car)
   ....
6. A lot of people were interested in the job. (the manager / interview / each / the people who applied)   ....
7. Not many people live in the north of the country. (most / the people / live / the south)
   ....*Most people*...
8. The club is mainly for younger people. (few / the members / over 25)
   ....
9. When the mail arrived, she looked through it hopefully, but (none / the letters / for her)
   ....

78.2 *Complete these sentences with* **most** *or* **most of.**

Example: ...*Most*.................tourists do not visit this part of the town.

1. I spend .... my spare time gardening.
2. The public transportation system is bad, but ....people have a car.
3. .... days I get up early.
4. We had a relaxing vacation. ....the time we lay on the beach.
5. The church is very old. .... it was built in the 12th century.
6. I bet .... you are tired after your long trip.

78.3 *Answer these questions using the word(s) in parentheses.*

Example: Do you like this music? (some)   *Some of it.*......................................

1. Did you watch the movie? (most)   ....
2. Did you take these photographs? (some)   ....
3. Have you read these books? (a few)   ....
4. Are those people Canadian? (most)   ....
5. How much of this luggage is yours? (all)   ....
6. How many of these people do you know? (not many)   ....
7. Does this furniture belong to you? (some)   ....
8. Have you spent all the money I gave you? (not all)   ....
9. How much of this money is yours? (half)   ....

UNIT 79
Both / both of, neither / neither of, either / either of

a We use **both, neither,** and **either** when we are talking about two things. You can use these words with a noun:

- **Both restaurants** are very good. (*not* the both restaurants)
- **Neither restaurant** is expensive.
- We can go to **either restaurant.** I don't care. (**either** = one or the other; it doesn't matter which one)
- I didn't like **either restaurant.** (not the one or the other)

b You can also use **both/neither/either** with **of....** When you use these words with **of,** you always need **the/these/those/my/your/his,** etc. You cannot say, "both of restaurants." You have to say "both of **the** restaurants," "both of **these** restaurants," etc.:

- **Both of these** restaurants are very good.
- **Neither of the** restaurants we went to was (*or* were) expensive.
- We can go to **either of those** restaurants. I don't mind.

With **both** you can leave out **of.** So you can say:

both my parents *or* both **of** my parents

c After **both of / neither of / either of** you can also use **us/you/them:**

- Can **either of you** speak Spanish?
- I wanted Tom and Ann to come, but **neither of them** wanted to.

You must say: "both **of**" before **us/you/them:**

- **Both of us** were very tired. (*not* Both us ...)

d After **neither of ...** you can use a singular or a plural verb:

- Neither of the children **wants** (*or* **want**) to go to bed.
- Neither of us **is** (*or* **are**) married.

e You can say **both...and..., neither...nor...,** and **either...or....** Study these examples:

- **Both** Tom **and** Ann were late.
- They were **both** tired **and** hungry.
- **Neither** Tom **nor** Ann came to the party.
- **He** said he would contact me, but he **neither** wrote **nor** called.
- I'm not sure where he is from. He's **either** Spanish **or** Italian.
- **Either** you apologize, **or** I'll never speak to you again.

f You can also use **both/neither/either** alone:

- "Is he British or American?" "**Neither.** He's Australian."
- "Do you want tea or coffee?" "**Either.** It doesn't matter."
- I couldn't decide which one to choose. I liked **both.**

For **I don't either** and **neither do I** see Unit 49c.

UNIT 79 Exercises

79.1 *Complete these sentences with* **both/neither/either.** *Sometimes you need* **of.**

Examples: There are two windows in my room. It was very warm so I had .**both of**............
them open.
"Do you want tea or coffee?" " .**Either**................ . It doesn't matter."

1. After the accident .... cars stopped. .... drivers
   got out and started shouting at each other. .... them were very
   angry.
2. It wasn't a very good soccer game. .... team played well.
3. A: Which of the two movies did you prefer? The first one or the second one?
   B: Actually, I didn't like .... them.
4. There are two ways to get downtown. You can take the local streets, or you can take the
   highway. You can go .... way.
5. .... these sweaters are very nice. I don't know which one to buy.
6. .... my parents are American. My father is Polish and my mother is
   Italian.
7. "Do you care which sandwich I take?" "No, take .... "
8. "Is today the 18th or the 19th?" " .... It's the 20th."
9. Tom and I hadn't eaten for a long time, so .... us were very hungry.
10. When the boat started to sink, we were really frightened because ....
    us could swim.
11. A: Did you go to Florida or Puerto Rico for your vacation?
    B: We went to ....: a week in Florida and a week in Puerto Rico.

79.2 *Make sentences with* **both . . . and . . . , neither . . . nor . . . ,** *and* **either . . . or . . . .**

Examples: Tom was late. So was Ann. ..**Both Tom and Ann were late.**..................
He didn't write. He didn't telephone. **He neither wrote nor telephoned.**

1. The hotel wasn't clean. And it wasn't comfortable.
   The hotel was neither...
2. It was a very boring movie. It was very long too.
   The movie was...
3. Is that man's name Richard? Or is it Robert? It's one of the two.
   That man's name ....
4. I don't have the time to take a vacation. And I don't have the money.
   I have...
5. We can leave today or we can leave tomorrow – whichever you prefer.
   We...
6. He gave up his job because he needed a change. Also because the pay was low.
   He gave up his job both ....
7. Laura doesn't smoke. And she doesn't eat meat.
   ....
8. The front of the house needs painting. The back needs painting too.
   ....

UNIT 80

Some and any
Some/any + -one/-body/-thing/-where

a In general we use **some** in positive sentences and **any** in negative sentences (but see also sections b and d):

- Ann has bought **some** new shoes.
- They don't have **any** children.
- I've got **something** in my eye.
- He's lazy. He **never** does **any** work.

We use **any** in the following sentences because the meaning is negative:

- He left home **without any money**. (He didn't have any money.)
- She **refused to say anything**. (She didn't say anything.)

b We often use **any/anyone/anything**, etc., after **if**:

- **If any** letters arrive for me, can you send them to this address?
- **If anyone** has any questions, I'll be glad to answer them.
- **If** you need **anything**, just ask.
- Buy some pears **if** you see **any**.

The following sentences are without **if**, but they have the idea of **if**:

- **Anyone** who wants to take the exam must give me their names before Friday. (= if there is anyone who . . .)
- I'll send on **any letters** that arrive for you. (= if there are any)

c In questions we usually use **any** (*not* some):

- Do you have **any** money?
- Has **anybody** seen Tom?

But we often use **some** in questions when we expect the answer "yes":

- What's wrong with your eye? Have you got **something** in it? (= I think you have something in your eye, and I expect you to say "yes")

We use **some** in questions, especially when we offer or ask for things:

- Would you like **some** tea?
- Can I have **some** of those apples?

d **Any** also has another meaning. **Any/anyone/anybody/anything/anywhere** can mean **it doesn't matter which/who/what/where**:

- You can catch **any of these buses**. They all go downtown. (= it doesn't matter which of these buses)
- Come and see me **any time** you want. (= it doesn't matter when)
- You can have **anything you want** for your birthday present.
- We left the door unlocked. **Anybody** could have come in.
- I'd rather go **anywhere** than stay at home during my vacation.
- "Sing a song." "Which song shall I sing?" "**Any song.** I don't care."

e **Someone/somebody/anyone/anybody** are singular words:

- **Someone wants** to see you.
- **Is** anybody there?

But we often use **they/them/their** after these words:

- If **anyone wants** to leave early, **they** can. (= he or she can)
- **Somebody has** spilled **their** (= his or her) coffee on the carpet.

For **some of** / **any of** see Unit 78. For **not . . . any** see Unit 81.

160

to move each tense back one

UNIT 80 Exercises

80.1 *Complete these sentences with* **some/any/someone/anyone/somebody/anybody/something/
anything/somewhere/anywhere.**

Examples: Ann bought ...**some**.......... new shoes.
The boy refused to tell us .**anything.**.....

1. Does ....mind if I smoke?
2. Would you like ....*something* to eat?
3. Do you live ...*anywhere*... near Jim?
4. The prisoners refused to eat ....*anything*.
5. There's ...*someone*... at the door. Can you go and see who it is?
6. We slept in the park because we didn't have ...*anywhere*... to stay. We didn't know
   .... we could stay with, and we didn't have ....money for a
   hotel.
7. Can I have ....*some*..... milk in my coffee, please?
8. Sue is very secretive. She never tells ...*anything anybody*... (*two words*).
9. Why are you looking under the bed? Have you lost ...*something*?
10. You can cash these travelers checks at ......*any*...... bank.
11. I haven't read ...*any*... of these books, but Tom has read ...*some* of them.
12. He left the house without saying .... to ....
13. Would you like ...*some*........... more coffee?
14. The film is really great. You can ask .... who has seen it.
15. This is a No Parking area. ...*anyone*..... who parks here will have to pay a fine.
16. Can you give me ....*some*........ information about places to see in the town?
17. With this special tourist bus ticket you can go ...*anywhere*...you like on...*any*......
    bus you like.

80.2 *Write sentences with* **if.**

Example: Perhaps someone will need help. If so, they can ask me.
If .*anyone needs help, they can ask me.*.........................

1. Perhaps someone will ring the doorbell. If so, don't let them in.
   If .... , don't let them in.
2. Perhaps someone will ask you some questions. If so, don't tell them anything.
   If ....
3. Perhaps someone saw the accident. If so, they should contact the police.
   If ....

80.3 *Complete these sentences. Use* **any/anyone/anybody/anything/anywhere.**

Example: I don't care what you tell him. *You can tell him anything you like.*....

1. I don't care what you wear to the party.   You can wear ......*anything*
2. I don't care where you sit.   You can...
3. It doesn't matter which day you come.   You ....
4. I don't care who you talk to.   You..
5. It doesn't matter which flight you travel on.   You..
6. I don't care who you marry.   ....
7. It doesn't matter what time you call.   ....

161

No/none/any
No/any + one/-body/-thing/-where

a No   none   no one   nobody   nothing   nowhere
We use these negative words especially at the beginning of a sentence or alone:
- **No one** (*or* **Nobody**) came to visit me when I was in the hospital.
- **No** system of government is perfect.
- "Where are you going?" "**Nowhere.** I'm staying here."
- **None** of these books are mine.
- "What did you do?" "**Nothing.**"

You can also use these words in the middle or at the end of a sentence. But don't use "not" with these words. They are already negative:
- I saw **nothing.** (*not* I didn't see nothing.)

In the middle or at the end of a sentence, we more often use: **not . . . any/anyone/anybody/anything/anywhere**:
- I did**n't** see **anything.** (= I saw nothing.)
- We do**n't** have **any** money. (= We have no money.)
- The station is**n't anywhere** near here. (= . . . is nowhere near here)
- She did**n't** tell **anyone** about her plans. (= She told no one)

Where there is another negative word, you don't need "not":
- **Nobody** tells me **anything.** (= People don't tell me anything.)

b No and **none**
We use **no** with a noun. **No** = **not a** or **not any**:
- We had to walk because there was **no bus.** (= there wasn't a bus)
- I can't talk to you now. I have **no time.** (= I don't have any time)
- There were **no stores** open. (= There weren't any stores open.)

We use **none** alone (without a noun):
- "How much money do you have?" "**None.**"

Or we use **none of**:

none of these shops   none of my money   none of it/us/you/them

After **none of** + a *plural* word ("none of **the girls** / none of **them**," etc.), you can use a singular or a plural verb. A plural verb is more usual, especially in spoken English:
- None of the **people** I met **were** English.

c After **no one/nobody** we often say **they/them/their**:
- **Nobody** called, did **they**? (= did he or she)
- **No one** in the class did **their** homework. (= his or her homework)

d You can use **any/no** with *comparative* (**any better** / **no bigger**, etc.):
- Do you feel **any better** today? (= Do you feel better at all? – *said to someone who felt sick yesterday*)
- We've waited long enough. I'm **not** waiting **any longer.** (= not even a minute longer)
- I expected your house to be very big, but it's **no bigger** than mine. (= not even a little bigger)

For **any** see also Unit 80.

UNIT 81   Exercises

81.1   *Answer these questions with* **none (of)/no one/nobody/nothing/nowhere**.

Example: What did you do? .*Nothing.*...

1. Where are you going?........................
2. How many children does he have? ....
3. What did you tell them?.....................

4. Who are you talking to?.....................
5. How much of this money is
   yours?..

Now write answers to these questions with **any/anyone/anybody/anything/anywhere**.

Example: "What did you do?   " *I didn't do anything.*............................... "

6. "Where are you going?"   "I .... "
7. "How many children do they have?"   "They .... "
8. "Who did you dance with?"   "I .... "
9. "What did they give you?"   " .... "

81.2   *Complete these sentences with* **no/none/no one/nobody/nothing/nowhere/any/anyone/anybody/anything/anywhere**.

Examples: There were .....*no*.............. stores open.   I don't want *anything*...... to eat.

1. The bus was completely empty. There wasn't ....on it.
2. "Where did you go for your vacation?"   " .... I stayed home."
3. I couldn't make an omelette because I had .... eggs.
4. I didn't say .... Not a word.
5. The accident looked serious, but fortunately .... was injured.
6. The town was still the same when I returned years later. .... had changed.
7. We took a few photographs, but .... of them were very good.
8. I can't find my watch .... I've looked all over the house.
9. "What did you have for breakfast?"   " .... I don't usually have ....
   for breakfast."
10. We canceled the party because .... of the people we invited could come.
11. .... intelligent person could do such a stupid thing.
12. There was complete silence in the room. .... said ....
13. "How many movie theaters are there in this town?"   " .... The last one
    closed six months ago."
14. The four of us wanted to go to a restaurant, but we couldn't because .... of
    us had .... money.

81.3   *Make sentences with* **any/no** + *a comparative*.

Example: I hear you weren't feeling well yesterday. Do you feel *any better*. today?

1. I'm going as fast as I can. I can't go ....
2. What makes you think Harry is old? He is .... than you.
3. I'm sorry I'm late, but I couldn't come ....
4. This restaurant is a little expensive. Is the other one .... ?
5. I have to stop for a rest. I can't walk ....

UNIT 82 Much, many, little, few, a lot, plenty

a **Much   many   few   little**
We use **much** and **little** with uncountable nouns:
   much time   **much** luck   **little** energy   **little** money

We use **many** and **few** with plural nouns:
   many friends   **many** people   **few** cars   **few** countries

b **A lot (of)   lots (of)   plenty (of)**
We use **a lot of / lots of / plenty of** with uncountable and plural nouns:

   a lot of luck   **lots of** time   **plenty of** money
   a lot of people   **lots of** books   **plenty of** ideas

Plenty = more than enough:
   ■ "Have some more to eat."   "No, thank you. I've had **plenty**."
   ■ There's no need to hurry. We have **plenty of time**.

c We use **much** and **many** mainly in negative sentences and questions:
   ■ We did**n't** spend **much** money.
   ■ Do you have **many** friends?
In positive sentences it is usually better to use **a lot (of)**. **Much** is not normally used in positive sentences:
   ■ We spent **a lot of** money. (*not* we spent much money)
   ■ There has been **a lot of** rain recently. (*not* much rain)
But we use **too much** and **so much** in positive sentences:
   ■ I can't drink this tea. There's **too much** sugar in it.

d **Little / a little / few / a few**
Little and **few** (without **a**) are negative ideas:
   ■ Hurry up! There's **little** time. (= not much, not enough time)
   ■ He's not popular. He has **few** friends. (= not many, not enough friends)
We often use **very** before **little** and **few** (**very little** and **very few**):
   ■ There's **very little** time.
   ■ He has **very few** friends.
"**A** little" and "**a** few" are more positive ideas. **A little / a few** = some, a small amount, or a small number:
   ■ Let's go and have a cup of coffee. We have **a little** time before the train leaves. (= some time, enough time to have a drink)
   ■ "Do you have any money?" "Yes, **a little**. Do you want to borrow some?"
   ■ I enjoy my life here. I have **a few** friends and we get together. (a few friends = not many but enough to have a good time)
   ■ "When did you last see Tom?" "**A few** days ago." (= some days ago)
But "**only a** little" and "**only a** few" have a negative meaning:
   ■ Hurry up! We **only** have **a little** time.
   ■ The town was very small. There were **only a few** houses.

164

UNIT 82   Exercises

82.1 *Complete these sentences with* **much, many,** *and* **a lot (of).** *Sometimes there are two possibilities.*

Examples: There weren't .. *many* .... people at the party I had seen before.
It cost me .. *a lot of* .... money to furnish this house.

1. We'll have to hurry. We don't have .... time.
2. Tom drinks .... milk – two quarts a day.
3. She is a very quiet person. She doesn't say ....
4. I drank .... coffee last night. Perhaps too ....
5. .... people do not like flying.
6. The woman was badly injured in the accident. She lost .... blood.
7. It's not a very lively town. There isn't .... to do.
8. This car is expensive to run. It uses .... gasoline.
9. Don't bother me. I have .... work to do.
10. He has so .... money, he doesn't know what to do with it.
11. She always puts .... salt on her food.
12. We didn't take .... pictures when we were on vacation.

82.2 *Make sentences with* **plenty (of).** *Use the word in parentheses (. . .).*

Example: We needn't hurry. (time)   We .. *have plenty of time.* ....

1. He has no financial problems. (money)   He has...
2. We don't need to go to a gas station. (gas)   We ....
3. Come and sit at our table. (room)   There is...
4. We can make omelettes for lunch. (eggs)   We ....
5. We'll easily find somewhere to stay. (hotels)   There ....
6. I can't believe you're still hungry. (to eat)   You've had.......................................
7. Why are you sitting there doing nothing? (things to do)   You ....

82.3 *Complete these sentences with* **little / a little / few / a few.**

Examples: Hurry! We have ..... *little* .... time.
I last saw Tom ..... *a few* .... days ago.

1. We didn't have any money, but Tom had ....
2. He doesn't speak much English. Only .... words.
3. Jane's father died .... years ago.
4. "Would you like some more coffee?"   "Yes, please, but only .... "
5. This town isn't very well known and there isn't much to see, so .... tourists come here.
6. I don't think Jill would be a good teacher. She has .... patience with children.
7. This is not the first time the car has broken down. It has happened .... times before.
8. The theater was almost empty. There were very........................ people there.
9. There is a shortage of water because there has been very .... rain.

UNIT 83 All, every, and whole

a **All everyone everybody everything**

We do not normally use **all** to mean **everyone/everybody**:

- **Everybody** enjoyed the party. (*not* All enjoyed . . .)
- Ann knows **everyone** on her street. (*not* . . . all on her street)

Sometimes you can use **all** to mean **everything**, but it is usually better to say **everything**:

- He thinks he knows **everything**. (*not* knows all)
- It was a terrible vacation. **Everything** went wrong. (*not* all went wrong)

But you can use **all** in the expression **all about**:

- They told us **all about** their vacation.

We also use **all** to mean **the only thing(s)**:

- **All** I've eaten today is a sandwich. (= the only thing I've eaten)

b We use a *singular* verb after **every/everyone/everybody/everything**:

- **Every seat** in the theater **was** taken.
- **Everybody looks** tired today.
- **Everything** she said **was** true.

But we often use **they/them/their** after **everyone/everybody**, especially in spoken English:

- Has **everyone** got **their** tickets? (= his or her ticket)
- **Everybody** said **they** would come. (= he or she would come)

c **All and whole**

We use **whole** mainly with singular nouns:

- Have you read **the whole book?** (= all the book, not just a part of it)
- He was very quiet. He didn't say a word **the whole evening**.
- She has spent **her whole life** in South America.

We say **the/my/her**, etc., before **whole**. Compare:

  the whole book / all **the** book   **her** whole life / all **her** life

You can also say "**a whole** . . . ":

- Jack ate **a whole loaf of bread** yesterday. (= a complete loaf)

We do not normally use **whole** with uncountable nouns:

- **all the money** (*not* the whole money)

d **Every/all/whole** with time words

We use **every** to say how often something happens. So we say **every day / every week / every Monday / every ten minutes / every three weeks**, etc.:

- We go out **every Friday night**.
- The buses run **every ten minutes**.
- Ann goes to see her mother **every three weeks**.

All day / the whole day = the complete day:

- We spent **all day / the whole day** on the beach.
- I've been trying to find you **all morning / the whole morning**.

Note that we say **all day / all week**, etc. (*not* all the day / all the week)

For **all** see also Units 78 and 102c.

UNIT 83 Exercises

83.1 *Complete these sentences with* **all, everything,** *or* **everyone/everybody**.

Examples: Ann knows *everyone (or everybody)* on her street.
...*All*............I've eaten today is a sandwich.

1. Tom is very popular. .... likes him.
2. .... was very kind to us. They did........................ they could to help us.
3. Jill doesn't do any of the housework. Her husband does ....
4. Margaret told me .... about her new job. It sounds very interesting.
5. Can .... write their names on a piece of paper, please?
6. I can't lend you any money. .... I've got is a dollar, and I need that.
7. I can't stand him. He disagrees with .... I say.
8. I didn't spend much money shopping. .... I bought was a pair of gloves.
9. Why are you always thinking about money? Money isn't ....
10. He didn't say where he was going. .... he said was that he was going away.
11. .... has their faults. Nobody is perfect.

83.2 *Make sentences with* **the whole**.

Example: He read the book from beginning to end.   *He read the whole book.*............

1. He opened a bottle of soda. When he finished drinking, there was no soda left in the
   bottle.   He drank the ....
2. The police came to our house. They were looking for something. They searched
   everywhere, every room.   They searched ....
3. She worked from early in the morning until late in the evening.
   ....
4. Everyone in Tim and Carol's family plays tennis. Tim and Carol play, and so do all their
   children.   The .... tennis.
5. Jack and Jill went to the beach for a week. It rained from the beginning of the week to the
   end.   It ....
6. It was a terrible fire. Nothing was left of the building afterward.
   .... destroyed in the fire.
7. Everyone on the team played well.   ....

Now make sentences for 3 and 5 again. This time use **all** *instead of* **whole**.

8. (3) She ....
9. (5) It ....

83.3 *Now say how often something happens. Use* **every** *with these periods of time:*

four years   ten minutes   four hours   six months   ~~five minutes~~

Example: There's good bus service to the city center. The buses run *every five minutes.*

1. Tom is sick in bed. He has some medicine. He has to take it..
2. The Olympic Games take place..
3. Everyone should have a checkup with the dentist ....
4. We live near a busy airport. A plane flies over the house ....

167

UNIT 84 Relative clauses (1) – clauses with who/that/which

a Study this example:

The man │ who lives next door │ is very friendly.
└─ *relative clause* ─┘

A *clause* is a part of a sentence. A *relative clause* tells us which person or thing (or what kind of person or thing) the speaker means:

- The man **who lives next door** . . . (**who lives next door** tells us which man)
- People **who live in Paris** . . . (**who live in Paris** tells us what kind of people)

We use **who** in a relative clause when we are talking about *people*. We use **who** instead of **he/she/they**:

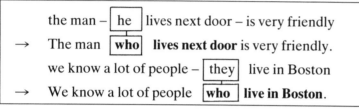

the man – │ he │ lives next door – is very friendly

→ The man │ **who** │ **lives next door** is very friendly.

we know a lot of people – │ they │ live in Boston

→ We know a lot of people │ **who** │ **live in Boston**.

- An architect is someone **who designs buildings**.
- What was the name of the man **who lent you the money**?
- The girl **who was injured in the accident** is now in the hospital.
- Anyone **who wants to take the exam** must sign up before next Friday.

It is also possible to use **that** instead of **who**:

- The man **that** lives next door is very friendly.

But sometimes you must use **who** for people – see Unit 87.

b When we are talking about *things*, we use **that** (not **who**) in a relative clause. We use **that** instead of **it/they**:

where are the eggs? – │ they │ were in the refrigerator

Where are the eggs │ **that** │ **were in the refrigerator?**

- I don't like stories **that have unhappy endings**.
- Jerry works for a company **that makes typewriters**.
- Everything **that happened** was my fault.
- The window **that was broken** has now been repaired.

You can also use **which** for things (but not for people):

- Where are the eggs **which** were in the refrigerator?

That is more usual than **which** in the sentences in this unit. But sometimes you must use **which** – see Unit 87.

c Remember that we use **who/that/which** instead of **he/she/they/it**:

- Do you know the man **who** lives next door? (*not* . . . who *he* lives . . .)

Now study the next unit for more information about relative clauses.

UNIT 84 Exercises

84.1 *Explain what these words mean. Choose the right meaning from the list and then write a sentence with* **who**. *Use a dictionary if necessary.*

he/she steals from a store	he/she breaks into a house and steals things
he/she doesn't eat meat	he/she fills prescriptions for medicine
~~he/she designs buildings~~	he/she buys something from a store

1. (an architect)   *An architect is someone who designs buildings.*
2. (a burglar)   A burglar is someone...
3. (a vegetarian)   A vegetarian ....
4. (a customer)   ....
5. (a shoplifter)   ....
6. (a pharmacist)   ....

84.2 *Read the two sentences and then write one sentence with the same meaning. Use a relative clause in your sentence.*

Example: A girl was injured in the accident. She is now in the hospital.
The girl *who was injured in the accident is now in the hospital.*

1. A man answered the phone. He told me you were out.
   The man...
2. A waitress served us. She was very impolite and impatient.
   The ....
3. Some boys were arrested. They have now been released.
   The boys ....

84.3 *The sentences in this exercise are not complete. Choose the most appropriate ending from the list and make it into a relative clause.*

he invented the telephone	~~it makes typewriters~~
she runs away from home	it gives you the meanings of words
they are never on time	it won the race
they stole my car	it can support life
they used to hang on that wall	it was found last week

1. Jerry works for a company *that (or which) makes typewriters.* ....
2. The book is about a girl ....
3. What was the name of the horse ....?
4. The police have caught the men ....
5. Alexander Bell was the man ....
6. Where are the pictures ....?
7. The police are still trying to identify the body ....
8. A dictionary is a book ....
9. I don't like people ....
10. It seems that Earth is the only planet ....

UNIT 85 Relative clauses (2) – clauses with or without **who/that**

a Look again at these examples from Unit 84:
- The man **who lives next door** is very friendly. (*or* **that** lives)
- Where are the eggs **that were in the refrigerator**? (*or* **which** were)

In these sentences **who** and **that** are *subjects* of the verbs in the relative clauses: the man lives next door, the eggs were in the refrigerator. You cannot leave out **who** or **that** in these sentences.

Sometimes **who** and **that** are *objects* of the verbs:

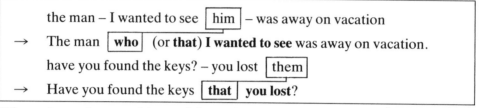

When **who** or **that** are objects of the verb in the relative clause, you can leave them out:
- **The man I wanted to see** was away on vacation. (*but not* The man I wanted to see *him* was away on vacation.)
- Have you found **the keys you lost**? (*but not* Have you found the keys you lost *them*?)
- **The dress Ann bought** doesn't fit her very well. (= the dress **that** Ann bought)
- **The woman Jerry is going to marry** is Mexican. (= the woman **who/that** Jerry is going to marry)
- Is there **anything I can do**? (= is there anything **that** I can do?)

b There are often prepositions (**in/at/with**, etc.) in relative clauses. Study the position of the prepositions in these sentences:

```
do you know the girl? – Tom is talking [to] her
→  Do you know the girl (who/that) Tom is talking [to] ?

the bed – I slept [in] it last night – wasn't very comfortable
→  The bed (that) I slept [in] last night wasn't very comfortable.
```

- The man **(who/that) I sat next to on the plane** talked all the time.
- Are these the books **(that) you have been looking for**?
- The girl **(who/that) he fell in love with** left him after a few weeks.

c You cannot use **what** instead of **that**:
- Everything **(that) he said** was true. (*not* everything what he said)
- I gave her **all the money (that) I had**. (*not* all . . . what I had)

What = the thing(s) that:
- Did you hear **what I said**? (= the words that I said)
- I won't tell anyone **what happened**. (= the thing that happened)

170

UNIT 85   Exercises

85.1 *The sentences in this exercise are not complete. Complete each one with a relative clause.*
Use the sentences in the box to make your relative clauses.

we met her yesterday	we wanted to visit it	Tom tells them
Tom recommended it	we had it for dinner	~~you lost them~~
Ann is wearing it	the police arrested him	I invited them to the party

1. Have you found the keys ...*you lost*...........................?
2. I like the dress ....
3. The museum .... was closed when we got there.
4. Most of the people .... couldn't come.
5. I didn't like that woman ....
6. The fish .... was really delicious.
7. We stayed at a hotel ....
8. The stories .... are usually very funny.
9. The man .... has now been released.

85.2 *Make a relative clause with a preposition.*

you were with her last night	I am living in it	~~I slept in it~~
they were talking about them	she is married to him	I work with them
we wanted to travel on it	I applied for it	we went to it

1. The bed .....*I slept in*.................... was too soft.
2. I didn't get the job ....
3. The man .... has been married twice before.
4. The party .... wasn't very enjoyable.
5. Who was that woman .... ?
6. The flight .... was fully booked.
7. I enjoy my job because I like the people ....
8. I wasn't interested in the things ....
9. The house .... is not in very good condition.

85.3 *Complete these sentences, where necessary, with **that, who,** or **what**. If it is possible to write*
***that** or leave it out, write (**that**) – in parentheses (. . .).*

Examples: Did you hear ..*what*..... I said?   Everything .*(that)*....he said was true.

1. She gives her children everything .... they want.
2. Tell me .... you want, and I'll try to help you.
3. Why do you blame me for everything .... goes wrong?
4. I won't be able to do very much, but I'll do the best .... I can.
5. I can't lend you any money. All .... I have is a dollar.
6. Susan is the only person .... understands me.
7. Why do you always disagree with everything .... I say?
8. I don't agree with .... you've just said.
9. This is an awful movie. It's the worst .... I've ever seen.

UNIT 86 Relative clauses (3) – **whose, whom,** and **where**

a Whose

We use **whose** in relative clauses instead of **his/her/their**:

> we saw some people – **their** car had broken down
>
> → We saw some people **whose** car had broken down.

We use **whose** mostly for people:

- A widow is a woman **whose husband is dead**. (**her** husband is dead)
- What's the name of the girl **whose car you borrowed**? (you borrowed **her** car)
- The other day I met someone **whose brother I went to school with**. (I went to school with **his** brother)

b

Whom is possible instead of **who** (for people) when it is the *object* of the verb in the relative clause (like the sentences in Unit 85):

- The man **whom I wanted to see** was away on vacation. (I wanted to see **him**)

You can also use **whom** with a preposition (**to/from/with whom**, etc.):

- The woman **with whom he fell in love** left him after a few weeks. (he fell in love **with her**)

But we do not often use **whom**. In spoken English we normally prefer **who** or **that** (or you can leave them out – see Unit 85):

- The man (**who/that**) **I wanted to see** . . .
- The woman (**who/that**) **he fell in love with** . . .

For **whom** see also Units 87 and 88.

c Where

You can use **where** in a relative clause to talk about places:

> the hotel – we stayed **there** – wasn't very clean
>
> → The hotel **where** **we stayed** wasn't very clean.

- I recently went back to **the town where I was born**. (*or* the town (that) I was born in)
- I would like to live in **a country where there is plenty of sunshine**.

d

We use **that** (or we leave it out) when we say **the day** / **the year** / **the time**, (etc.) **that something happened**:

- Do you still remember **the day (that) we first met**?
- **The last time (that) I saw her**, she looked very well.
- I haven't seen them since **the year (that) they got married**.

e

You can say **the reason why something happens** or **the reason that something happens**. You can also leave out **why** and **that**:

- **The reason (why/that) I'm calling you** is to invite you to a party.

172

UNIT 86 Exercises

86.1 *You were on vacation with a friend of yours. You met some people who had some bad experiences during their vacation. You met:*

1. some people / their car broke down
2. a man / his wife got sick and was taken to the hospital
3. a woman / her husband was arrested by the police
4. a girl / her passport was stolen
5. a couple / their luggage disappeared

You can't recall the names of these people. Ask your friend, making sentences with **whose**.

1. *What was the name of the people whose car broke down*?
2. What was the name of the man...?
3. What..?
4. ....?
5. ....?

86.2 *The sentences in this exercise are not complete. Complete them with* **where** .... *Use the sentences in the box to make your relative clauses.*

I can buy postcards there	~~I was born there~~
she had bought it there	we spent our vacation there
people are buried there	we can have a really good meal there

1. I recently went back to the town ..*where I was born.*....................................
2. The dress didn't fit her, so she took it back to the store..................................
3. Do you know a restaurant ....?
4. Is there a store near here..?
5. The place .... was really beautiful.
6. A cemetery is a place ....

86.3 *Complete the sentences with a relative clause. Use the sentences in the box to make your relative clauses.*

(her) dog bit me	they don't have a car (for this reason)
John is staying (there)	I didn't write to you (for this reason)
~~we first met (on that day)~~	World War II ended (in that year)
(his/her) parents are dead	you called (that evening)

1. Do you remember the day .*(that) we first met*......................................?
2. An orphan is a child..
3. The reason .... was that I didn't know your address.
4. Unfortunately I wasn't home the evening ....
5. I protested to the woman ....
6. The reason .... is that they can't afford one.
7. Do you know the name of the hotel ....?
8. Nineteen forty-five was the year ....

173

UNIT 87 Relative clauses (4) – "extra information" clauses (1)

a Look again at these examples from Units 84 and 85:
- The man **who lives next door** is very friendly.
- Jerry works for a company **that makes typewriters**.
- Have you found the keys **(that) you lost**?

In these examples, the relative clauses tell us *which person or thing (or what kind of person or thing)* the speaker means:

"The man **who lives next door**" tells us *which* man.

"a company **that makes typewriters**" tells us *what kind* of company.

"the keys **(that) you lost**" tells us *which* keys.

But not all relative clauses are like this. For example:
- Tom's father, **who is 78**, goes swimming every day.
- The house at the end of the street, **which has been empty for two years**, has just been sold.

In these examples the relative clauses (**who is 78** and **which has been empty for two years**) do *not* tell us which person or thing the speaker means. *We already know* which person or thing is meant: "**Tom's father**" and "the house **at the end of the street**." The relative clauses in these sentences give us *extra information* about the person or thing.

b In these "extra information" relative clauses you have to use **who** for people and **which** for things. You cannot use **that**, and you cannot leave out **who** or **which**.

When you write clauses like this, you have to put *commas* (,) at the beginning and at the end of the clause. Study these examples:
- Mr. Yates, **who has worked for the same company all his life,** is retiring next month.
- The strike at the car factory, **which lasted ten days,** is now over.

When the clause comes at the end of the sentence, you have to put a **comma** before the clause:
- Yesterday I met John, **who told me he was getting married.**
- She told me her address, **which I wrote down on a piece of paper.**

Remember that we use **who/which** instead of **he/she/it/they**:
- Last night we went to Ann's party, **which** we enjoyed very much. (*not* which we enjoyed *it* very much)

c You can also use **whose, whom,** and **where** in relative clauses with "extra information":
- Martin, **whose mother is Spanish**, speaks both Spanish and English fluently.
- Mr. Hill is going to Canada, **where his son has been living for five years**.
- My sister, **whom** (or **who**) **you once met**, is visiting us next week.

For more information about **whose, whom,** and **where** see Unit 86.

See also the next unit for "extra information" relative clauses.

UNIT 87 Exercises

87.1 *Write these sentences again, giving extra information in a relative clause. Sometimes the relative clause is in the middle of the sentence, sometimes at the end. Use the sentence in parentheses (. . .) to make your relative clauses.*

Examples: Tom's father goes swimming every day. (Tom's father is 78.)
Tom's father, who is 78, goes swimming every day.
She told me her address. (I wrote her address down on a piece of paper.)
She told me her address, which I wrote down on a piece of paper.

1. She showed me a photograph of her son. (Her son is a police officer.)
   She showed me a photograph of her son, ...
2. We decided not to swim in the ocean. (The ocean looked rather dirty.)
   We ....
3. The new stadium will be opened next month. (The stadium holds 90,000 people.)
   The ....
4. Joan is one of my closest friends. (I have known Joan for eight years.)
   ....
5. That man over there is an artist. (I don't remember his name.) (*use* **whose**)
   ....
6. Opposite our house there is a nice park. (There are some beautiful trees in this park.)
   (*use* **where**) ....
7. The storm caused a lot of damage. (Nobody had been expecting the storm.)
   ....
8. The mail carrier was late this morning. (The mail carrier is nearly always on time.)
   ....
9. We often go to visit our friends in Baltimore. (Baltimore is only 30 miles away.)
   ....
10. Mr. Edwards has gone into the hospital for some tests. (His health hasn't been good
    recently). (*use* **whose**) ....
11. Jack looks much nicer without his beard. (His beard made him look much older.)
    ....
12. I went to see the doctor. (The doctor told me to rest for a few days.)
    ....
13. Thank you for your letter. (I was very happy to get your letter.)
    ....
14. A friend of mine helped me to get a job. (His mother is the manager of a company.) (*use*
    whose) ....
15. Next weekend I'm going to Montreal. (My sister lives in Montreal.) (*use* **where**)
    ....
16. The population of London is now falling. (London was once the largest city in the
    world.) ....
17. I looked up at the moon. (The moon was very bright that evening.)
    ....
18. We spent a pleasant day by the lake. (We had a picnic by the lake.) (*use* **where**)
    ....

UNIT 88 Relative clauses (5) – "extra information" clauses (2)

You should study Unit 87 before you study this unit.

a *Prepositions* + **whom/which**

In "extra information" clauses you can use a preposition before **whom** (for people) and **which** (for things). So you can say "**to** whom / **with** whom / **about** which / **for** which," etc.:

- Mr. Carter, **to whom** I spoke last night, is very interested in our plan.
- Fortunately we had a map, **without which** we would have gotten lost.

But in spoken English we often keep the preposition after the verb in the relative clause. When we do this, we normally use **who** (*not* whom):

- This is Mr. Carter, **who** I was telling you **about**.
- Yesterday we visited the National Museum, **which** I'd never been **to** before.

b **All of/most of**, etc. + **whom/which**   Study these examples:

> Jack has three brothers. All of them are married. (*2 sentences*)
> → Jack has three brothers, **all of whom** are married. (*1 sentence*)
>
> Ann has a lot of books. She hasn't read most of them. (*2 sentences*)
> → Ann has a lot of books, **most of which** she hasn't read. (*1 sentence*)

You can also say:

none of/many of/much of/(a) few of/some of
any of/half of/each of/both of/neither of } + **whom** (people)
either of/one of/two of, etc.   } + **which** (things)

- He tried on three jackets, **none of which** fit him.
- They've got three cars, **two of which** they never use.
- Sue has a lot of friends, **many of whom** she went to school with.
- Two men, **neither of whom** I had seen before, came into my office.

c **Which** (*not* what)

Study this example:

| Jim passed his driving test. | | This | surprised everybody. (*2 sentences*) |

| Jim passed his driving test, | | **which** | surprised everybody. (*1 sentence*) |
                                             — *relative clause* —

In this example **which** = the fact that he passed his driving test. You *cannot* use **what** instead of **which** in sentences like this:

- She couldn't come to the party, **which was a pity**. (*not* . . . what was a pity)
- The weather was very good, **which we hadn't expected**. (*not* . . . what we hadn't expected)

For **what** see Unit 85c.

176

UNIT 88   Exercises

88.1 *Write these sentences again, giving extra information in a relative clause. Use the sentences in parentheses (. . .) to make your relative clauses.*

Example: Mr. Carter is interested in our plan. (I spoke to him on the phone last night.)
Mr. Carter, who I spoke to on the phone last night, is interested in our plan.
or: Mr. Carter, to whom I spoke on the phone last night, is interested in our plan.

1. This is a photograph of our friends. (We went on vacation with them.)
   This is ....
2. The wedding took place last Friday. (Only members of the family were invited to it.)
   The ....
3. I've just bought some books about astronomy. (I'm very interested in astronomy.)
   ....

88.2 *Make sentences with* **all of**/**most of**, *etc.* + **whom**/**which**.

Example: Jack has three brothers. All of them are married.
Jack has three brothers, all of whom are married. ....

1. They gave us a lot of information. Most of it was useless.
   They gave...
2. There were a lot of people at the party. I had met only a few of them before.
   ....
3. I have sent him two letters. Neither of them has arrived.
   ....
4. Norman won $50,000. He gave half of it to his parents.
   ....
5. Ten people applied for the job. None of them were qualified.
   ....
6. Tom made a number of suggestions. Most of them were very helpful.
   ....

88.3 *Complete these sentences, giving extra information in a relative clause. Use the sentences in the box to make your relative clauses.*

this means I can't leave the country	this was very nice of him
this makes it difficult to contact her	this was perfectly true
this makes it difficult to sleep	~~this was a shame~~
I thought this was very rude of them	

1. She couldn't come to the party, *which was a shame.* ....
2. Jill doesn't have a phone, ...
3. They said they didn't have any money, ...
4. I haven't got a passport, ...
5. He offered to let me stay in his house, ...
6. They didn't thank us for the meal before they left, ...
7. The part of town where I live is very noisy at night, ...

177

UNIT 89

-ing and -ed clauses ("the woman talking to Tom," "the man injured in the accident")

a A *clause* is a part of a sentence. Some clauses begin with **-ing** or **-ed**:

- Do you know the woman | talking to Tom | ? (**-ing** clause)

- The man | injured in the accident | was taken to the hospital. (**-ed** clause)

b We use **-ing** clauses to say what someone (or something) is doing or was doing at a particular time:

- Do you know the woman **talking to Tom**? (the woman **is talking** to Tom)
- The police officers **investigating the robbery** are looking for three men. (the police officers **are investigating** the robbery)
- I was awakened by a bell **ringing**. (the bell **was ringing**)
- Who was that man **standing outside**? (the man **was standing** outside)
- Can you hear someone **singing**? (someone **is singing**)

For **see/hear someone doing something** see Unit 63.

When you are talking about *things* (and sometimes people), you can use an **-ing** clause for permanent characteristics (what something does all the time, not just at a particular time):

- The road **joining the two villages** is very narrow. (the road **joins** the two villages)
- I live in a pleasant room **overlooking the garden**. (the room **overlooks** the garden)

c **-ed** clauses have a *passive* meaning:

- The man **injured in the accident** was taken to the hospital. (the man **was injured** in the accident)
- None of the people **invited to the party** can come. (the people **have been invited** to the party)

Injured and **invited** are *past participles*. Many verbs have irregular past participles that do not end in **-ed**. For example: **stolen/made/bought/written**, etc.:

- The money **stolen in the robbery** was never found. (the money **was stolen** in the robbery)
- Most of the goods **made in this factory** are exported. (the goods **are made** in this factory)

For a full list of irregular verbs see Appendix 2.

d We often use **-ing** and **-ed** clauses after **there is / there was**, etc.:

- **Is there** anybody **waiting** to see me?
- **There were** some children **swimming** in the river.
- When I arrived, **there was** a big red car **parked** outside the house.

For more information about **-ing** clauses see Unit 64.

178

UNIT 89   Exercises

89.1 *Rewrite the sentences. Each time use the information in parentheses (. . .) to make an* **-ing** *clause.*

Example: That woman is Australian. (she is talking to Tom)
.*That woman talking to Tom is Australian.*...

1. A plane crashed into the ocean yesterday. (it was carrying 28 passengers)
   A plane ....yesterday.
2. When I was walking home, there was a man. (he was following me)
   When ....
3. I was awakened by the baby. (she was crying)
   I...
4. At the end of the street there is a path. (the path leads to the river)
   At ....
5. Some paintings were stolen from the gallery. (they belong to the artist)
   Some...

89.2 *This time make an* **-ed** *clause.*

Example: The man was taken to the hospital. (he was injured in the accident)
The man injured in the accident was taken to the hospital............

1. The window has now been repaired. (it was broken in last night's storm)
   The window...repaired.
2. Most of the suggestions were not very practical. (they were made at the meeting)
   ....
3. The paintings haven't been found yet. (they were stolen from the museum)
   ....
4. Did you hear about the boy? (he was knocked down on his way to school this morning)
   Did ....

89.3 *Complete these sentences with the following verbs. Put the verb in the correct form:*

blow   **call**   ~~invite~~   **live**   **offer**   **mail**   **read**   ~~ring~~   **sit**   **study**
wait   **work**

1. I was awakened by a bell .*ringing*...........
2. None of the people .*invited*.........to the party can come.
3. Tom has a brother ....in a bank in New York and a sister ....
   economics at a university in California.
4. Somebody .... Jack phoned while you were out.
5. All letters ....today should arrive tomorrow.
6. When I entered the waiting room there was nobody .... except for a young
   man .... by the window ....a magazine.
7. A few days after the interview, I received a letter ....me the job.
8. There was a tree ....down in the storm last night.
9. Sometimes life must be very unpleasant for people ....near airports.

UNIT 90 Adjectives ending in -ing and -ed (boring/bored, etc.)

a There are many pairs of adjectives ending in **-ing** and **-ed**. For example: **boring** and **bored**. Study this example situation:

Jane has been doing the same job for a very long time. Every day she does exactly the same thing over and over. She doesn't enjoy it any more and would like to do something different.

Jane's job is **boring**.
Jane is **bored** (with her job).

Someone is **-ed** if something (or someone) is **-ing**. Or, if something is **-ing**, it makes you **-ed**. So:

- Jane is bor**ed** because her job is bor**ing**.
- Jane's job is bor**ing**, so Jane is bor**ed**. (*not* Jane is boring)

Now study these examples:

Someone is **interested** because something (or someone) is **interesting**:
- Tom is interest**ed** in politics. (*not* interesting in politics)
- Tom finds politics interest**ing**.
- Are you interest**ed** in buying a car?
- Did you meet anyone interest**ing** at the party?

Someone is **surprised** because something is **surprising**:
- Everyone was surpris**ed** that she passed the exam.
- It was surpris**ing** that she passed the exam.

Someone is **disappointed** because something is **disappointing**:
- I was disappoint**ed** with the movie. I expected it to be much better.
- The movie was disappoint**ing**. I expected it to be much better.

Someone is **tired** because something is **tiring**:
- He is always very tir**ed** when he gets home from work.
- He has a very tir**ing** job.

b Other pairs of adjectives ending in **-ing** and **-ed** are:

fascinating	fascinated	horrifying	horrified
exciting	excited	terrifying	terrified
amusing	amused	frightening	frightened
amazing	amazed	depressing	depressed
astonishing	astonished	worrying	worried
shocking	shocked	annoying	annoyed
disgusting	disgusted	exhausting	exhausted
embarrassing	embarrassed	satisfying	satisfied
confusing	confused		

UNIT 90   Exercises

90.1 *Complete two sentences for each situation. Use an adjective ending in* **-ing** *or* **-ed** *to complete each sentence.*

Example: The movie wasn't as good as we had expected.   (disappoint-)
   a) The movie was .*disappointing*.... .
   b) We were *disappointed*.... with the movie.

1. It's been raining all day. I hate this weather.   (depress-)
   a) This weather is ....   b) This weather makes me ....
2. Astronomy is one of Tom's main interests.   (interest-)
   a) Tom is .... in astronomy.
   b) He finds astronomy very ....
3. I turned off the television in the middle of the program.   (bor-)
   a) The program was ....   b) I was ....
4. Ann is going to Indonesia next month. She has never been there before.   (excit-)
   a) She is really .... about going.
   b) It will be an .... experience for her.
5. Diana teaches young children. It's a hard job.   (exhaust-)
   a) She often finds her job ....
   b) At the end of the day's work she is often ....

90.2 *Choose the right adjective.*

Example: I was ~~disappointing~~ / disappointed with the movie. I had expected it to be better.

1. We were all horrifying/horrified when we heard about the disaster.
2. It's sometimes embarrassing/embarrassed when you have to ask people for money.
3. Are you interesting/interested in soccer?
4. I enjoyed the soccer game. It was very exciting/excited.
5. It was a really terrifying/terrified experience. Afterward everybody was very shocking/shocked.
6. I had never expected to be offered the job. I was really amazing/amazed when I got it.
7. The kitchen hadn't been cleaned for ages. It was really disgusting/disgusted.
8. Do you get embarrassing/embarrassed easily?

90.3 *Complete these sentences with an adjective ending in* **-ing** *or* **-ed**. *The first letter(s) of the adjective are given each time.*

Example: Jane finds her job b.*oring*............. . She wants to do something different.

1. I seldom visit art galleries. I'm not very in........................ in art.
2. We went for a very long walk. It was very ti........................ .
3. Why do you always look so b........................? Is your life really so b........................?
4. He's one of the most b........................ people I've ever met. He never stops talking and never says anything in........................ .
5. I was as........................ when I heard they were getting divorced. They had always seemed so happy together.
6. I'm starting a new job next week. I'm really ex........................ about it.

181

UNIT 91

Adjectives:
Word order ("a **nice new** house")
After verbs ("Do you **feel tired?**")

a Sometimes we use two or more adjectives together:

- Tom lives in a **nice new** house.
- In the kitchen there was a **beautiful large round wooden** table.

Adjectives like **new/large/round/wooden** are *fact* adjectives. They give us objective information about something (age, size, color, etc.). Adjectives like **nice/beautiful** are *opinion* adjectives. They tell us what someone thinks of something.
Opinion adjectives usually go before *fact* adjectives:

	opinion	*fact*	
a	**nice**	**sunny**	day
	delicious	**hot**	soup
an	**intelligent**	**young**	man
a	**beautiful**	**large round wooden**	table

b Sometimes there are two or more *fact* adjectives. Very often (but not always) we put *fact* adjectives in this order:

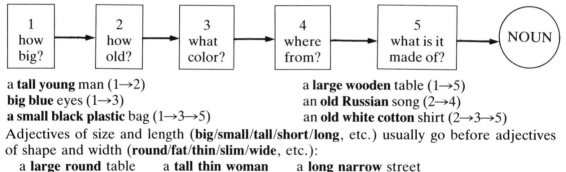

a **tall young** man (1→2)   a **large wooden** table (1→5)
big blue eyes (1→3)   an **old Russian** song (2→4)
a small black plastic bag (1→3→5)   an **old white cotton** shirt (2→3→5)

Adjectives of size and length (**big/small/tall/short/long**, etc.) usually go before adjectives of shape and width (**round/fat/thin/slim/wide**, etc.):

a **large round** table   a **tall thin** woman   a **long narrow** street

c We also use adjectives after some verbs, especially **be/get/become**:

Are you **tired?**   **Be careful!**   I'm **getting hungry.**

We also use adjectives after: **feel   smell   taste   sound   seem   look**:

- Do you **feel tired?**
- Dinner **smells good**.
- This coffee **tastes strong**.
- Tom **sounded angry** when I spoke to him on the phone.
- Your friend **seems** very **nice**.

But after other verbs you must use an *adverb* (see also Units 92 and 93):

- **Drive carefully!** (*not* drive careful)
- Susan **plays** the piano very **well**. (*not* plays . . . very good)
- Tom **shouted** at me **angrily**. (*not* shouted . . . angry)

Look   We use an adjective after **look** when it means **seem**:

- Tom **looked sad** when I saw him.

But after **look at** we use an adverb:

- Tom **looked at me sadly**. (*not* looked at me sad)

UNIT 91   Exercises

91.1 *Put the adjectives in parentheses (. . .) in the correct position.*

Example: a beautiful table (wooden round) *A beautiful round wooden table* ....

1. an unusual ring (gold)   ....
2. an old lady (nice)   ....
3. a good-looking man (young)   ....
4. a modern house (attractive)   ....
5. black gloves (leather)   ....
6. an American movie (old)   ....
7. a large nose (red)   ....
8. a sunny day (lovely)   ....
9. a hot bath (nice)   ....
10. an ugly dress (orange)   ....
11. a red car (old/little)   ....
12. a metal box (black/small)   ....
13. a long face (thin)   ....
14. a wide avenue (long)   ....
15. a big cat (fat/black)   ....
16. a little village (old/lovely)   ....
17. long hair (blonde/beautiful)   ....
18. an old painting (interesting/French)   ....

91.2 *Complete each sentence with a verb and an adjective from the box.*

feel	look	~~seemed~~	awful	fine	interesting
smell	sounded	tastes	nice	~~upset~~	wet

1. Ann *seemed upset* .... this morning. Do you know what was wrong?
2. I can't eat this. I've just tried it and it ....
3. Jim told me about his new job last night. It .... very .... ,
   much better than his old job.
4. I wasn't very well yesterday, but I .... today.
5. What beautiful flowers! They .... too.
6. You................................ . Have you been out in the rain?

91.3 *Choose the right word: adjective or adverb.*

Examples: The dinner smells good/~~well~~.   Drive ~~careful~~/carefully!

1. Please shut the door quiet/quietly.
2. Can you be quiet/quietly, please?
3. This soup tastes nice/nicely.
4. Tom cooks very good/well.
5. Don't go up that ladder. It doesn't look safe/safely.
6. We were relieved that he arrived safe/safely after his long trip.
7. Do you feel nervous/nervously before exams?
8. Hurry up! You're always so slow/slowly.
9. She looked at me angry/angrily when I interrupted her.

UNIT 92

Adjectives and adverbs (1)
(quick/quickly)

a Study these examples:
- Our vacation was too short – the time went **quickly**.
- The driver of the car was **seriously** injured in the accident.

Quickly and **seriously** are *adverbs*. Many adverbs are made from an adjective + **-ly**:

adjective:	quick	serious	careful	quiet	heavy	bad
adverb:	quick**ly**	serious**ly**	careful**ly**	quiet**ly**	heavi**ly**	bad**ly**

For spelling rules see Appendix 3. For **hard/fast/well** see Unit 93.

Not all words ending in **-ly** are adverbs. Some adjectives end in **-ly** too. For example:
friendly   lively   elderly   lonely   silly   lovely

b *Adjective or adverb?*
An adjective tells us more about a *noun*. We use adjectives before nouns and after a few verbs (especially **be**):
- Tom is a **careful driver**.
- **Be quiet**, please!
- We didn't go out because of the **heavy rain**.
- I was disappointed that my exam results **were** so **bad**.

For adjectives after **look/smell/feel**, etc., see Unit 91c.

An adverb tells us more about a *verb*. An adverb tells us in what way someone does something or in what way something happens:
- Tom **drove carefully** along the narrow road. (*not* drove careful)
- **Speak quietly**, please! (*not* speak quiet)
- We didn't go out because it was **raining heavily**. (*not* raining heavy)
- I was disappointed that I **did** so **badly** on the exam. (*not* did so bad)

Compare: She speaks **perfect English**.   (*adjective + noun*)

She **speaks** English **perfectly**.   (*verb + object + adverb*)

c We also use adverbs before *adjectives* and *other adverbs*. For example:

reasonably cheap	(*adverb + adjective*)
terribly sorry	(*adverb + adjective*)
incredibly quickly	(*adverb + adverb*)

- It's a **reasonably cheap** restaurant and the food is **extremely good**.
- Oh, I'm **terribly sorry**. I didn't mean to push you.
- Maria learns languages **incredibly quickly**.
- I was **bitterly disappointed** that I didn't get the job.
- The examination was **surprisingly easy**.

You can use an adverb before a *past participle* (**injured/organized**, etc.):
- The meeting was very **badly organized**.
- The driver of the car was **seriously injured** in the accident.
- The building was **totally destroyed** in the fire.

UNIT 92   Exercises

92.1 *Decide whether the underlined words are right or wrong. Correct the wrong words.*

Examples: The driver of the car was serious injured.   *WRONG - seriously*
Be quiet, please! I'm trying to concentrate.   *RIGHT*

1. I waited nervous in the waiting room before the interview.   ....
2. Why were you so unfriendly when I saw you yesterday?   ....
3. It rained continuous for three days.   ....
4. Alice and Stan are very happy married.   ....
5. Tom's French is not very good, but his German is almost fluent.   ....
6. Eva lived in the U.S. for five years, so she speaks very well English.   ....
7. Everybody at the party was very colorful dressed.   ....
8. Ann likes wearing colorful clothes.   ....
9. Sue is terrible upset about losing her job.   ....

92.2 *Complete the sentences with adverbs. The first letter(s) of each adverb are given.*

Example: We didn't go out because it was raining h.*eavily*.............. .

1. We had to wait for a long time, but we didn't complain. We waited pat....................... .
2. I lost the tennis match because I played very ba....................... .
3. I don't think he trusted me. He looked at me so sus....................... .
4. Sorry, I didn't mean to kick you. I didn't do it int....................... .
5. Nobody knew he was coming. He arrived unex....................... .
6. Jill has just gotten a job in a store, but she won't be staying there long. She is only working there tem....................... until she can find another job.
7. My French isn't very good, but I can understand per....................... if people speak sl....................... and cl....................... .
8. I had very little difficulty finding an apartment. I found one quite ea....................... .

92.3 *Choose two words (one from each box) to complete each sentence.*

absolutely	~~reasonably~~	badly		~~cheap~~	enormous	planned
completely	seriously	fully		changed	ill	quiet
extremely	unusually	slightly		damaged	insured	sorry

1. I thought the restaurant would be expensive, but it was *reasonably cheap*............ .
2. George's mother is .... in the hospital.
3. The fire destroyed our house, but luckily we were ....
4. What a big house! It's ....
5. It wasn't a serious accident. The car was only .. ..
6. A lot of things went wrong during our vacation because it was ....
7. The children are normally very lively but they're .... today.
8. When I returned home after 20 years, everything had ....
9. I'm .... about losing your book. I'll buy you another one.

185

UNIT 93 Adjectives and adverbs (2) (good/well, fast/hard/late, hardly)

a **Good/well** **Good** is an *adjective*. The *adverb* is **well**:

- Your **English** is very **good.**   You **speak** English **well.**
- Susan is a **good pianist.**   She **plays** the piano **well.**

We often use **well** with *past participles* (**dressed/known**, etc.):

well dressed (*not* good dressed)   **well known**   **well educated**

But **well** is also an *adjective* with the meaning "in good health":

- "How are you today?"   "I'm very **well**, thanks." (*not* I'm very good)

b **Fast/hard/late** These words are both adjectives and adverbs:

adjective	*adverb*
Jack is a very **fast runner.**	Jack can **run** very **fast.**
Ann is a **hard worker.**	Ann **works hard.** (*not* works hardly)
The train **was late.**	I **got up late** this morning.

The adverb **lately** = recently:

- Have you seen Tom **lately**?

c **Hardly** has a completely different meaning from **hard**:

Hardly = almost not. Study these examples:

- George asked Carol to marry him. She was surprised because they had only known each other for two days. She said: "We can't get married now! We **hardly** know each other." (= we know each other very little; we almost don't know each other)
- Why was Tom so unfriendly at the party last night? He **hardly** spoke to me. (= he spoke to me very little)

We often use **hardly** with **can/could**:

- Your writing is terrible. I **can hardly** read it. (= I can read it but only with a lot of difficulty)
- My leg was hurting me. I **could hardly** walk.

We also use **hardly** with **any/anyone/anything/anywhere**:

- "How much money do you have?"   "**Hardly any.**" (= almost none; very little)
- The exam results were very bad. **Hardly anyone** passed. (= almost no one passed; very few people passed)
- She ate **hardly anything** because she didn't feel hungry. (= she ate almost nothing; she ate very little)

Note that you can say:

- She ate **hardly anything**.   *or*   She **hardly** ate **anything**.
- We have **hardly any** food.   *or*   We **hardly** have **any** food.
- We've done **hardly any** work.   *or*   We've **hardly** done **any** work.

Hardly ever = almost never:

- I'm nearly always at home in the evenings. I **hardly ever** go out.

UNIT 93 Exercises

93.1 *Decide whether the underlined words are right or wrong. Correct the wrong words.*

Examples: We lost the game because we didn't play very <u>good</u>. *WRONG – well*
Ann has been working very <u>hard</u> recently. *RIGHT*

1. Give my best wishes to your parents. I hope they are <u>well</u>. ....
2. The children behaved themselves very <u>good</u>. ....
3. I tried <u>hardly</u> to remember his name but I couldn't. ....
4. The company's financial situation is not <u>well</u> at present. ....
5. Jack has started his own business. Everything is going quite <u>good</u>. ....
6. Don't walk so <u>fast</u>! Can't you walk more slowly? ....
7. See you soon! Don't work too <u>hard</u>. ....

93.2 *Finish these sentences with* **well** + *one of the following words:*

balanced   ~~behaved~~   dressed   informed   kept   known

1. The children were very good. They were *well behaved.*
2. Many people have heard of him. He is quite well ....
3. Their garden is neat and tidy. It is very ....
4. You should eat different types of food. You should have a .... diet.
5. Ann knows a lot about many things. She is a .... woman.
6. His clothes were old and torn. He wasn't very ....

93.3 *Make sentences with* **hardly**. *Use the words in parentheses (. . .).*

Example: George and I have only met once. (know / each other) *We hardly know each other.*

1. I'm very tired this morning. (slept / last night)   I .... night.
2. You're speaking very quietly. (can / hear)   I can .... you.
3. I met Keith a few days ago. I hadn't seen him for a long time. He looks very different now. (recognized)   I ....
4. They were really shocked when they heard the news. (could / speak)
   ....

93.4 *Complete these sentences with* **hardly** + **any/anyone/anything/anywhere/ever.**

Example: I'll have to go shopping. We have *..hardly any..* food.

1. I listen to the radio a lot, but I .... watch television.
2. The weather was good during our vacation. There was .... rain.
3. He is not very popular. .... likes him.
4. It's crowded in here. There's .... to sit down.
5. We used to be good friends, but we .... see each other now.
6. I hate this town. There's .... to do and .... to go.
7. I enjoyed driving this morning. There was .... traffic.

So and **such**

a Study these examples:
- I didn't enjoy the book. The story was **so** stupid.
- I didn't enjoy the book. It was **such** a stupid story.

> We use **so** with an adjective *without* a noun: **so stupid**
> We use **such** with an adjective *with* a noun: **such a stupid story**

You can also use **so** with an adverb:
- He's difficult to understand because he speaks **so quickly**.

b So and **such** make the meaning of the adjective stronger:
- It's a beautiful day, isn't it? It's **so warm**. (= really warm)
- We enjoyed our vacation. We had **such a good time**. (= a really good time)

Compare **so** and **such** in these sentences:
- I like Tom and Ann. They are **so nice**.
- I like Tom and Ann. They are **such** nice **people**. (*not* so nice people)

We often say **so . . . that . . .** and **such . . . that . . .** :
- I was **so tired that** I went to bed at seven o'clock.
- She worked **so hard that** she made herself sick.
- It was **such beautiful weather that** we spent the whole day in the park.
- The book was **so good that** I couldn't put it down.
  It was **such a good book that** I couldn't put it down.

You can leave out **that** in these sentences:
- I was so tired (that) I went to bed at 7 o'clock.

c In these sentences we use **so** and **such** in a different way:
- I expected the weather to be much cooler. I didn't expect it to be **so warm**. (= as warm as it is)
- I'm tired because I got up at 6 o'clock. I don't usually get up **so early**. (= as early as 6 o'clock)
- Hurry up! Don't walk **so slowly**. (= as slowly as you are walking)
- I was surprised when Jack told me the house was built 100

  years ago. { I didn't realize it was **so old**.
  { I didn't realize it was **such an old house**. (= as old as it is)

d We say: **so long** but "**such a long time**"; **so far** but "**such a long way**"; **so many**, **so much** but "**such a lot** (of)":
- I haven't seen him for **so long** that I've forgotten what he looks like. (*or* . . . for **such a long time** . . .)
- I didn't know you lived **so far** from the city. (*or* . . . **such a long way** from . . .)
- Why did you buy **so much** food? (*or* . . . **such a lot of** food?)

UNIT 94 Exercises

94.1 *Put in* **so** *or* **such**.

Examples: Come on! Don't walk ..*so*.......... slowly!
I've never read ..*such*...... a stupid book.

1. I was surprised that he looked ....well after his recent illness.
2. They've got................ a lot of money, they don't know what to do with it.
3. She is a very attractive young woman. She's got .... beautiful eyes.
4. Everything is................ expensive these days, isn't it?
5. Why did you ask them .... stupid questions?
6. It was .... a boring movie that I fell asleep in the middle of it.
7. The wind was ....strong, it was difficult to walk.
8. The food at the hotel was very bad. I've never eaten................ awful food.

94.2 *Make a sentence with* **so** *from two sentences.*

Example: She worked very hard. She made herself sick.
..*She worked so hard (that) she made herself sick.*...........................

1. I was very excited about going away. I couldn't sleep.
I was so ....
2. The water was very dirty. We decided not to go swimming.
....
3. She speaks English very well. You would think it was her native language.
....

94.3 *Use* **such** *instead of* **so**.

Example: The book was so good that I couldn't put it down.
..*It was such a good book that I couldn't put it down.*...................

1. The road is so narrow that it is difficult for two cars to pass each other.
It is..
2. The weather was so warm that I didn't need a coat.
It..
3. His feet are so big that he has trouble finding shoes to fit him.
He has..
4. Why do you put so much sugar in your coffee?
Why ....

94.4 *Complete these sentences.*

Example: We had a lot of problems.   We hadn't expected to have so *many problems.*.....

1. It's a long way from your house to the airport.
I didn't know it was so ....
2. It took us a long time to get home this evening.
It doesn't usually take us so..
3. You've got a lot of furniture in this room.
Why have you got so ....?

UNIT 95 Enough and too

a The position of **enough**:

Enough goes *after* adjectives and adverbs:

- He didn't get the job because he wasn't **experienced enough**. (*not* enough experienced)
- You won't pass the exam if you don't work **hard enough**.
- She can't get married yet. She's not **old enough**.

Enough goes *before* nouns:

- He didn't get the job because he didn't have **enough experience**. (*not* experience enough)
- I'd like to take a vacation, but I don't have **enough money**.
- Some of us had to sit on the floor because there weren't **enough chairs**.

You can also use **enough** alone (without a noun):

- I'll lend you some money if you don't have **enough**.

b After **enough** and **too** you can say **for someone/something**:

- I don't have enough money **for a vacation**.
- He wasn't experienced enough **for the job**.
- This shirt is too big **for me**. I need a smaller size.

But we do not usually say "enough/too . . . for doing something." We use the *infinitive* after **enough** and **too**. So we say "**enough** money **to do** something," "old **enough to do** something," "**too** young **to do** something," etc.:

- I don't have **enough money to take** a vacation. (*not* for taking)
- He wasn't **experienced enough to do** the job.
- She's only sixteen. She's not **old enough to get** married. (*or* She's **too young to get** married.)
- Let's take a taxi. It's **too far to walk**.
- There weren't **enough chairs** for everyone **to sit down**.
- The weather wasn't **nice enough to go** swimming.
- She spoke **too quickly** for us **to understand**.

c We say:

- The food was so hot that we couldn't eat **it**.

and: The food was very hot. We couldn't eat **it**.

or we say:

- The food was **too hot to eat**. (*without* "it")

Here are some more examples like this:

- That picture is **too heavy to hang** on the wall.
- I had to carry my wallet in my hand. It was **too big to put** in my pocket.
- The water wasn't **clean enough to swim in**.

190

UNIT 95   Exercises

95.1 *Complete these sentences using* **enough** *with one of the following words:*

big   ~~**old**~~   **warm**   **well**   **cups**   **money**   **qualifications**   **room**   **time**

1. She can't get married yet. She's not *old enough* .
2. Tom would like to buy a car, but he doesn't have ....
3. I couldn't make coffee for everybody. There weren't ....
4. Are you ....? Or shall I turn on the heat?
5. It's only a small car. There isn't .... for all of you.
6. George didn't feel.. to go to work this morning.
7. I didn't finish the exam. I didn't have ....
8. Do you think I've got .... to apply for the job?
9. Try this jacket on and see if it's .... for you.

95.2 *Answer these questions using the words in parentheses (. . .).*

Example: "Is she getting married." (not old enough)
   "No, *she isn't old enough to get married.* "

1. "Why can't you talk to me now?" (too busy)   "I'm too .... now."
2. "Let's go to the movies." (too late)   "No, it's .... movies."
3. "Why don't we sit outside?" (not warm enough)
   "It's not.. "
4. "Would you like to be a politician?" (too nice)
   "No, I'm .... "
5. "Are you going away on vacation this year?" (not enough money)
   "No, I don't have.. "
6. "Shall we take a picture?" (too dark)   "No, ... "
7. "Did you hear what he was saying?" (too far away)
   "No, we .... "
8. "Can she make herself understood (in English)?" (not enough English)
   "No, she doesn't speak .... "
9. "Does Harry work?" (too lazy)   "No, he's .... "

95.3 *Make one sentence (using* **too** *or* **enough***) from the two sentences given.*

Example: We couldn't eat the food. It was too hot. *The food was too hot (for us) to eat.*

1. I can't drink this coffee. It's too hot.   This coffee is ....
2. Nobody could move the piano. It was too heavy.
   The piano ....
3. I can't wear this coat in winter. It's not warm enough.
   This coat ....
4. Don't stand on that chair. It's not strong enough.
   That chair..
5. Six people can't fit in this car. It's not big enough for six people.
   This car ....

191

a Compare these two sentences:

> Jim doesn't speak very clearly.
> - A **It is difficult to understand him**.
> - B **He is difficult to understand**.
>
> Sentences A and B have the same meaning. But note that we say "He is difficult **to understand**." (*not* He is difficult to understand *him*.)

You can use the structure in sentence B after **difficult/easy/impossible/hard** and after a few other adjectives:

- ■ Your writing is almost **impossible to read**. (*not* . . . to read it)
  (= It is almost impossible to read your writing.)
- ■ Do you think this water is **safe to drink**? (*not* . . . to drink it)
- ■ Jill is very **interesting to talk to**. (*not* . . . to talk to her)

You can also use this structure with an *adjective + noun*:

- ■ This is a very **difficult question** to answer. (*not* . . . to answer it)
- ■ Jill is an **interesting person** to talk to.
- ■ I enjoyed the soccer game. It was an **exciting game** to watch.

b We use the *infinitive* after **the first / the second / the third**, etc., and also after **the next** and **the last**:

- ■ Who was **the first** person **to reach** the South Pole?
- ■ If I have any more news, you'll be **the first to know**.
- ■ **The next** plane **to arrive** at gate 4 will be Flight 61 from Buenos Aires.
- ■ Who was **the last** person **to leave** the building last night?

c You can use the *infinitive* after a number of adjectives to say how someone feels about something. For example:

- ■ I was **sorry to hear** that your father is ill.
- ■ Was Tom **surprised to see** you when you visited him?
- ■ I was **delighted to get** your letter last week.

Other adjectives you can use in this way include:

happy	pleased	disappointed	amazed
glad	sad	relieved	astonished

d Note the structure (**it is**) **nice of someone to do something**. This structure is possible after a number of adjectives, including:

nice	mean	silly	polite	generous
kind	stupid	clever	careless	foolish

- ■ It was **nice of you to take** me to the airport. Thank you very much.
- ■ It was **careless of Jack to leave** the door unlocked when he went out.
- ■ It's **stupid of him to give** up his job when he needs the money.
- ■ It was very **generous of Ann to lend** us the money.

UNIT 96   Exercises

96.1 *Write these sentences in another way, beginning as shown.*

Example: It is difficult to understand him.   He *is difficult to understand.* ....

1. It's easy to find our house.   Our house is ....
2. It was very hard to open the window.   The window ....
3. It's impossible to translate some words.   Some words ....
4. It's not very difficult to make bread.   Bread ....
5. It's not safe to stand on that chair.   That chair ....
6. It's difficult to explain some grammatical rules.
   Some grammatical rules ....
7. It's hard to find a good restaurant in this town.
   A good restaurant ....

96.2 *Use the following words to complete each sentence:*

first man/walk   **first/complain**   **last/arrive**   **last person/see**   ~~next train/arrive~~

1. The *next train to arrive*..... at platform 2 will be the 7:45 to Chicago.
2. When anything goes wrong, Mary is always ....
3. Nobody has seen Keith for days. Who was .... him?
4. Neil Armstrong was ....on the moon.
5. We always have to wait for her. She's always ....

96.3 *Use the following words to complete these sentences:*

~~delighted/get~~   **astonished/find**   **sorry/hear**   **happy/see**   **glad/hear**

1. I was really *delighted to get*... your letter last week.
2. Thank you for your letter. I'm ....that you're doing well.
3. When I walked into my bedroom, I was ....a complete stranger
   sleeping in my bed.
4. Hello! I'm so glad you could come. I'm really ....you again.
5. I'm .... that your mother is ill. I hope she gets better soon.

96.4 *Make sentences using the words in parentheses (. . .).*

Example: Jack left the door unlocked when he went out.   (careless)
   It was careless of Jack to leave the door unlocked when he went out.

1. Sue offered to help me.   (kind)
   It was ....me.
2. You make the same mistake over and over.   (careless)
   It's ....
3. She went out in the rain without a raincoat.   (stupid)
   It was ....
4. Don and Jenny invited me to stay with them for a few days.   (nice)
   It..
5. He left without saying thank you.   (not polite)
   It wasn't ....

UNIT 97 Comparison (1) – cheaper, more expensive, etc.

a Study these examples:

> Let's go by car. It's **cheaper**.
> Don't go by train. It's **more expensive**.
>
> **Cheaper** and **more expensive** are *comparative* forms.

After comparatives we use **than**:
- It's cheaper to go by car **than** to go by train.

For **than** see also Unit 99.

b We use **-er** for the comparative of short adjectives and adverbs:

cheap/cheap**er**   hard/hard**er**   large/larg**er**   thin/thin**ner**
- This jacket is too small. I need a **larger** size.
- Ann works **harder** than most of her friends.

We prefer **-er** with some two-syllable adjectives, especially adjectives ending in **-y**. For example:

lucky/luck**ier**   funny/funn**ier**   easy/eas**ier**   pretty/prett**ier**
and also: **quiet**/quiet**er**   **narrow**/narrow**er**   **simple**/simpl**er**
- The examination was **easier** than we expected.
- It's too noisy here. Can we go somewhere **quieter?**

For spelling rules see Appendix 3.

c We use **more . . .** (*not* -er) for other two-syllable adjectives and longer adjectives:

more modern   **more serious**   **more expensive**   **more comfortable**
- **More expensive** hotels are usually **more comfortable** than cheap**er** ones.
- Her illness was **more serious** than we first thought.

We also use **more . . .** for adverbs that end in **-ly**:

more slowly   **more seriously**   **more quietly**   **more carefully**
- Could you speak **more slowly**, please?

We also say **more often**:
- I don't play tennis much now. I used to play **more often**.

But we say **earlier** (*not* more early):
- You're always tired in the mornings. You should go to bed **earlier**.

d Before the comparative of adjectives and adverbs you can use:

a (little) bit   **a little**   **much**   **a lot**   **far** (= a lot)
- Let's go by car. It's **much** (*or* **a lot**) **cheaper**.
- Don't go by train. It's **much** (*or* **a lot**) **more expensive**.
- Ann works **a lot** (*or* **much**) **harder** than most of her friends.
- Could you speak **a (little) bit** (*or* **a little**) **more slowly?**
- Her illness was **far more serious** than we first thought.

UNIT 97   Exercises

97.1 *Complete these sentences. Each time use the comparative form of one of the following adjectives or adverbs:*

crowded	early	easily	expensive	interested	~~large~~	near	often
quiet	thin						

1. This jacket is too small. I need a .. *larger* .... size.
2. You look .... Have you lost weight?
3. He's not so enthusiastic about his studies. He's .... in having a good time.
4. You'll find your way around the town .... if you have a map.
5. You're making too much noise. Can you be a little bit .... ?
6. There were a lot of people in the cafe. It was .... than usual.
7. You're late. I expected you to be here ....
8. You hardly ever write to me. Why don't you write a little .... ?
9. The hotel was surprisingly cheap. I expected it to be much ....
10. It's a shame you live so far away. I wish you lived ....

97.2 *Complete these sentences. Use the comparative of the words in parentheses (. . .) + **than**.*

Example: Her illness was *more serious than* .... we first thought.   (serious)

1. Sorry I'm late. It took me .... to get here .... I expected.   (long)
2. My toothache is .... it was yesterday.   (painful)
3. She looks about 20, but in fact she's much .... she looks.   (old)
4. The problem is not so complicated. It's .... you think.   (simple)
5. Your English has improved. You speak a lot .... you did when we last met.   (fluently)
6. Health and happiness are .... money.   (important)
7. We always go camping when we go on vacation. It's much .... staying in a hotel.   (cheap)
8. I like the country. It's .... and .... living in the city.   (healthy/peaceful)

97.3 *This exercise is similar, but this time you also need to use **a bit / a little / much / a lot / far**. Use **than** where necessary.*

Example: Her illness was *much more serious than* .... we first thought. (much / serious)

1. It's .... today .... it was yesterday.   (a little / warm)
2. You're driving too fast. Can you drive .... ?   (a bit / slowly)
3. A: Did you enjoy your visit to the museum?
    B: Yes, I found it .... I expected.   (far / interesting)
4. I prefer this armchair. It's .... the other one. (much / comfortable)
5. You looked depressed this morning, but you look .... now. (a little / happy)
6. This apartment is too small. I need something ....   (much / big)
7. It's .... to learn a foreign language in the country where it is spoken. (a lot / easy)

195

Comparison (2)

a

Some adjectives and adverbs have irregular comparative forms:

good/well	**better**	Let me ask him. I know him **better** than you do.
		The garden looks **better** since you tidied it up.
bad/badly	**worse**	"Is your headache better?" "No, it's **worse**."
		The situation was much **worse** than we expected.
far	**further**	I'm very tired. I can't walk much **further**.
	(*or* **farther**)	(*or* . . . much **farther**.)

Further (*but not* farther) can also mean **more** or **additional**:
- Let me know immediately if you hear any **further** news. (= any more news)

Note the comparative words **more** and **less**:
- I smoke **more** than I used to.
- We've got **less** time than I thought.

b

Older and **elder**

The comparative of **old** is **older**:
- Tom looks **older** than he really is. (*not* elder)

We use **elder** when we are talking about members of a family. We say **(my) elder brother/ sister/son/daughter** (**older** is also possible):
- My **elder** (*or* **older**) **brother** is a pilot.

We use **elder** only before a noun:
- My brother is **older** than me. (*not* elder than me)

For **eldest** see Unit 100c.

c

Sometimes you can use two comparatives together. For example: **harder and harder, more and more, more and more difficult**. We use this structure to say that something is changing continuously:
- It's becoming **harder and harder** to find a job.
- Your English is improving. It's getting **better and better**.
- It's becoming **more and more difficult** to find a job.
- These days **more and more** people are learning English.

d

Note the structure **the** + *comparative* **the better**. For example:
- "What time shall we leave?" "**The sooner the better**." (= it will be best if we leave as soon as possible)
- "What size box do you want?" "**The bigger the better**." (= it will be best if the box is as big as possible)

We also use **the . . . the . . .** (with two comparatives) to say that one thing depends on another thing:
- **The warmer** the weather, **the better** I feel.
- **The earlier** we leave, **the sooner** we will arrive.
- **The more expensive** the hotel, **the better** the service.
- **The more** electricity you use, **the higher** your bill will be.
- **The more** you have, **the more** you want.

UNIT 98 Exercises

98.1 *Complete these sentences using these words:* **better   worse   further   older   elder**
You have to use some of these words more than once. Use **than** *where necessary.*

Example: Let me ask him. I know him **better than**.... you do.

1. We complained about the food in our hotel. But instead of improving, it got
   ....
2. Your work isn't very good. I'm sure you can do .... this.
3. Ann's younger sister is still in school. Her .... sister is a nurse.
4. Our team played really badly this afternoon. We played .... we have ever
   played before.
5. You're standing too near the camera. Can you move a little .... away?
6. "Is Jim younger than Tom?"   "No, he's ...."
7. The damage to our car wasn't so bad. It could have been much ....
8. If you need any .... information, please contact our head office.

98.2 *Use the structure* **. . . and . . .** *(see section c).*

Examples: It's becoming . **harder and harder**.... to find a job.   (hard)
It's becoming **more and more difficult**.. to find a job.   (difficult)

1. As I waited for my interview, I became ....   (nervous)
2. That hole in your sweater is getting ....   (big)
3. The suitcase seemed to get .... as I carried it along the
   road.   (heavy)
4. As the day wore on, the weather got ....   (bad)
5. As the conversation continued, he became ....   (talkative)
6. Traveling is becoming ....   (expensive)
7. Since she has been in the U.S., her English has gotten ....
   (good)

98.3 *Write sentences with* **the . . . the . . . .** *Choose a half sentence from box A to go with a half
sentence from box B.*

A the earlier we leave	B the faster you'll learn
the longer he waited	the more you have to pay
the more I got to know him	the sooner we'll arrive
the more you practice your English	the more profit you'll make
the longer the telephone call	the more impatient he became
the more goods you sell	the more I liked him

1. The earlier we leave, *the sooner we'll arrive.*................................
2. ....
3. ....
4. ....
5. ....
6. ....

a Study this example situation:

Joe, Henry, and Arthur are all millionaires. They are all very rich. Joe has $10 million, Henry has $6 million, and Arthur has $2 million. So:

Henry is rich.
He is **richer than** Arthur.
But he is**n't as rich as** Joe. (= Joe is **richer than** Henry is)

Here are some more examples of **not as ... as**:

- Sue is**n't as old as** she looks. (= she looks **older than** she is)
- The shopping center was**n't as crowded** this morning **as** it usually is. (= it is usually **more crowded**)
- Jim did**n't** do **as well** on his exam **as** he had hoped. (= he had hoped to do **better**)
- "The weather's better today, isn't it?" "Yes, it's **not as cold.**" (= yesterday was **colder**)
- I do**n't** know **as many** people **as** you do. (= you know **more** people)

You can also say "not **so** ... as" (instead of "not **as** ... as"):

- Henry isn't **so** rich as Joe.

b You can also use **as ... as** (but not "so ... as") in positive sentences and in questions:

- I'm sorry I'm late. I got here **as fast as** I could.
- There's plenty of food, so eat **as much as** you like.
- Let's walk. It's **just as quick as** taking the bus.
- Can you send me the money **as soon as** possible, please?

We also say **twice as ... as, three times as ... as**, etc.

- Gasoline is **twice as expensive as** it was a few years ago.
- Their house is about **three times as big as** ours.

c We say **the same as** (*not* the same like):

- Ann's salary is **the same as** mine. (*or* Ann gets **the same** salary **as** me.)
- Tom is **the same** age **as** George.
- "What would you like to drink?" "I'll have **the same as** last time."

d After **than** and **as** it is more usual to say **me/him/her/them/us** when there is no verb. Compare these sentences:

- You are taller **than I am**. *but:* You are taller **than me**.
- They have more money **than we have**. *but:* They have more money **than us**.
- I can't run as fast **as he can**. *but:* I can't run as fast **as him**.

UNIT 99 Exercises

99.1 *Complete the sentences using* **as . . . as.**

Examples: I'm very tall, but you are taller. I'm not *as tall as you.*.................................
Ann works reasonably hard, but she used to work much harder.
Ann doesn't *work as hard as she used to.*.................................

1. My salary is high, but yours is higher. My salary isn't ....
2. You know a little bit about cars, but I know more. You don't...........................
3. I still smoke, but I used to smoke a lot more. I don't ....
4. I still feel tired, but I felt a lot more tired yesterday.
   I don't ....
5. They've lived here for a long time, but we've lived here longer.
   They haven't ....
6. I was a little nervous before the interview, but usually I'm a lot more nervous.
   I wasn't ....
7. The weather is still unpleasant today, but yesterday it was worse.
   The weather isn't...

99.2 *Rewrite these sentences so that they have the same meaning. Begin as shown.*

Example: Jack is younger than he looks. Jack isn't *as old as he looks.*........................

1. It's warmer today than yesterday. It isn't ....
2. The station was nearer than I thought. The station wasn't ....
3. I go out less than I used to. I don't ....
4. The hotel is cheaper than I expected. The hotel isn't................................
5. There were fewer people at this meeting than at the last one.
   There weren't ....
6. The exam was easier than we expected.
   The exam wasn't ....

99.3 *Complete these sentences using* **just as** *with one of the following words:*

> **bad   comfortable   expensive   ~~quick~~   well-qualified**

1. Let's walk. It's *just as quick as*............. taking the bus.
2. I'm going to sleep on the floor. It's .... sleeping in that bed.
3. Why did she get the job? I'm .... her.
4. I thought he was nice, but he's .... everybody else.
5. You won't find a cheaper restaurant than this. They'll all be ....

99.4 *Make sentences with* **the same as.**

Example: (Tom / same age / George) *Tom is the same age as George.*.......................

1. (your hair / same color / mine) Your hair ....
2. (I arrived here / same time / you) ....
3. (you made / same mistake / I made) ....

UNIT 100 Superlatives – **the longest, the most enjoyable**, etc.

a Study these examples:

> What is **the longest** river in the world?
> What was **the most enjoyable** vacation you've ever had?
>
> **Longest** and **most enjoyable** are *superlative* forms.

b We use **-est** or **most**... to form the superlative of adjectives and adverbs. In general we use **-est** for shorter words and **most**...for longer words. (The rules are the same as those for the comparative – see Unit 97.) For example:

long/longest	**hot**/hottest	**easy**/easiest	**hard**/hardest
but: **most** famous	**most** boring	**most** difficult	**most** expensive

For spelling rules see Appendix 3.
- Yesterday was **the hottest** day of the year.
- That was **the most boring** movie I've ever seen.
- "Why did you stay at that hotel?" "It was **the cheapest** we could find."
- She is a really nice person – one of **the nicest** people I know.

Note the irregular superlatives **best** and **worst**:
- That was a delicious meal. It's one of **the best** I've ever had.
- Why does he always come to see me at **the worst** possible moment?

Don't forget that we normally use **the** with superlatives: "**the** best," "**the** most boring," etc.

c **Oldest** and **eldest**
The superlative of **old** is **oldest**:
- That house over there is **the oldest** building in the town. (*not* the eldest)

We use **eldest** when we are talking about the members of a family (**oldest** is also possible):
- **My eldest** (*or* **oldest**) **son** is 13 years old.
- Are you **the eldest** (*or* **oldest**) in your family?

d After superlatives, we use **in** with places (towns, buildings, etc.):
- What's the longest river **in the world**? (*not* of the world)
- We were lucky to have one of the nicest rooms **in the hotel**.

Also: (the best ...) **in the class** / **in the company**, etc.
But: the happiest day **of my life**, the hottest day **of the year**.

Note that we often use the *present perfect* (**I have done**) after a superlative (see also Unit 14a):
- What's the **best** movie **you've ever seen**?
- That was the **most delicious** meal **I've had** in a long time.

e We sometimes use **most** + adjective (*without* the) to mean **very**:
- The book you lent me was **most interesting**. (= very interesting)
- Thank you for the money. It was **most generous** of you. (= very generous)

UNIT 100   Exercises

100.1 *Complete the sentences with a superlative and preposition.*

Example: It's a very nice room.   It's .the. nicest. room. in........ the hotel.

1. It's a very cheap restaurant.   It's .... town.
2. It was a very happy day.   It was .... my life.
3. She's a very intelligent student.   She .... the school.
4. It's a very valuable painting.   It .... the gallery.

In the following sentences use **one of the** + *superlative.*
Example: It's a very nice room. It's *one. of. the. nicest. rooms. in..* the hotel.

5. He's a very rich man.   He's one .... the world.
6. It's a very old castle.   It's............................... France.
7. She's a very good student.   She .... the class.
8. It was a very bad experience.   It was .... my life.
9. He's a very dangerous criminal.   He .... the country.

100.2 *Read these sentences and then write a new sentence with the same meaning. Use a superlative each time and begin each sentence as shown.*

Example: I've never seen such a boring movie.   It's *the. most. boring. movie. I've. ever. seen.*

1. I've never heard such a funny story.   That's the .... heard.
2. He's never made such a bad mistake.   It's...
3. I haven't tasted such good coffee in a long time.
   That's .... time.
4. I've never slept in such an uncomfortable bed.
   This is ....
5. I've never had such a big meal.   It's ....
6. I've never met such a generous person as Ann.
   Ann is ....
7. I've never had such a good friend as you.   You...
8. I haven't had to make such a difficult decision in years.
   This is .... years.

100.3 *Here are some questions for you to answer. But first write the questions using the words in parentheses (. . .). Then answer them.*

1. (what / large / city / your country?)   What *is. the. largest. city. in. your. country.?......*
2. (who / famous singer / your country?)   Who .... your country?
3. (what / popular sport / your country?)   What...
4. (what / expensive thing / you / ever bought?)   ....
5. (what / happy / day / your life?)   What was ....
6. (what / stupid thing / you / ever done?)   ....
7. (who / intelligent person / you know?)   .... you know?
8. (who / beautiful person / you know?)   ....

UNIT 101 Word order (1) – verb + object; place and time

a *Verb + object*

The *verb* and the *object* of the verb normally go together. We do *not* usually put other words between them:

	verb	*+ object*	
I	**like**	**children**	very much. (*not* I like very much children.)
Did you	**see**	**Norman**	yesterday?
Ann often	**plays**	**tennis.**	

Here are some more examples. Notice how each time the verb and the object go together:

- Do you **clean the house** every weekend? (*not* Do you clean every weekend the house?)
- Everybody **enjoyed the party** very much. (*not* Everybody enjoyed very much the party.)
- Our guide **spoke English** fluently. (*not* . . . spoke fluently English.)
- I not only lost all my money – I also **lost my passport**. (*not* I lost also my passport.)
- At the end of the street you'll **see a supermarket** on your left. (*not* . . . see on your left a supermarket.)

For the position of words like **also** and **often** before the verb, see Unit 102.

b *Place* and *time*

We usually say the *place* (**where?**) before the *time* (**when?** / **how often?** / **how long?**):

	place	*time*	
Tom walks	**to work**	**every morning.**	(*not* Tom walks every morning to work.)
She has been	**in Canada**	**since April.**	
We arrived	**at the airport**	**early.**	

Here are some more examples:

- I'm going **to Paris on Monday**. (*not* I'm going on Monday to Paris.)
- Don't be late. Make sure you're **here by 8 o'clock**.
- Why weren't you **at home last night**?
- You really shouldn't go **to bed so late**.

It is often possible to put the time at the beginning of the sentence:

- **On Monday** I'm going to Paris.
- **Every morning** Tom walks to work.

Note that you *cannot* use **early** or **late** at the beginning of the sentence in this way.

There is more information about word order in Unit 102.

UNIT 101   Exercises

101.1 *Decide whether the word order is right or wrong. Correct the sentences that are wrong.*

Examples: I like children very much.   *RIGHT*.......
            Tom walks every morning to work.   *WRONG.-.to work every morning*

1. Jim doesn't like very much baseball.   ....
2. Ann drives every day her car to work.   ....
3. When I heard the news, I called Tom immediately.   ....
4. Maria speaks very well English.   ....
5. After eating quickly my dinner, I went out.   ....
6. You watch all the time television. Can't you do something else?   ....
7. Liz smokes about 20 cigarettes every day.   ....
8. I think I'll go early to bed tonight.   ....
9. You should go to the dentist every six months.   ....
10. When I heard the alarm, I got immediately out of bed. ....
11. Did you learn a lot of things at school today?   ....
12. We went last night to the movies.   ....

101.2 *Put the parts of a sentence in the correct order. The first nine sentences are like those in section a.*

Example: (children / very much / I like)   *I.like.children.very.much.*.........................

1. (she won / easily / the game)   She won...
2. (again / please don't ask / that question)   Please ....
3. (tennis / every weekend / does Ken play?)   Does ....
4. (quietly / the door / I closed)   I...
5. (his name / after a few minutes / I remembered)   ....
6. (a letter to her parents / Ann writes / every week)   ....
7. (at the top of the page / your name / please write)   ....
8. (some interesting books / we found / in the library)
    ....
9. (across from the park / a new hotel / they are building)
    ....

The next six sentences are like those in section b.

10. (to the bank / every Friday / I go)   I go ....
11. (home / why did you come / so late?)   Why...
12. (around town / all morning / I've been walking)
    ....
13. (recently / to the theater / have you been?)   ....
14. (to London / for a few days next week / I'm going) ....
    ....
15. (on Saturday night / I didn't see you / at the party) ....
    ....

U N I T
102 Word order (2) – adverbs with the verb

a We put some adverbs (for example **always, also, probably**) with the verb in the middle of a sentence:

- Tom **always goes** to work by car.
- We were feeling very tired. We **were also** hungry.
- Your car **has probably been** stolen.

b Study these rules for the position of adverbs in the middle of a sentence. (They are only general rules, so there are exceptions.)

i) If the verb is one word (**goes, cooked**, etc.), we usually put the adverb *before* the verb:

	adverb	*verb*	
Tom	always	goes	to work by car.

- I cleaned the house and **also cooked** dinner. (*not* cooked also)
- Jack **hardly ever watches** television and **rarely reads** newspapers.
- She **almost fell** over as she came down the stairs.

Note that these adverbs (**always/often/also**, etc.) go before **have to**:
- We **always have to** wait a long time for the bus.

But adverbs go *after* **am/is/are/was/were**:
- We were feeling very tired. We **were also** hungry.
- Why are you always late? You**'re never** on time.
- The traffic **isn't usually** as bad as it was this morning.

ii) Sometimes a verb is two or more words (**can remember, doesn't smoke, has been stolen**, etc.). We usually put the adverb after the first part of the verb:

	verb 1	*adverb*	*verb 2*	
I	can	never	remember	his name.
Ann	doesn't	usually	smoke.	
	Are you	definitely	going	to the party tomorrow?
Your car	has	probably	been	stolen.

- My parents **have always lived** in Chicago.
- Jill can't cook. She **can't even boil** an egg.
- The house **was only built** a year ago and it**'s already falling** down.

In negative sentences **probably** goes before the negative. So we say:
- I **probably** won**'t** see you.   *or*   I will **probably not** see you.
  (*but not* I won't probably see you.)

c We also use **all** and **both** in these positions:
- We **all felt** sick after the meal.
- Jack and Tom **have both applied** for the job.
- We **are all going** out to eat tonight.
- My parents **are both** teachers.

UNIT 102 Exercises

102.1 *Decide whether the underlined words are in the right position or not. Correct the sentences that are wrong.*

Examples: Tom goes always to work by car.   *WRONG – Tom always goes*
              I cleaned the house and also cooked dinner.   *RIGHT......*

1. I have a good memory for faces, but I always forget names.   ....
2. Those tourists over there probably are French.   ....
3. Amy gets hardly ever angry.   ....
4. We both were astonished when we heard the news.   *We were both astonished*
5. I soon found the keys I had lost.   ....
6. I did some shopping and I went also to the bank.   ....
7. Jim has always to hurry in the morning because he gets up so late.   ....
8. The baby is very good. She seldom cries during the night.   ....
9. I usually am very tired when I get home from work.   ....
10. I usually take a bath when I get home from work.   ....

102.2 *Rewrite the sentences to include the word in parentheses (. . .).*

Example: Ann doesn't smoke. (usually)   *Ann doesn't usually smoke.*...................

1. Have you been arrested? (ever)   Have..
2. I don't have to work on Saturdays. (usually)   I...
3. Does Tom sing when he's taking a shower? (always)   ....
4. I'll be home late tonight. (probably)   ....
5. We are going away tomorrow. (all)   ....
6. (Don't take me seriously.) I was joking. (only)   I...
7. Did you enjoy the party? (both)   ....
8. (I've got a lot of housework to do.) I must write some letters. (also)
   I...

102.3 *Put the words in parentheses into the sentences in the correct order.*

Example: I *..can never remember.* his name.   (remember / never / can)

1. I *...usually take...* sugar in my tea.   (take / usually)
2. "Where's Jim?" "He ....home early."   (gone / has / probably)
3. Ann .... very generous.   (is / always)
4. John and Carol *...were both born...*in Vancouver.   (both / were / born)
5. Tim is a good pianist. He *...can also sing...*very well.   (sing / also / can)
6. Our television set *...often breaks...* down.   (often / breaks)
7. We *...always have to...* a long time for the bus.   (have / always / to wait)
8. My eyesight isn't very good. I *...can only read...* with glasses.   (read / can / only)
9. I *...will probably be...*early tomorrow.   (probably / leaving / will / be)
10. I'm afraid I .... able to come to the party.   (probably / be / won't)
11. If we hadn't taken the same train, we ....each other.   (never / met / might / have)

205

UNIT
103
Still and yet
Anymore / any longer / no longer

---

a **Still** and **yet**

We use **still** to say that a situation or action is continuing. **Still** usually goes in the middle of the sentence with the verb (see Unit 102b for the exact position):

- It's 10:00 and Tom is **still** in bed.
- "Have you given up smoking?" "No, I **still** smoke."
- Are you **still** living in the same house, or have you moved?
- When I went to bed, Ann was **still** working.
- Do you **still** want to go to the party, or have you changed your mind?

We use **yet** when we ask if something has happened or when we say that something has not happened. We use **yet** mainly in questions and negative sentences. **Yet** usually goes at the end of the sentence:

- I'm hungry. Is dinner ready **yet**?
- Have you finished writing that letter **yet**?
- It's 10:00 and Tom hasn't gotten up **yet**. (*or* . . . isn't up **yet**.)
- We don't know where we're going on our vacation **yet**.

We often use **yet** with the *present perfect* ("**Have** you **finished** writing that letter **yet**?"). See also Unit 15b.

Now compare **still** and **yet** in these sentences:

- Jack lost his job a year ago and he **is still** unemployed.
  Jack lost his job a year ago and **hasn't found** another job **yet**.
- **Is** it **still raining**?
  Has it **stopped** raining **yet**?

Still is also possible in *negative* sentences:

- He said he would be here an hour ago, and he **still** hasn't come.

This is similar to "he hasn't come **yet**." But **still . . . not** shows a stronger feeling of surprise or impatience. Compare:

- She has**n't** written to me **yet**. (but I expect she will write soon)
- She **still** has**n't** written to me. (she should have written before now)

b We use **not . . . anymore, not . . . any longer**, and **no longer** to say that a situation has changed. **Anymore** and **any longer** go at the end of the sentence:

- Mr. Davis doesn't work here **anymore** (*or* **any longer**). He left about six months ago.
- We were good friends once, but we aren't friends **anymore** (*or* **any longer**).

No longer goes in the middle of the sentence (see Unit 102b):

- We are **no longer** friends.
- She **no longer** loves him.

We do not normally use **no more** in this way:

- He is **no longer** a student. (*not* He is no more a student.)

UNIT 103   Exercises

103.1 *Ask some questions about a friend, Dave. You haven't seen Dave for a very long time. When you last saw him:*

~~1. he was living on Market Street~~   4. he had a beard
2. he was single   5. he wanted to be a politician
3. he was working in a factory   6. he smoked lot

You meet someone who has met Dave recently. Ask questions about Dave, using **still**.
1. *Is he still living on Market Street?*   4. ....
2. .... single?   5. ....
3. ....   6. ....

103.2 *Write sentences with* **yet**.

Example: It's still raining. (stopped)   *It hasn't stopped raining yet.*...................

1. George is still here. (gone)   He...
2. The concert is still going on. (finished)   It ....
3. The children are still asleep. (woken up)   ....
4. Ann is still on vacation. (come back)   ....
5. Linda is still up. (gone to bed)   ....
6. We're still waiting for him to reply to our letter. (replied)
   ....
7. I'm still thinking about what color to paint the wall. (decided)
   ....

103.3 *Use* **still** *and* **not . . . anymore**.

Example: Tom used to play tennis and soccer.   (still / tennis but . . .)
   He still plays tennis, but he doesn't play soccer anymore....................

1. Jack used to have long hair and a beard. (still / long hair but . . .)
   He .... , but ....
2. She was in the hospital and she was in critical condition. (still / hospital but . . .)
   .... , but ....
3. She was a student, and she was studying economics. (still / a student but . . .)
   ....
4. I was feeling tired and sick. (still / tired but . . .)
   ....
5. He was a good player, and he was the best on the team. (still / good player but . . .)
   ....
6. I used to like George and Ken. (still / George but . . .)
   ....

Now use **no longer** *instead of* **not . . . anymore** *in sentences 1–4.*

7. (1) *He no longer has a beard.*   9. (3) She ....
8. (2) ....   10. (4) ....

UNIT 104

Although / though / even though
In spite of / despite

---

a Study this example situation:

Last year Jack and Jill spent their vacation at the beach.
It rained a lot, but they enjoyed themselves. You can say:

Although it rained a lot, they enjoyed themselves.
(= It rained a lot, *but* they . . .) *or:*

In spite of
Despite } **the rain**, they enjoyed themselves.

---

b After **although** we use a *subject + verb*:
- **Although she smokes** 20 cigarettes a day, she seems quite healthy.
- **Although it rained** a lot, we enjoyed our vacation.
- I didn't get the job, **although I had** all the necessary qualifications.

After **in spite of** (or **despite**) we use a *noun,* a *pronoun* (**this/that/what**, etc.), or **-ing**:
- **In spite of the rain**, we enjoyed our vacation.
- I didn't get the job, **despite my qualifications**.
- She wasn't well, but **in spite of this** she went to work.
- **Despite what** I said last night, I still love you.
- I'm not tired, **in spite of working** hard all day.

Note that we say "in spite **of**," but **despite** (without **of**).
You can also say **in spite of / despite the fact that . . .** :
- **In spite of the fact that** I was tired, I couldn't sleep.
- She seems healthy, **despite the fact that** she smokes 20 cigarettes a day.

Compare **although** and **in spite of / despite**:
- **Although the traffic was** bad, I arrived on time.
  In spite of the traffic, I arrived on time.
- I couldn't sleep, **although I was** very tired.
  I couldn't sleep, **despite being** very tired.

---

c Sometimes we use **though** instead of **although**:
- I didn't get the job, **though** I had all the necessary qualifications.

In spoken English we often use **though** at the end of a sentence:
- The house isn't very nice. I like the garden **though**. (= but I like the garden)
- I see him every day. I've never spoken to him **though**. (= but I've never spoken to him)

Even though is a stronger form of **although**:
- **Even though** I was really tired, I couldn't sleep.

UNIT 104   Exercises

104.1 *Complete these sentences. Each time use* **although** + *a sentence from the box.*

I didn't speak the language	~~he has a very responsible job~~
I had never seen him before	we don't like her very much
it was quite cold	he had promised to be on time

1. *Although he has a very responsible job*., he isn't particularly well paid.
2. Although ...., I recognized him from a photograph.
3. I didn't wear a coat, ...
4. We thought we'd better invite her to the party, ...
5. ...., I managed to make myself understood.
6. He was late, ...

104.2 *Complete these sentences with* **although** *or* **in spite of**.

Example: .*Although*................ it rained a lot, we enjoyed our vacation.

1. .... all my careful plans, a lot of things went wrong.
2. ....I had planned everything carefully, a lot of things went wrong.
3. I love music, ... I can't play a musical instrument.
4. ....being very tired, we kept on walking.
5. The heat was turned all the way up, but .... this the house was still cold.
6. Keith decided to quit his job, ... I advised him not to.

104.3 *Read these sentences and then write a new sentence with the same meaning. Use the word(s) in parentheses (. . .) in your sentences.*

Example: I couldn't sleep, although I was tired.   (despite)
   I couldn't sleep despite being tired.(or despite the fact (that) I was tired)..

1. Although he's got a French name, he is in fact American.   (despite)
   Despite ....
2. In spite of her injured foot, she managed to walk home.   (although)
   ....
3. I decided to accept the job, although the salary was low.   (in spite of)
   I decided ....
4. We lost the match, although we were the better team.   (despite)
   ....
5. In spite of not having eaten for 24 hours, I didn't feel hungry.   (even though)
   ....

104.4 *Use the words in parentheses to make a sentence with* **though** *at the end.*

Example: The house isn't very nice. (like / garden) *I like the garden though.*..........

1. She's very nice. (don't like / husband)   I ....
2. It's very warm. (a bit windy)   It ....
3. We didn't like the food. (ate)   We ....

UNIT 105 Even

a Study this example:

> Our football team lost yesterday. We all played badly. Bill is our best player, but yesterday **even Bill** played badly.
>
> We use **even** to say that something is unusual or surprising. We say **even Bill** . . . because he is a good player and it is unusual for him to play badly. If he played badly, it must have been a bad day for the team.

- These photographs aren't very good. **Even I** could take better photographs than these. (I'm certainly not a good photographer, so they must be bad.)
- It's a very rich country. **Even the poorest people** own cars. (so the rich people must be very rich)
- She always wears a coat – **even in summer**.
- Nobody would lend him the money – **not even his best friend**. (*or* **Even** his best friend would**n't** lend him the money.)

b Very often we use **even** with the verb in the middle of a sentence (see Unit 102b for the exact position):

- Don has traveled all over the world. He has **even** been to the Antarctic. (It's very unusual to go to the Antarctic, so he must have traveled a lot.)
- He always wears a tie. He **even** wears a tie in bed!
- They are very rich. They **even** have their own private jet.

Here are some examples with **not even**:

- I can't cook. I can**'t even** boil an egg. (so I certainly can't cook, because boiling an egg is very simple)
- They weren't very friendly to us. They did**n't even** say hello.
- She's in good shape. She's just run five miles and she's **not even** out of breath.

c You can use **even** with *comparatives* (**hotter / more surprised**, etc.):

- It was very hot yesterday, but today it's **even hotter**.
- I got up at 6:00, but Carol got up **even earlier**.
- I knew I didn't have much money, but I've got **even less** than I thought.
- I was surprised to get a letter from her. I was **even more surprised** when she appeared at my door the next day.

d You can use **even** with **if, when,** and **though**:

- I'll probably see you tomorrow. But **even if** I don't, we're sure to see each other before the weekend.
- She never shouts, **even when** she's angry. (you expect people to shout when they are angry)
- He has bought a car, **even though** he can't drive.

For **if** and **when** see Unit 9c. For **even though** see Unit 104.

UNIT 105   Exercises

105.1 *Complete a conversation. Use* **even** *or* **not even**.

Example: A: We lost the game. The whole team played badly.
     B: Really? ..*Even*..... Bill?   A: Yes, *even Bill played badly.*........

1. A: Everyone was on time for work this morning.
   B: Really? .... Sue?   A: Yes,...
2. A: Everyone makes mistakes sometimes.
   B: Really? .... you?   A: Yes,...
3. A: The whole country is going on strike.
   B: Really? .... the police?   A: Yes,...
4. A: Nobody knows where Peter has gone.
   B: Really? Not .... his wife?   A: No,...
5. A: Everybody passed the exam.
   B: Really? .... George?   A: Yes,...

105.2 *Make sentences with* **even**. *Use the words in parentheses (. . .).*

Example: He wears a tie all the time. (in bed)   *He even wears a tie in bed.*..................

1. They painted the whole room white. (the floor)
   They .... white.
2. He has to work every day. (on Sundays)   He..
3. You could hear the noise from a long way away. (from the next street)
   ....
4. They have the window open all the time. (when it's freezing)
   ....

Use **not even**.
Example: She didn't say anything to me. (hello)   *She didn't even say hello.*...............

5. I can't remember anything about her. (her name)   I..
6. There isn't anything in this town. (a movie theater)   There..
7. I haven't eaten anything today. (a piece of bread)   ....
8. He didn't tell anyone where he was going. (his wife)
   ....
9. I don't know anyone on our block. (the people next door)
   ....

105.3 *Complete these sentences with* **even** + *a comparative.*

Example: It was very hot yesterday, but today it's .*even hotter*......... .

1. We found a very cheap hotel, but the one Jack found was ....
2. That's a very good idea, but I have an .... one.
3. The cafe is always crowded, but today it's .... than usual.
4. This church is 500 years old, but the house next to it is ....
5. I did very little work for the exam, but you did ....

UNIT 106

As (time) – "I watched her as she worked."   As (reason) – "As I was feeling tired, I went to bed."

a **As** *(time): two things happening together*
You can use **as** when two things happen at the same time or over the same period of time:
- I watched her **as** she opened the letter.
- **As** they walked along the street, they looked in the store windows.
- Turn off the light **as** you go out, please.

We use **as** especially for two *short* actions happening at the same time:
- George arrived **as** I left. (= he arrived and I left at the same time)
- We all waved goodbye to Tom **as** he drove away in his car.

You can also use **just as** (= exactly at that moment):
- George arrived **just as** I left.
- **Just as** I sat down, the phone rang.

We also use **as** when two *changes* happen over the same period of time:
- **As the day wore on,** the weather got worse.
- I began to enjoy the job more **as I got used to it.**

b **As** *(time): one thing happening during another*
You can say that you did something **as** you were doing something else (= in the middle of doing something else).

When we use **as** in this way, both actions are usually quite short:
- The man slipped **as he was getting off the train.**
- Jill burned herself **as she was taking the cake out of the oven.**
- The thief was seen **as he was climbing over the wall.**

You can also use **just as:**
- **Just as we were going out,** it started to rain.
- I had to leave **just as the conversation was getting interesting.**

For the *past continuous* (**was getting** / **were going**, etc.) see Unit 12.

Note that we use **as** only if two actions happen *together*. Do *not* use **as** if one action follows another:
- **When** I got home, I took a bath. (*not* as I got home)

c **As** *(reason)*
As sometimes means "because":
- **As** I was feeling tired, I went to bed early. (= because I was feeling tired)
- **As** they live near us, we see them quite often.
- **As** tomorrow is a national holiday, all the stores will be closed.
- **As** we had nothing better to do, we watched television the whole evening.

For **as** and **like** see Unit 107. For **as . . . as** see Unit 99.

UNIT 106   Exercises

106.1 *Make one sentence with* **as** *(time) from each pair of sentences.*

Example: She opened the letter. I watched her. *I watched her as she opened the letter.*

1. We posed for the photograph. We smiled.
   We smiled ....
2. He explained what I had to do. I listened carefully.
   I ....
3. The two teams ran onto the field. The crowd cheered.
   The crowd ....
4. She passed me on the street. She didn't look at me.

   ....

In the following sentences use **just as**.
Example: I sat down. Just at that moment the phone rang.
   The phone rang just as I sat down. ....

5. We arrived at the beach. Just at that moment it started to rain.
   It started ....
6. I took the photograph. Just at that moment you moved.

   ....

In these sentences, one thing happens during another.
Example: Jill was taking the cakes out of the oven. She burned herself.
   Jill burned herself as she was taking the cakes out of the oven. ....

7. Tom was climbing out of the window. He fell.
   Tom fell ....
8. We were driving along the road. A dog ran out in front of the car.
   A dog ....
9. She was getting out of the car. She dropped her bag.

   ....

106.2 *Join a sentence from box A with a sentence from box B. Begin each of your sentences with* **as** *(reason).*

A ~~tomorrow is a national holiday~~ there isn't anything to eat in the house it was a nice day we didn't want to wake anyone up the door was open I didn't have enough money for a taxi	B I walked in I had to walk home we came in very quietly ~~the stores will be closed~~ let's go out to eat we decided to go for a walk

1. *As tomorrow is a national holiday, the stores will be closed.* ....
2. As ....
3. ....
4. ....
5. ....
6. ....

Like and as

a **Like** = similar to / the same as / for example:

- What a beautiful house! It's **like a palace**. (*not* as a palace)
- "What does George do?" "He's a teacher, **like me**." (*not* as me)
- Why do you always talk about boring things **like your job**?
- Be careful! The floor was just waxed. It's **like walking** on ice.
- It's raining again. I hate weather **like this**.

Like is a *preposition*. So it is followed by a *noun* ("like **a palace** / like **your job**"), a *pronoun* ("like **me** / like **this**"), or **-ing** ("like walk**ing**").
You can also say "**like** (someone/something) **-ing**":

- "What's that noise?" "It sounds **like a baby crying**."

b We use **as** before a *subject* + *verb*:

- Don't move anything. Leave everything **as it is**.

Compare **like** and **as** in these sentences:

- You should have done it **like this**. (**like** + *pronoun*)
- You should have done it **as I showed** you. (**as** + *subject* + *verb*)

But we use **such as** (= for example) without a verb:

- Some sports, **such as auto racing**, can be dangerous.

Note that we say **as usual**:

- You're late **as usual**.

c **As** + *subject* + *verb* can have other meanings. For example:

- Do **as you are told**! (= Do what you are told.)
- They did **as they promised**. (= They did what they promised.)

You can also say **as you know** / **as we expected** / **as I said** / **as I thought**, etc.:

- **As you know**, it's Tom's birthday next week. (= you know this already)
- Ann failed her driving test, **as we expected**.

d **As** can also be a *preposition* (which means you can use it with a *noun*), but the meaning is different from **like**.

We use **like** when we *compare* things:

- She looks beautiful – **like a princess**. (she isn't really a princess)
- Everyone is sick at home. Our house is **like a hospital**. (it isn't really a hospital)

We use **as** + *noun* to say what something *really is or was* (especially when we talk about someone's job or how we use something):

- A few years ago I worked **as a waiter**. (I really was a waiter)
- Sue has just found a job **as a sales clerk**.
- During the war this hotel was used **as a hospital**. (so it really was a hospital)
- We don't have a car, so we use the garage **as a workshop**.
- The news of her death came **as a great shock**. (it really was a shock)

UNIT 107   Exercises

107.1 *Complete these sentences with* **like** *or* **as**. *The sentences in this exercise are like those in sections a, b, and c.*

Examples: This house is beautiful. It's ..*like*..... a palace.
            Ann failed her driving test, ...*as*........ we expected.

1. Do you think Ann looks .... her mother?
2. He really gets on my nerves. I can't stand people .... him.
3. Why didn't you do it .... I told you to do it?
4. "Where does Bill work?"   "He works in a bank, ... most of his friends."
5. He never listens. Talking to him is .... talking to a wall.
6. .... I said yesterday, I'm thinking of going to Mexico.
7. Carol's idea seemed a good one, so we did .... she suggested.
8. It's a difficult problem. I never know what to do in situations .... this.
9. I'll call you tomorrow evening .... usual, okay?
10. This tea is terrible. It tastes .... water.
11. Suddenly there was a terrible noise. It was .... a bomb exploding.
12. She's a really good swimmer. She swims .... a fish.

107.2 *Choose* **like** *or* **as** *(preposition – see section d).*

Examples: She looks beautiful this evening – ..*like*..... a princess.
            A few years ago I worked ..*as*........ a waiter in a restaurant.

1. He's been studying English for a few years, but he still speaks .... a beginner.
2. My feet are really cold. They're .... blocks of ice.
3. Margaret once had a part-time job .... a tourist guide.
4. We don't need all the bedrooms in the house, so we use one of them .... a study.
5. Her house is full of lots of interesting things. It's .... a museum.
6. Have you ever worked .... a construction worker on a building site?
7. The news that he was getting married came .... a complete surprise to me.
8. He's 35, but he sometimes behaves .... a child.

107.3 *There are sentences of all types in this exercise. Put in* **like** *or* **as**.

1. Your English is very fluent. I wish I could speak _____ you.
2. You don't have to take my advice if you don't want to. You can do .... you like.
3. He wastes too much time doing things .... sitting in cafes all day.
4. There's no need to change your clothes. You can go out .... you are.
5. The weather's terrible for the middle of summer. It's .... winter.
6. She decided to give up her job .... a journalist and become a teacher.
7. I think I prefer this room .... it was, before we decorated it.
8. When we asked Jack to help us, he agreed immediately, ... I knew he would.
9. While we were on vacation, we spent most of our time on sports .... sailing, water skiing, and swimming.
10. Ann's been working .... a waitress for the last few weeks.

UNIT 108 As if

a You can use **as if** to say how someone or something **looks/sounds/feels**, etc.:
- The house **looked as if** nobody was living in it.
- Ann **sounds as if** she's got a cold, doesn't she?
- I've just come back from vacation, but I feel tired and depressed. I don't **feel as if** I've had a vacation.

Compare:
- You look **tired**. (**look** + *adjective*)
  You look **as if you haven't slept**. (**look** + **as if** + *subject* + *verb*)
- Tom sounded **worried**. (**sound** + *adjective*)
  Tom sounded **as if he was** worried. (**sound** + **as if** + *subject* + *verb*)

You can use **as though** instead of **as if**:
- Ann sounds **as though** she's got a cold.

b You can also say **It looks/sounds/smells as if** (or **as though**):
- Tom is very late, isn't he? **It looks as if** he isn't coming.
- We took an umbrella because **it looked as if** it was going to rain.
- Do you hear that music next door? **It sounds as if** they are having a party, doesn't it?
- **It smells as though** someone has been smoking in here.

After **It looks/sounds/smells**, many people use **like** instead of **as if / as though**:
- It looks **like** Tom isn't coming.

c You can also use **as if** with other verbs to say how someone does something:
- He **ran as if** he were running for his life.
- After the interruption, she **continued talking as if** nothing had happened.
- When I told them my plan, they **looked at me as if** I were insane.

d After **as if** we sometimes use the *past* when we are talking about the *present*. For example:
- I don't like Norman. He talks as if he **knew** everything.

The meaning is *not* past in this sentence. We use the past (''as if he **knew**'') because the idea is *not real*: Norman does *not* know everything. We use the past in the same way in **if** sentences and after **wish** (see Unit 35).

When we use the past in this way, we use **were** instead of **was**:
- Harry's only 50. Why do you talk about him **as if he were** (*or* **was**) an old man?
- They treat me **as if I were** (*or* **was**) their own son. (I'm not their son.)

UNIT 108 Exercises

108.1 *Use the sentences in the box to make sentences with* **as if**.

she had hurt her leg	he hadn't washed in ages	~~you need a good rest~~
she was enjoying it	she was going to throw it at him	he was calling long distance
you've seen a ghost	they hadn't eaten for a week	I'm going to be sick

1. Tom looks very tired. You say to him: You look *as if you need a good rest.*
2. When you talked to Jack on the phone last night, you couldn't hear him very well. He
   sounded ....
3. Carol had a bored expression on her face during the concert.
   She didn't look ....
4. You could smell him from a long way away. He needed a bath badly.
   He smelled ....
5. Your friend comes into the room looking absolutely terrified. His face is white.
   You say: What's the matter? You look ....
6. You've just eaten a whole box of candy. Now you are feeling sick.
   You say: I feel ....
7. When you saw Sue, she was walking in a strange way.
   She looked ....
8. They were extremely hungry and ate their dinner very quickly.
   They ate their dinner ....
9. Ann and Tom were having an argument. She was very angry. Suddenly she picked up a
   plate. She looked ....

108.2 *Make sentences beginning* **It looks/sounds as if** *(or* **like***)* . . .

~~he isn't going to come~~	you had a good time	there's been an accident
we'll have to walk home	it's going to rain	they are having an argument

1. Tom hasn't arrived yet and it's late.   You say: *It looks as if (or like) he isn't going to come.*
2. The sky is full of black clouds.   You say: It...
3. You hear two people shouting at each other next door.   You say: It sounds ....
   ....
4. There is an ambulance, some police officers, and two damaged cars at the side of the
   road.   You say: ....
5. You and your friend have just missed the last bus home.   You say: ....
   ....
6. Sue and Dave have just been telling you about all the interesting things they did on their
   vacation.   You say: ....

108.3 *These sentences are like the ones in section d. Complete each sentence.*

Example: Norman doesn't know everything, but he talks *as if he knew everything.*

1. I'm not a child, but sometimes you talk to me .... a child.
2. She doesn't know me, so why did she smile at me...
3. He's not my boss, but sometimes he acts...

a **At** We use **at** with times:

at 5 o'clock   **at** 11:45   **at** midnight   **at** lunchtime
- Carol usually leaves work **at five o'clock**.

But we usually leave out **at** when we ask (At) **what time . . . ?**:
- **What time** are you going out this evening?

We also use **at** in these expressions:

at night	I don't like going out **at night**.
at Christmas / at Easter (public holiday periods)	We give each other presents **at Christmas**.
at the moment / at present	Ms. King is busy **at the moment / at present**.
at the same time	Ann and I arrived **at the same time**.
at the age of . . .	Tom left school **at the age of 16 / at 16**.
at the beginning of . . .	I'm going away **at the beginning of May**.
at the end of . . .	**At the end of the concert**, there was great applause.

b **On** We use **on** with dates and days:

on March 12th   **on** Friday(s)   **on** Christmas Day (*but* **at** Christmas)
- They got married **on March 12th**.

We also say:
on Friday morning(s)   **on** Sunday afternoon(s)   **on** Monday evening(s)
on Saturday night(s), etc.   **on** weekends
- I usually go out **on Monday evenings**.
- What are you doing **on the weekend**?

c **In** We use **in** for longer periods of time (for example: months/years/seasons):

in April   **in** 1968   **in** (the) winter
in the 18th century   **in** the 1970s   **in** the Middle Ages
- They got married **in 1968**.

We also say:
in the morning(s) / **in** the afternoon(s) / **in** the evening(s)
- I'll see you **in the morning**. (*but* I'll see you **on Friday morning**.)

d We do not use **at/on/in** before **last** and **next**:
- I'll see you **next** Friday.   - They got married **last** March.

e **In** + a period of time = a time in the future:
- The train will be leaving **in a few minutes**. (= a few minutes from now)
- Jack went away. He'll be back **in a week**. (= a week from now)
- They are getting married **in six months**. (= six months from now)

You can also say "in six months' **time**," "in a week's **time**," etc.:
- They are getting married **in six months' time**.

We also use **in** to say how long it takes to do something:
- I learned to drive **in four weeks**. (= it took me four weeks to learn)

UNIT 109   Exercises

109.1 *Complete the sentences. Each time use* **at, on,** *or* **in** *with one of the phrases from the box.*

the 1920s	1917	~~the 15th century~~	about five minutes	the same time
Saturdays	night	the age of five	July 21, 1969	the moment

1. Columbus discovered America *in the 15th century.*
2. The first man landed on the moon *on July 21 1969*
3. In Britain soccer matches are usually played *on Sat*
4. You can see the stars *at night* if the sky is clear.
5. In many countries, children have to start school *at the age of five*
6. Jazz became popular in the United States *in the 1920s*
7. It's difficult to listen when everyone is speaking *at the same time*
8. The Russian Revolution took place *in 1917*
9. Tom isn't here *at the moment* He'll be back *in about 5 min*

109.2 *Put in the correct prepositions:* **at, on,** *or* **in.**

Examples: The concert starts ....**at**........ 7:45.   I learned to drive ....**in**........ four weeks.

1. The course begins ...*on*... January 7th and ends ...*on*... March 10th.
2. I went to bed ...*at*... midnight and got up ...*at*... 6:30 the next morning.
3. We traveled overnight to Paris and arrived ...*at*... 5:00 ...*in*... the morning.
4. Mozart was born in Salzburg ...*in*... 1756.
5. Are you doing anything special ...*on*... the weekend?
6. Hurry up! We've got to go ...*in*... five minutes.
7. I haven't seen Ann for a few days. I last saw her ...*on*... Tuesday.
8. I'll call you ...*on*... Tuesday morning ...*at*... about 10:00, okay?
9. I might not be home ...*in*... the morning. Can you call ...*in*... the afternoon instead?
10. Tom's grandmother died ...*in*... 1977 ...*at*... the age of 79.
11. I get paid ...*at*... the end of the month.
12. Jack's brother is an engineer, but he's unemployed ...*at*... the moment.
13. The price of electricity is going up ...*in*... October.
14. ...*On*... Sunday afternoons I usually go for a walk in the park.
15. There are usually a lot of parties ...*on*... New Year's Eve.
16. I like walking around town ...*at*... night. It's always so peaceful.
17. Tom doesn't see his parents very often these days – usually only ...*at*... Christmas and sometimes ...*in*... the summer for a few days.
18. ...*At*... the end of a course, the students usually have a party.
19. I've been invited to a wedding ...*on*... February 14.
20. I'm just going out to do some shopping. I'll be back ...*in*... half an hour.
21. Ann works hard during the week, so she likes to relax ...*on*... weekends.
22. It was a short book and easy to read. I read it ...*in*... a day.
23. Carol got married ...*at*... 17, which is rather young to get married.
24. Would you like to go to the movies ...*on*... Friday night?
25. The telephone rang and the doorbell rang ...*at*... the same time.
26. Mary and Henry always go out for dinner ...*on*... their wedding anniversary.
27. Mr. Davis is 63. He'll be retiring from his job ...*in*... two years' time.

UNIT 110 For, during, and while

a For and during

We use **for** + a period of time to say *how long* something goes on:

for **six years**   for **two hours**   for **a week**

- I've lived in this house **for six years**.
- We watched television **for two hours** last night.
- Ann is going away **for a week** in September.
- Where have you been? I've been waiting **for hours**.
- Are you going away **for the weekend**?

You cannot use **during** in this way:

- It rained **for** three days without stopping. (*not* during three days)

We use **during** + *noun* to say *when* something happens (*not* how long):

during **the movie**   during **our vacation**   during **the night**

- I fell asleep **during the movie**.
- We met a lot of interesting people **during our vacation**.
- The ground is wet. It must have rained **during the night**.
- I'll call you some time **during the afternoon**.

b During and while

We use **during** + *noun*. We use **while** + *subject* + *verb*. Compare:

		noun
I fell asleep	**during**	**the movie.**
		subject + verb
I fell asleep	**while**	**I was watching** television.

Compare **during** and **while** in these examples:

- We met a lot of interesting people **during our vacation**.
  We met a lot of interesting people **while we were** on vacation.
- Robert suddenly began to feel sick **during the exam**.
  Robert suddenly began to feel sick **while he was taking** the exam.

Here are some more examples of **while**:

- We saw Ann **while we were waiting** for the bus.
- **While you were** out, there was a phone call for you.
- Tom read a book **while I watched** television.

When you are talking about the future, use the *present* (*not* will) after **while**:

- I'm going to Toronto next week. I hope to see Tom **while I'm** there.
- What are you going to do **while** you **are** waiting?

See also Unit 9a.

For **while -ing** see Unit 64b. For **for** and **since** see Unit 19b.

UNIT 110   Exercises

110.1 *Put in* **for** *or* **during**.

Examples: It rained ...*for*........ three days without stopping.
I fell asleep *during*.... the movie.

1. I waited for you ...*for*....... half an hour and then decided that you weren't coming.
2. He hasn't lived in Haiti all his life. He lived in France ...*for*...... four years.
3. Production at the factory was seriously affected ...*during*.....the strike.
4. I felt really sick last week. I couldn't eat anything ......*for*.... three days.
5. When we were at the theater last night, we met Ann...*during*.... intermission.
6. Sue was very angry after our argument. She didn't speak to me ...*for*.......a week.
7. We usually go out on weekends, but we don't often go out ...*during*....the week.
8. Jack started a new job a few weeks ago. Before that he was out of work ...*for*.........six months.

110.2 *Put in* **while** *or* **during**.

Examples: We met a lot of people ..*while*...... we were on vacation.
We met a lot of people *during*... our vacation.

1. I met Sue *while*.... I was waiting for the bus.
2. ...*While*... we were in Paris, we stayed at a very comfortable hotel.
3. ...*During*...our stay in Paris, we visited a lot of museums and galleries.
4. The phone rang three times ...*while*... we were having dinner last night.
5. I had been away for many years. ...*During*...that time, many things had changed.
6. What did she say about me ...*while*....I was out of the room?
7. Jack read a lot of books and magazines ...*while*...he was sick.
8. I went out for dinner last night. Unfortunately I began to feel sick ...*during*...the meal.
9. Many interesting suggestions were made ...*during*... the meeting.
10. Please don't interrupt me ...*while*....I'm speaking.
11. There were many interruptions ...*during*...the President's speech.
12. Can you set the table ...*while*. I get dinner ready?

110.3 *Now use your own ideas to complete these sentences.*

Examples: I fell asleep while *I was reading the newspaper.*.......................
I didn't sleep very well. I kept waking up during *the night.*........................

1. I fell asleep during ......*the English class*.........................
2. The lights suddenly went out while ...*we were watching the pieces of art*...
3. I hurt my arm while ......*playing tennis*.........................
4. The students looked bored during ...*the Math lecture*...
5. Can you wait here while ...*I am cooking supper*...................?
6. It rained a lot during ......*the day*.........................
7. I fell off my chair during......*the sleep*...*game*...
8. It started to rain while......*we were picking mushrooms*...
9. She burned herself while ......*baking the cakes*..

221

UNIT 111
By and until
By the time . . .

a **By** (+ *a time*) = not later than:
- I mailed the letter today, so they should receive it **by Monday**.
  (= *on or before* Monday, on Monday *at the latest*)
- We'd better hurry. We have to be home **by 5 o'clock** (= at or before 5 o'clock, at 5 o'clock at the latest)
- Where's Ann? She should be here **by now**. (= now or before now; so she should have already arrived)

You cannot use **until** with this meaning:
- Tell me **by Friday** whether or not you can come to the party.
  (*not* Tell me until Friday)

We use **until** (or **till**) to say how long a situation continues:
- "Shall we go now?"   "No, let's wait **until** (or **till**) **it stops raining**."
- I was tired this morning, so I stayed in bed **until half past ten**.

Compare **until** and **by** in these sentences:
- Sue will be away **until Monday**. (so she'll come back on Monday)
- Sue will be back **by Monday**. (= she'll be back on or before Monday, on Monday at the latest)
- I'll be working **until 11 o'clock**. (so I'll stop working at 11 o'clock)
- I'll have finished my work **by 11 o'clock** (= I'll finish my work at or before 11 o'clock, at 11 o'clock at the latest)

b You can also say **by the time (something happens), ...** Study these examples carefully:
- It's not worth going shopping now. **By the time we get to the stores**, they will be closed. (= they will close between now and the time we get there)
- (*from a letter*) I'm flying to the United States this evening. So **by the time you receive this letter**, I'll probably be in New York. (= I will arrive in New York between now and the time you receive this letter.)

When you are talking about the past, you can use **By the time (something happened), . . .**
- Tom's car broke down on the way to the party last night. **By the time he arrived**, most of the guests had left. (= It took him a long time to get to the party and most of the guests left during this time.)
- I had a lot of work to do yesterday evening. **By the time I finished**, I was very tired. (= It took me a long time to do the work and I became more and more tired during this time.)
- It took them a long time to find a place to park their car. **By the time they got to the theater**, the play had already started.

You can also use **by then** or **by that time**:
- Tom finally arrived at the party at midnight. But **by then** (*or* **by that time**), most of the guests had left.

UNIT 111   Exercises

111.1 *Make sentences with* **by**:

Example: I have to be home no later than 5:00.   *I have to be at home by 5:00.*

1. I have to be at the airport no later than 10:30.
   I have to be at the airport ....
2. Let me know no later than Saturday whether you can come to the party.
   Let me know ....
3. Please make sure that you are here no later than 2:00.
   Please ....
4. If you want to take the exam, you have to register no later than April 3.
   If..
5. If we leave now, we should be in Winnipeg no later than lunchtime.
   If..

111.2 *Put in* **by** *or* **until**.

Examples: Tom went away. He'll be away *until* Monday.
   Sorry, but I've got to go. I have to be home *by* 5:00.

1. I've been offered a job. I haven't decided yet whether to accept it or not. I have to decide
   by Thursday.
2. I think I'll wait *until* Thursday before making a decision.
3. A: I hear you're writing a book. Have you finished it yet?
   B: Not quite, but I hope to finish it *by* the end of this month.
4. A: I'm going out now. I'll be back at 4:30. Will you still be here?
   B: I don't think so. I'll probably have gone *by* then.
5. I'm moving into my new apartment next week. I'm staying with a friend *until* then.
6. A: Do you think I'll still be unemployed this time next year?
   B: No, of course not. I'm sure you'll have found a job *by* that time.

111.3 *Read these situations and then complete the sentences using* **By the time . . . .**

Example: Tom was invited to a party, but he got there much later than he intended.
   By the time he got to the party, most of the guests had left.

1. I had to catch a train, but it took me longer than expected to get to the station.
   By the time I arrived at the station, my train had left.
2. I saw two men who looked as if they were trying to steal a car. So I called the police. But
   it was some time before the police arrived.
   by the time police arrived, the two men had disappeared.
3. A man escaped from prison last night. It was a long time before the guards discovered
   what had happened. *By the time the guards discov. what had happened*
   By the time the guards, the escaped prisoner was miles away.
4. I intended to go to the movies after finishing my work. But I finished my work much later
   than expected. *work*
   By the time I finished my, it was too late to go to the movies.

223

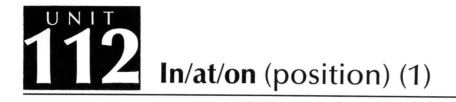

UNIT 112 In/at/on (position) (1)

a **In**   Study these examples:

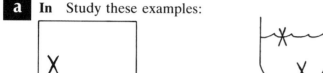

in a room / **in** a building
in a garden / **in** a park
in a town / **in** a country

in the water
in the ocean
in a river

in a row / **in** a line

- There's no one **in the room** / **in the building** / **in the store**.
- The children are playing **in the garden** / **in the park**.
- When we were **in Italy**, we spent a few days **in Venice**. (*not* at Venice)
- Robert lives **in a small village in the mountains**.
- She keeps her money **in her bag** / **in her purse**.
- What do you have **in your hand** / **in your mouth**?
- Look at that girl swimming **in the water** / **in the ocean** / **in the river**!
- When I go to the movies, I prefer to sit **in the front row**.
- Have you read this article **in the newspaper?**

Note that we say:

> (sit) **in an armchair** (*but* **on** a **chair**)
> **in a photograph / in a picture / in a mirror**   **in the sky**

- Who is the woman **in that photograph?** (*not* on that photograph)
- It was a beautiful day. There wasn't a cloud **in the sky**.
- Don't sit **in that armchair**. It's broken.

b **In (the) front of   In (the) back of**

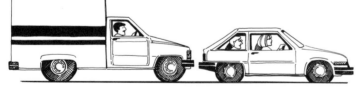

- The car is **in front of** the truck. (but not *in* the truck!)
- The truck is **in back of** (= behind) the car. (but not *in* the car!)
- The woman is in **the** front of the car. (*in* the car)
- The man is in **the** back (of the car). (*in* the car)

We say **in the front** / **in the back** of a car, room, theater, group of people, etc.:

- I was sitting **in the back** of the car when we crashed.
- Let's sit **in the front** (of the theater).
- John was standing **in the back** of the crowd.

but: **on** the front/back of a piece of paper, photograph, envelope,
etc.:   Write your name **on the back** of this piece of paper.

c **At** Study these examples:

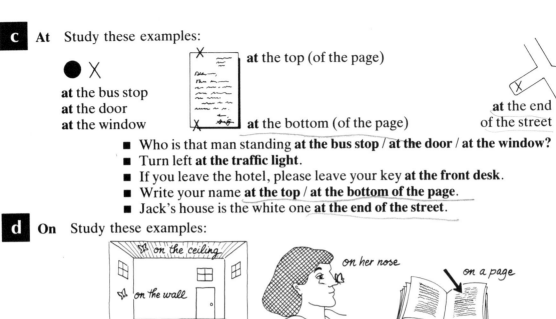

at the bus stop
at the door
at the window

at the top (of the page)

at the bottom (of the page)

at the end
of the street

- Who is that man standing **at the bus stop** / **at the door** / **at the window**?
- Turn left **at the traffic light**.
- If you leave the hotel, please leave your key **at the front desk**.
- Write your name **at the top** / **at the bottom of the page**.
- Jack's house is the white one **at the end of the street**.

d **On** Study these examples:

on the ceiling

on the wall

on the floor

on her nose

on a page

- Don't sit **on the floor** / **on the ground** / **on the grass**!
- There's a butterfly **on the wall** / **on the ceiling** / **on your nose**.
- **Have you seen the notice on the bulletin board**?
- The book you are looking for is **on the top shelf** / **on the table**.
- There's a report of the soccer game **on page 7** of the newspaper.
- Don't sit **on that chair**. It's broken. (*but* sit **in** an **armchair**)

Note that we say:

> **on the left** / **on the right** (*or* **on** the left- / right-**hand side**)
> **on** the ground **floor** / **on** the first **floor** / **on** the second **floor**, etc.

- In Britain people drive **on the left**. (*or* **. . . on the left-hand side**)
- Our apartment is **on the second floor** of the building.

We use **on** with small islands:
- Tom spent his vacation **on a small island** off the coast of Scotland.

We also say that a place is **on the coast** / **on a river** / **on a road**:

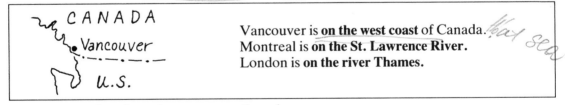

CANADA
Vancouver
U.S.

Vancouver is **on the west coast** of Canada.
Montreal is **on the St. Lawrence River**.
London is **on the river Thames**.

We say that a place is **on the way** to another place:
- We stopped for lunch in a pretty village **on the way** to Rome.

e **In/at/on the corner** We say "**in the corner** of a **room**," but "**at the corner** (*or* **on the corner**) of a **street**":
- The television is **in the corner** of the room.
- There is a telephone booth **at/on the corner** of the street.

UNIT 112 Exercises

112.1 *Answer questions about the pictures. Use **in**, **at**, or **on** with the words in parentheses (. . .).*

1. Where's the label? (bottle) ....*On*..... the bottle.
2. Where's the man standing? (gate) ...*at*..
3. Where's Tom sitting? (armchair) ...*in*..
   Where's the picture? (wall) ....*on*...
4. Where's Ann standing? (top / stairs) ...*at*.......................................
   And where's the cat? (bottom / stairs) ....*at*...................................
5. What's George doing? (looking / mirror) He's.....*at himself in the mirror*
6. Tom lives in this building. Where's his apartment? (third floor) .....*on*......
7. Where are the children? (back / car) ...*in the back of the car*........
8. Tom is at the movies. Where's he sitting? (back) ...*in the back*......
9. Where's the post office? (left) ...*on the*......And the bank? (right) ...*on the*...
10. Where's the notice? (door) .....*on*..
11. Where is the woman standing? (corner) ...*at / on*............................
12. Where is the man standing? (corner) ...*in*....................................

112.2 *Complete these sentences. Each time use* **in, at**, *or* **on** *with one of the phrases from the box.*

the front row	~~New York~~	the west coast
the third floor	the back of the class	the Swiss Alps
my way to work	the back of the envelope	the window
the right	the front page of the newspaper	

1. The headquarters of the United Nations is *in New York* .
2. In most countries people drive *on the right* .
3. I usually buy a newspaper *on my way* in the morning.
4. Last year we had a great skiing vacation *in the Swiss Alps*
5. San Francisco is *on the west* of the United States.
6. She spends all day sitting *at the window* and watching what is happening outside.
7. I have to walk up a lot of stairs every day. My apartment is *on the third floor* and there is no elevator.
8. I read about the accident. There was a story *on the front page* .
9. We went to the theater last night. We had seats *in the front row*
10. I couldn't hear the teacher very well. She had a soft voice, and I was sitting *in the back of the class*
11. When you send a letter, it is a good idea to write your name and address *on the back of the envelope*

112.3 *Complete these sentences with* **in, at**, *or* **on**.

Examples: Turn left ...*at*... the traffic light.
You'll find the cups ...*on*... the top shelf.

1. I'll meet you ...*at, on*... the corner (of the street) at 10:00.
2. We got stuck in a traffic jam ...*on*... the way to the airport.
3. There was an accident ...*at*... the intersection this morning. ?
4. Look at those beautiful horses ...*in*... that field!
5. I can't find Tom ...*in*... this photograph. Is he ...*in*... it?
6. ...*at*... the end of the road there is a path leading to the river.
7. I wouldn't like an office job. I couldn't spend the whole day sitting ...*at*... a desk.
8. Do you take sugar ...*in*... your coffee?
9. Ann's brother lives ...*in*... a small town ...*on*... the coast of Maine.
10. You'll find the sports results ...*on*... the back page of the newspaper.
11. Sue and Dave got married ...*in*... Denver four years ago.
12. Paris is ...*on*... the river Seine.
13. Mr. Black's office is ...*on*... the fifth floor. When you get off the elevator, it's the third door ...*on*... your left.
14. We normally use the front entrance to the building, but there's another entrance ...*in*... the back.
15. If you want to get away from modern life, you should go and live ...*on*... a small island in the middle of the ocean.
16. The man the police are looking for has a scar ...*on*... his right cheek.
17. I wasn't sure whether I had come to the right apartment because there was no name ...*on*... the door.

UNIT 113 In/at/on (position) (2)

a We say that someone is **at** an event. For example: "**at** a party / **at** a concert / **at** a conference / **at** the movies / **at** a football game":

- Were there many people **at the party** / **at the meeting?**
- I saw Jack **at the football game** / **at the concert** on Saturday.

b We say:

at work	**at** an airport	**at** sea	**in** bed	**on** a farm
at a station	**at** the seashore		**in** prison/jail	**in** the hospital

- I'll be **at work** until 5:30.
- Can you meet me **at the airport?**
- Have you ever worked **on a farm?**
- Tom's father is **in the hospital**.

You can say **be home / stay home** with or without **at**:

- We'll be out during the day but we'll **be (at) home** all evening.
- I didn't go out last night. I **stayed (at) home**.

c You can be **in** or **at** college/school. Use **at college** or **at school** when you are thinking of the college/school as a place or when you give the name of a college/school:

- Dan will be **in college** / **in school** for two more years.
- Tom is away **at college** right now, but he'll be home for the summer.
- She's majoring in economics **at Los Angeles City College**.

d You can often use **in** or **at** with buildings. You can stay **in a hotel** or **at a hotel**; you can eat **in a restaurant** or **at a restaurant**. We usually say **at** when we say where an event takes place (for example: a concert, a movie, a meeting, a sports event, etc.):

- We went to a concert **at the Arts Center**.
- The meeting took place **at the company's main office**.
- "Where were you last night?" "**At the theater**."

We say **at someone's house**:

- I was **at Tom's house** last night. (*or* I was **at Tom's** last night.)

We use **in** when we are thinking about the building itself:

- The rooms **in** Tom's house are very small.
- I enjoyed the movie, but it was very cold **in the theater**.

e We usually say **in** with towns and villages:

- Tom's parents live **in St. Louis**. (*not* "at St. Louis")

But you can use **at** when the town or village is a point on a journey:

- Do you know if this train stops **at Smithtown?**
- We stopped **at** a pretty town on the way to Los Angeles.

f We say **arrive IN** a country or town:

- When did he **arrive in Japan** / **in Tokyo?**

We say **arrive AT** with other places (buildings, etc.) or events:

- What time did he **arrive at school** / **at work** / **at the hotel** / **at the party?**

We say **arrive home** (without a preposition):

- When did he **arrive home?**

UNIT 113 Exercises

113.1 *Complete these sentences. Use* **in, at,** *or* **on** *with one of the words or phrases from the box.*

bed	sea	the National Theatre	a farm	the hospital
school	prison	the airport	the movie theater	~~the station~~

1. My train arrives at 11:30. Can you meet me .*at the station*.....?
2. I didn't feel very well when I woke up, so I stayed .....*in bed*.........
3. My favorite movie, *Gone With the Wind*, is playing .....*at the movie*.........downtown.
4. Many people are ....*in prison*............ for crimes that they did not commit.
5. I like the country and the fresh air. I think I'd like to work .....*on a farm*.......
6. Did you get along well with your teachers when you were .....*in school*.........?
7. We went to see a play .....*at the N....*........when we were in London.
8. Linda was injured in a car accident a few days ago. She is still .....*in the hospital*....
9. It was a very long voyage. We were ....*at sea*...... for ten weeks.
10. Our flight was delayed. We had to wait ....*at the airport*....for four hours.

113.2 *Complete these sentences with* **in** *or* **at.**

Example: Were there many people ....*at*................ the concert?

1. I didn't see you .....*at*... the party on Saturday. Where were you?
2. It was a very slow train. It stopped ...*at*...... every little station.
3. He speaks French quite well. He studied ...*in*.... Paris for a year.
4. Tom's sick. He wasn't .....*at*....work today. He was ...?...... home ....*in*.... bed.
5. The exhibition .*at*.......the art gallery finished on Saturday. ?
6. There will be a public meeting ....*at*... the Town Hall next week, to discuss the plan to build a new highway.
7. I haven't seen Ken for some time. I last saw him ....*at*....Dave's wedding.
8. Paul is a student ....*at*... Central Community College.
9. Don't call tomorrow evening. I won't be .... home. I'll be ...*at*.... Ann's.
10. It's always too hot ..*in*....... Linda's house. She has the heat on too high.
11. Jane is an anthropology student.....*in*....college. ?
    at

113.3 *Complete these sentences with a preposition, if a preposition is necessary.*

Example: What time did you arrive ...*at*..... the station?

1. After many years away, he arrived back ...*in*..... Italy a month ago.
2. The train from Rome arrives ...*at*...... platform 4.
3. What time do you expect to arrive ...*in*.... Mexico City?
4. What time do you expect to arrive ...*at*.... the hotel?
5. What time do you usually arrive ....home in the evening?
6. What time do you usually arrive ...*at*..... work in the morning?
7. We arrived ....*in*.... the town with nowhere to stay.
8. When we arrived ...*at*... the theater, there was a long line outside.
9. It's a strange feeling when you first arrive ....*in*.... a foreign country.
10. I arrived .... home feeling very tired.

229

UNIT 114

To, been to, into
By car/in my car

---

a **To** We say **go/come/travel** (etc.) **to** a place or event. For example:

go to Brazil	**come to** the U.S.	**return to** Italy
fly to Tokyo	**walk to** work	**drive to** the airport
go to the bank	**go to** a party	**go to** a concert
be sent to prison	**be taken to** the hospital	**go to** bed

but! arrive in (handwritten)

We say **get to** (*but* **arrive in/at** – (see Unit 113f):
- What time did you **get to** Montreal / work / the party?

We say **go home / come home / get home**, etc. (with no preposition):
- I'm tired. Let's **go home**. ■ What time did you **get home** last night?

b **Been to** **I have been to** (a place) = I have visited a place; I went there, but now I have come back (see also Unit 13d):
- Have you ever **been to Japan**? ■ I've **been to Buenos Aires** twice.
- Ann has never **been to a football game** in her life.
- Jack has plenty of money. He has just **been to the bank**.

c **Into** "Go **into** / come **into**," etc. = **enter** (a room / building, etc.):
- I opened the door and **went into the room**.
- Don't wait outside! **Come into the house**.
- The man the police were chasing **ran into a store**.
- A bird **flew into the room** through the window.

INTO

d **By car** / **in my** car We use **by . . .** to say how we travel:

by car	by train	by plane	by boat/ship	by bus	by bicycle
also:	by rail	by air	by sea	by subway	

- "How did you go to Paris?" "**By plane**."
- Sue usually goes to work **by bicycle** / **by car** / **by bus** / **by train**.

But we say "**on foot**":
- Did you come here **by** car or **on** foot?

But you cannot use **by** if you say "**my** car / **the** train / **a** taxi," etc. We say "**in my** car" (*not* by my car), "**on the** train" (*not* by the train).

> We use **in** for cars and taxis:
> **in my** car **in Tom's** car **in the** car **in a** car **in a** taxi
> We say **get in(to) / get out of** a car or taxi:
> He **got into** the car and drove off. (*or* He got **in** the car . . .)
>
> We use **on** for bicycles and public transportation (buses, trains, etc.):
> **on my** bicycle **on the** bus **on the** 6:45 train **on a** big ship
> We say **get on / get off** a bicycle, bus, or train:
> Quick! **Get on** the train. It's ready to leave.

230

UNIT 114 Exercises

114.1 *Complete these sentences with* **in, to, into, on,** *or* **by.** *If no preposition is necessary, leave the sentence as it is.*

Examples: When are you going ....*to*........ Argentina?
  Tom usually goes ....*to*...... work ...*by*..... car.

1. I'm tired. I'm going ...*to*........ bed.
2. What time are you going .... home?
3. I decided not to go .....*by*....car. I went....*on*..... my bike instead.
4. We went ...*to*...... a very good party last night. We didn't get .... home until 3 a.m.
5. I saw Jane this morning. She was ...*on*..... a bus that passed me.
6. Sorry I'm late. I missed the bus, so I had to come....*on*.... foot.
7. The quickest way to get around New York is ...*by*..... subway.
8. I have to go ....*to*........ the bank today to change some money.
9. I had lost my key, but I managed to climb...*into*..... the house through a window.
10. Marcel has just returned ......*to*..... France after two years in Canada.
11. I didn't feel like walking, so I came home ...*in*......a taxi.

114.2 *Use* **been to.** *Write questions asking someone if they have been to these places.*

Example: (Australia) *Have you been to Australia?*...............................

1. (Africa) Have ....
2. (Japan) ....
3. (Rome) ....
4. (Moscow) ....
5. (Canada) ....
6. (Puerto Rico) ....

Now choose four of these places and say whether you have been to them. Answer in the way shown.
Example: (Australia) *I've been to Australia once/twice/many times, etc.*
  or I've never been to Australia....................................

7. I've ....
8. ....
9. ....
10. ....

114.3 *Write sentences using* **get into/out of/on/off.**

Example: You were walking home. A friend passed you in his car. He saw you, stopped, and offered you a lift. He opened the door. What did you do? *I got into the car.*

1. You were waiting for your bus. At last your bus arrived. The doors opened. What did you do then? I got ...*on the bus*...... .
2. You drove home in your car. You arrived at your house and parked the car. What did you do then? I...*went home*... *got out of*
3. You were traveling by train to Vancouver. When the train arrived at Vancouver, what did you do? *I got off the train*
4. You needed a taxi. After a few minutes a taxi stopped for you. You opened the door. What did you do then? ...*got into*...........
5. You were riding your bike. There was a big hill, and you didn't have the energy to pedal up it. What did you do? ......*got off*.......... and pushed it up the hill.

Study this list of *nouns + preposition*. Sometimes other prepositions are possible – a good dictionary will give you more information.

a **check FOR** (a sum of money):
- They sent me a **check for** $100.

a **demand** / a **need FOR** something:
- The company closed down because there wasn't enough **demand for** its product.

a **reason FOR** something:
- The train was late but no one knew the **reason for** the delay.

a **rise** / an **increase** / a **fall** / a **decrease IN** something:
- There has been an **increase in** automobile accidents lately.

an **advantage** / a **disadvantage OF** something:
- The **advantage of** living alone is that you can do what you like.

but we say "**there is** an advantage **in** (or **to**) doing something":
- There are many advantages **in** (or **to**) living alone.

a **cause OF** something:
- Nobody knows what the **cause of** the explosion was.

a **photograph** / a **picture OF** someone/something:
- He always keeps a **photograph of** his wife in his wallet.

damage TO something:
- The accident was my fault, so I paid for the **damage to** the other car.

an **invitation TO** a party / a wedding, etc.:
- Did you get an **invitation to** the party?

a **reaction TO** something:
- I was surprised at her **reaction to** what I said.

a **solution TO** a problem / an **answer TO** a question / a **reply TO** a letter / a **key TO** a door:
- Do you think we'll find a **solution to** this problem?
- The **answer to** your question is "No"!

an **attitude TO/TOWARD** someone/something:
- His **attitude to/toward** his job is very negative.

a **relationship** / a **connection** / **contact WITH** someone/something:
- Do you have a good **relationship with** your parents?
- The police want to question a man in **connection with** the robbery.

but: a **relationship** / a **connection** / a **difference BETWEEN** two things:
- The police have said that there is no **connection between** the two murders.
- There are some **differences between** British English and American English.

UNIT 115   Exercises

115.1 *Read the sentence and then complete the following sentence with the same meaning.*

Example: What caused the explosion?   What was the cause *of the explosion* ......?

1. We're trying to solve the problem.   We're trying to find a solution... *to* ....
2. Ann gets along well with her brother.   Ann has a good relationship ... *with* ....
3. Prices have increased a lot. There has been a big increase ... *in* ....
4. I don't know how to answer your question.   I can't think of an answer ... *to* ....
5. Nobody wants to buy shoes like these anymore.
   There is no demand ...... *for* ....
6. I think that being married has some advantages.
   I think that there are some advantages ... *in* ....
7. The number of people without jobs has fallen this year.
   There has been a fall..... *in the number* ....
8. I don't think that a new highway is necessary.
   I don't think that there is any need .... *for* ....

115.2 *Complete these sentences with the correct preposition.*

Example: There are some differences *between* British English and American English.

1. I just received an invitation ... *to* .... a wedding next week.
2. The cause ... *of* .... the fire in the hotel last night is still unknown.
3. Ann showed me a photograph ...... *of* .... the hotel where she stayed on her vacation.
4. Money isn't the solution ..... *to* .... every problem.
5. The company has rejected the workers' demands .... *for* .... an increase ..... *in* ....
   pay.
6. The two companies are completely independent. There is no connection ..... *between* ......
   them.
7. When I opened the envelope, I was delighted to find a check ..... *for* .... $500.
8. Have you seen this picture ...... *of* .... the town as it looked 100 years ago?
9. Sorry I haven't written to you for so long. The reason ..... *for* ...... this is that I've been
   sick.
10. The advantage .... *of* ....having a car is that you don't have to rely on public
    transportation.
11. There are many advantages ... *in* .... being able to speak a foreign language.
12. There has been a sharp rise ..... *in* ...... the cost of living in the past few years.
13. The front door is locked. Do you have the key.......... *to* .... the back door?
14. Bill and I used to be good friends, but I don't have much contact ... *with* ....him now.
15. I've never met Carol, but I've seen a picture ..... *of* ...... her.
16. It wasn't a serious accident. The damage ..... *to* ....the car was only slight.
17. Tom's reaction .... *to* .... my suggestion was not very enthusiastic.
18. What were George's reasons ..... *for* ...... giving up his job?
19. The fact that he got a job in the company has no connection ..... *with* ......the fact that his
    father is the managing director.
20. When he left home, his attitude *toward* his parents seemed to change.
21. I wrote to Sue last month, but I still haven't received a reply.... *to* .... my letter.

233

Preposition + noun ("**by** mistake," "**on** television," etc.)

Students often use the wrong preposition before the words in this unit, so study this list carefully:

to **pay BY check** (*but* to **pay IN cash** *or* to **pay cash**):
- Did you **pay by check** or **in cash**?

(to do something) **BY accident** / **BY mistake** / **BY chance**:
- We hadn't arranged to meet. We met **by chance**.

a **play BY Shakespeare** / a **painting BY Rembrandt** / a **novel BY Tolstoy**, etc.:
- Have you read any books **by Tolstoy**? (= any books written by Tolstoy?)

(to be/to fall) **IN love WITH** someone:
- Have you ever been **in love with** anyone?

IN (my) **opinion**:
- **In my opinion** the film wasn't very good.

IN time (= soon enough for something/soon enough to do something):
- Will you be home **in time for dinner**? (= soon enough for dinner)
- We got to the station **just in time to catch** the train.

ON time (= punctual, not late)
- The 11:45 train left **on time**. (= it left at 11:45)
- The conference was well organized. Everything began on time.

(to be) **ON fire**:
- Look! That car is **on fire**.

(to be) **ON the telephone** / **ON the phone**:
- I've never met her but I've spoken to her **on the phone**.

ON television / **ON the radio**:
- I didn't watch the game **on television**. I listened to it **on the radio**.

(to be/to go) **ON a diet**:
- I've put on a lot of weight. I'll have to go **on a diet**.

(to be/to go) **ON strike**:
- There are no trains today. The railroad workers are **on strike**.

(to be/to go) **ON vacation** / **ON business** / **ON a trip** / **ON a tour** / **ON a cruise** / **ON an expedition**, etc.
- Did you go to Paris **on business** or **on vacation**?
- One day I'd like to go **on a world tour**.

but you can also say "go **to a place FOR a** vacation / **FOR my** vacation":
- Tom has gone to France **for a** vacation.
- Where are you going **for your** vacation this year?

(to go/to come) **FOR a walk** / **FOR a swim** / **FOR a meal**, etc.:
- She always goes **for a walk** with her dog in the morning.
- After work we went to the restaurant **for a meal**.

(to have something) **FOR breakfast** / **FOR lunch** / **FOR dinner**:
- What did you have **for lunch**?

Unit 116 Exercises

116.1 *Complete these sentences. Use a preposition with a word or phrase from the box.*

mistake	time	~~a meal~~	a swim	strike
the phone	television	Shakespeare	time	love
business	a diet	breakfast	check	

1. After work we went to a restaurant *for a meal.*
2. The factory has closed because the workers have gone ...*on strike*...
3. I didn't mean to take your umbrella. I took it ...*by mistake*...
4. I got up late this morning and had to rush. All I had ...*for breakfast*... was a cup of tea.
5. I feel lazy tonight. Is there anything worth watching ...*on TV*...?
6. The train service is very good. The trains always run ...*on time*...
7. They fell ...*in love*... with each other immediately and were married in weeks.
8. It was an extremely hot day, so we went ...*for a swim*... in the lake.
9. Jim's job involves a lot of traveling. He often goes to other cities ...*on business*...
10. I didn't have any money on me, so I paid ...*by check*...
11. George has put on a lot of weight recently. I think he should go ...*on a diet*...
12. I washed your shirt this morning, so it should be dry ...*in time*... for you to wear it this evening.
13. I can never reach Sue. Whenever I call, she's always ...*on the phone*...
14. *Hamlet* and *Macbeth* are plays ...*by*...

116.2 *Complete these sentences with the correct preposition.*

Example: We hadn't arranged to meet. We met ...**by**... chance.

1. I'm hungry. What's ...*for*... dinner this evening?
2. ...*In*... my opinion, violent movies shouldn't be shown .... TV.
3. I think I need some exercise. Do you want to go ...*for*... a walk?
4. A dog ran across the street in front of the car, but I managed to stop just ...*in*... time.
5. Do you know any songs ...*by*... the Beatles?
6. I'd better not eat too much. I'm supposed to be ...*on*... a diet.
7. There was panic when people realized the building was ...*on*... fire.
8. Next month I'm going to Mexico ...*for*... a short vacation.
9. Where did you go ...*on*... your vacation last year?
10. I won't be at work next week. I'll be ...*on*... vacation.
11. I wouldn't like to go ...*on*... a cruise. I think I'd get bored.
12. The store clerk wouldn't accept my check and insisted that I pay ...*in*... cash.
13. Ann reads a lot of books ...*by*... American writers.
14. Did you hear the news this morning ...*on*... the radio?
15. Please don't be late for the meeting. We want to begin ...*on*... time.
16. I would like to get up ...*in*... time to have a big breakfast before going to work.
17. It was only ...*by*... accident that I found out who the man really was.
18. When we went to Rome, we went ...*on*... a tour around the city.
19. I wouldn't like his job. He spends most of his time talking ...*on*... the telephone.
20. When I was 14, I went ...*on*... a trip to France.
21. Ann liked the dress, but ...*in*... my opinion it didn't look very good on her.

235

UNIT 117

Adjective + preposition (1)

Study these groups of *adjectives + preposition*. Sometimes other prepositions are possible – a good dictionary will give you more information.

---

nice/kind/good/generous/mean/stupid/silly/intelligent/sensible/(im)polite/rude/unreasonable OF someone (to do something):

- Thank you. It was very **nice/kind of you** to help me.
- It's **stupid of her** to go out without a coat. She'll catch cold.

but: (to be) **nice/kind/good/generous/mean/(im)polite/rude/(un)pleasant/(un)friendly/cruel TO** someone:

- She has always been very **nice/kind to** me. (*not* with me)
- Why were you so **rude/unfriendly to** Bill?

angry/annoyed/furious { **ABOUT** something
{ **WITH** someone **FOR** doing something:

- What are you so **angry/annoyed about?**
- They were furious **with me for** not inviting them to the party.

delighted/pleased/satisfied/disappointed WITH something:

- I was **delighted with** the present you gave me.
- Were you **disappointed with** your exam results?

bored/fed up WITH something:

- You get **bored with** doing the same thing every day.
- I'm **fed up with** doing the dishes all the time.

surprised/shocked/amazed/astonished AT/BY something:

- Everybody was **surprised at/by** the news.
- I was **shocked at/by** the condition of the building.

excited/worried/upset ABOUT something:

- Are you **excited about** going on vacation next week?
- Ann is **upset about** not being invited to the party.

afraid/frightened/terrified/scared OF someone/something:

- "Are you **afraid of** dogs?" "Yes, I'm **terrified of** them."

proud/ashamed OF someone/something:

- I'm not **ashamed of** what I did. In fact I'm quite **proud of** it.

jealous/envious/suspicious OF someone/something:

- Why are you always **so jealous of** other people?
- He didn't trust me. He was **suspicious of** my intentions.

aware/conscious OF something:

- "Did you know they were married?" "No, I wasn't **aware of** that."

good/bad/excellent/brilliant AT (doing) something:

- I'm not very **good at** repairing things.

married/engaged TO someone:

- Linda is **married to** an American. (*not* with an American)

236

UNIT 117   Exercises

117.1 *Say how you feel about George in each situation.*

Example: George has kept you waiting for hours. (annoyed)   *I'm annoyed with him.*

1. George hasn't been eating well recently. (worried)   I'm ....*worried about*.... him.
2. George has been telling lies about you. (angry)   I'm ....*angry*.... him.
3. George is much better at everything than you are. (jealous)   ....*of*....
4. George is big, strong, aggressive, and violent. (afraid)   ....*of*....
5. You've had enough of George. (fed up)   I'm ....*with*....

117.2 *Complete these sentences with the correct preposition.*

Example: I was delighted .*with*.... the present you sent me.

1. It's very nice ...*of*........ you to let me use your car. Thank you very much.
2. Why are you always so impolite ....*to*...... your parents? Can't you be nice ...*to*....... them?
3. It wasn't very polite .....*of*...... him to leave without saying thank you.
4. I can't understand people who are cruel ......*to*...... animals.
5. Why do you always get so annoyed ....*about*.... little things?
6. The people next door are annoyed ...*with*.... us ....*for*.... making so much noise last night.
7. We enjoyed our vacation, but we were disappointed ....*with*.... the hotel.
8. I was surprised ....*at/by*... the way he behaved. It was out of character.
9. She doesn't go out at night very much. She's afraid ......*of*.....the dark.
10. I've been trying to learn Spanish, but I'm not satisfied ....*with*....my progress.
11. Jill starts her new job on Monday. She's very excited ....*about*....it.
12. I was shocked ...*at/by*... what you said. You should be ashamed ....*of*...... yourself.
13. Did you know that Linda is engaged ....*to*...... a friend of mine?
14. I had never seen so many people before. I was astonished ....*at/by*...the crowds.
15. Bill has been doing the same job for too long. He's bored ....*with*....it.
16. These days everybody is aware ....*of*........ the dangers of smoking.
17. Are you still upset ...*about*...what I said to you yesterday?
18. She's very nice, but I wouldn't like to be married ....*to*........her.
19. Mr. Davis spends a lot of time gardening. His garden is very well-kept, and he's very proud ...*of*........ it.

117.3 *Write sentences about yourself. Are you good at these things or not? Use:*

brilliant   very good   pretty good   not very good

Examples: (repairing things) *I'm not very good at repairing things.*
(tennis) *I'm pretty good at tennis.*

1. (repairing things)   ....
2. (tennis)   ....
3. (remembering people's names)   ....
4. (telling jokes)   ....
5. (languages)   ....

237

Study this list of *adjectives + preposition*:

---

sorry ABOUT something:
- I'm **sorry about** the noise last night. We were having a party.

but: **sorry FOR doing something:**
- I'm **sorry for shouting** at you yesterday.

You can also say:
- I'm **sorry I shouted** at you yesterday.

(to **feel**/to **be**) **sorry FOR** someone:
- I **feel sorry for** George. He has no friends and no money.

crazy ABOUT something:
- Ann is **crazy about** Westerns. She'd go to the movies every night if a Western were playing.

impressed BY/WITH someone/something:
- I wasn't very **impressed by/with** the movie.

famous FOR something:
- The Italian city of Florence is **famous for** its art treasures.

responsible FOR something:
- Who was **responsible for** all that noise last night?

different FROM someone/something (in informal English we sometimes say **different THAN**):
- The movie was quite **different from** what I expected.

interested IN something:
- Are you **interested in** art and architecture?

capable/incapable OF something:
- I'm sure you are **capable of** passing the examination.

fond OF someone/something:
- Mary is very **fond of** animals. She has three cats and two dogs.

full OF something:
- The letter I wrote was **full of** mistakes.

short OF something:
- I'm a little **short of** money. Can you lend me some?

tired OF something:
- Come on, let's go! I'm **tired of** waiting.

similar TO something:
- Your writing is **similar to** mine.

crowded WITH (people, etc.):
- The city was **crowded with** tourists.

UNIT 118   Exercises

118.1 *Complete the sentences. Each time use the most appropriate word in the box with the correct preposition.*

different	full	~~sorry~~	responsible	interested
short	similar	tired	capable	impressed

1. I don't feel *..sorry for..............* George. All his problems are his own fault.
2. I can't stop to talk to you now. I'm a little *.....short of..........* time.
3. "Do you want to watch the football game on television?"   "No, thanks. I'm not *.....interested in...............* football."
4. Your shoes are *.....similar to.........* mine, but they're not exactly the same.
5. My new job is a completely new experience for me. It's very *...different from....* what I did before.
6. The human race is now *.....capable of............* destroying the whole world with nuclear weapons.
7. We've got plenty of things to eat. The refrigerator is *....full of th......* food.
8. I wasn't very *....impressed with....* the service in the restaurant. We had to wait a long time before getting our food.
9. Can't we have something different to eat for a change? I'm *.....tired of.........* having the same thing day after day.
10. The editor is *.....respons for.......* what appears in the newspaper.

118.2 *Complete these sentences with the correct preposition.*

Example: Sorry *.about.....* the noise last night. We were having a party.

1. I'd rather not go to an Indian restaurant. I'm not crazy *.....about......* Indian food.
2. Ann is very fond *....of........* her younger brother.
3. This part of town is always very lively at night. It's usually crowded *....with.......* people.
4. In the closet I found a box full *.....of.........* old letters.
5. I felt sorry *....for........* the children when we went on vacation. It rained every day, and they had to spend most of the time indoors.
6. He said he was sorry *....about.....* the situation, but that there was nothing he could do.
7. France is famous *....for......* its food.
8. They looked bored. I don't think they were interested *.....in........* what I was saying.
9. Joe failed his driving test many times. He isn't capable *....of.........* driving a car.
10. The man we interviewed for the job was quite intelligent, but we weren't very impressed *....with....* his appearance.
11. Traveling is great at first, but you get tired *.....of......* it after a while.
12. Do you know anyone who might be interested *.....in......* buying an old car?
13. Our house is similar *....to.....* theirs, but I think ours is a little bigger.
14. Sue and I come from the same country, but my accent is different *....from...* hers.
15. The police are responsible *....for....* maintaining law and order.
16. We're short *.....of.....* staff in our office at the moment. There aren't enough people to do the work that has to be done.
17. I'm sorry *...about..* the smell in this room. It's just been painted.

Verb + preposition (1)

Study this list of *verbs + preposition*:

---

apologize (TO someone) **FOR** something (see also Unit 57a):
- When I realized I was wrong, I **apologized to** him **for** my mistake.

apply FOR a job / admission to a university, etc.:
- I think you'd be good at this job. Why don't you **apply for** it?

believe IN something:
- Do you **believe in** God? (= Do you believe that God exists?)
- I **believe in** saying what I think. (= I believe that it is a good thing to say what I think.)

belong TO someone:
- Who does this coat **belong to?**

care ABOUT someone/something (= think someone/something is important):
- He is very selfish. He doesn't **care about** other people.

care FOR someone/something:
   i)   = like something (usually in questions and negative sentences):
- Would you **care for** a cup of coffee? (= Would you like . . . ?)
- I don't **care for** hot weather. (= I don't like . . .)
   ii)   = look after someone:
- She is very old. She needs someone to **care for** her.

take care OF someone/something (= look after):
- Have a nice vacation. **Take care of** yourself!
- Will you **take care of** the children while I'm away?

collide WITH someone/something:
- There was an accident this morning. A bus **collided with** a car.

complain (TO someone) **ABOUT** someone/something:
- We **complained to** the manager of the restaurant **about** the food.

concentrate ON something:
- Don't look out the window. **Concentrate on** your work!

consist OF something:
- We had an enormous meal. It **consisted of** seven courses.

crash/drive/bump/run INTO someone/something:
- He lost control of the car and **crashed into** a wall.

depend ON someone/something:
- "What time will you arrive?" "I don't know. It **depends on** the traffic."

You can leave out **on** before question words (**when/where/how**, etc.):
- "Are you going to buy it?" "It **depends** (on) **how much** it is."

die OF an illness:
- "What did he **die of?**" "A heart attack."

UNIT 119   Exercises

119.1 *Complete the sentences. Each time use one of the following words with the correct preposition:*   **belong**   **applied**   ~~**apologized**~~   **die**   **concentrate**   **believe**   **crashed**   **depends**

1. When I realized that I had taken the wrong umbrella, I immediately *apologized for* my mistake.
2. I was driving along when the car in front of me stopped suddenly. Unfortunately I couldn't stop in time and *crashed into* the back of it.
3. "Does this bag *belong to* you?"   "No, it isn't mine."
4. Don't try and do two things at once. *Concentrate* one thing at a time.
5. Jane is still unemployed. She has *applied for* several jobs but hasn't had any luck yet.
6. "Are you playing tennis tomorrow?"   "I hope so, but it *depends on* the weather."
7. If you smoke, there is a greater chance that you will *die of* lung cancer.
8. I don't *believe in* ghosts. I think people only imagine that they see them.

119.2 *Complete these sentences with a preposition (if a preposition is necessary).*

Example: There was an accident this morning. A bus collided *with* a car.

1. He loves to complain. He complains *about* everything.
2. Our neighbors complained *to* us *about* the noise we made last night.
3. She doesn't have a job. She depends *on* her parents for money.
4. You were very rude to Tom. Don't you think you should apologize *to* him?
5. Are you going to apologize *for* what you did?
6. Jill and I ran *into* each other downtown yesterday afternoon.
7. He decided to give up sports in order to concentrate *on* his studies.
8. I don't believe *in* working hard. It's not worth it.
9. A soccer team consists *of* 11 players.
10. It is terrible that some people are dying *of* hunger while others eat too much.
11. As I was going out of the room, I collided *with* someone who was coming in.
12. There was an awful noise as the car crashed *into* the tree.
13. Do you belong *to* a political party?
14. I don't know whether I'll go out tonight. It depends *on* how I feel.

119.3 *Put in the correct preposition after* **care**.

Example: He's very selfish. He doesn't care *about* other people.

1. Are you hungry? Would you care *for* something to eat?
2. He doesn't care *about* the exam. He's not worried whether he passes or fails.
3. Please let me borrow your camera. I promise I'll take good care *of* it.
4. I don't care *about* money. It's not important to me.
5. Don't worry about arranging our vacation. I'll take care *of* that.
6. "Do you like this coat?"   "No, I don't care *for* the color."

241

Verb + preposition (2)

Study this list of *verbs + preposition*:

---

dream ABOUT someone/something:
- I **dreamed about** you last night.

dream OF being something / doing something (= imagine):
- I often **dream of** being rich.

also: "**(I) wouldn't dream (of** doing something)":
- "Don't tell anyone what I said."   "No, **I wouldn't dream of** it."

happen TO someone/something:
- A strange thing **happened to** me the other day.
- What **happened to** that gold watch you used to have?

hear ABOUT something (= be told about something):
- Did you **hear about** the fight in the club on Saturday night?
- Have you **heard about** Jane? She's getting married.

hear OF someone/something (= know that someone/something exists):
- "Who is Tom Brown?" "I have no idea. I've never **heard of** him."
- Have you **heard of** a company called "Smith Electronics"?

hear FROM someone (= receive a letter / telephone call from someone):
- "Have you **heard from** Ann recently?"   "Yes, she wrote to me last week."

laugh/smile AT someone/something:
- I look stupid with this haircut. Everyone will **laugh at** me.

listen TO someone/something:
- We spent the evening **listening to** records.

live ON money/food:
- George's salary is very low. It isn't enough to **live on.**

look AT someone/something (= look in the direction of):
- Why are you **looking at** me like that?

also: **have a look AT, stare AT, glance AT**

look FOR someone/something (= try to find):
- I've lost my keys. Can you help me **look for** them?

look AFTER someone/something (= take care of):
- She's very old. She needs someone to **look after** her.

meet WITH someone (= have a meeting with):
- Our representatives **met with** the president of the company.

pay (someone) **FOR** something:
- I didn't have enough money to **pay for** the meal.

but: **pay a bill / a fine / $50 / a fare / taxes,** etc. (no preposition)

rely ON someone/something:
- You can **rely on** Jack. He always keeps his promises.

UNIT 120   Exercises

120.1 *Complete these sentences. Each time use one of the following words with a preposition:*

rely   listen   ~~look~~   live   laughing   glanced   paid   happened

1. Where's the newspaper? I want to ...*look at*............. the television guide.
2. I haven't seen Susan for ages. I wonder what's ....*happened to*........ her.
3. You must ...*listen to*... this record. You'll love it.
4. I ......*glanced* the newspaper to see if there was anything interesting in it.
5. When you went to the theater with Paul, who ....*paid for* the tickets?
6. The bus service isn't very good. You can't......*rely on*...... it.
7. What are you ....*laughing at*? I don't understand what's funny.
8. It's a very inexpensive country. You can ...*live on*...... very little money there.

120.2 *Complete these sentences with a preposition (if a preposition is necessary).*

Example: She smiled ...*at*....... me as she passed me in the street.

1. Don't listen ....*to*.... what he says. He's stupid.
2. What happened ....*to*....... the picture that used to be on that wall?
3. A: You wouldn't go away without telling me, would you?
   B: Of course not. I wouldn't dream ...*of*........ it.
4. I dreamed ....*about*.. Ann last night. We were dancing together at a party when she suddenly hit me. Then I woke up.
5. The accident was my fault, so I had to pay ....*for*... the damage.
6. I didn't have enough money to pay ....the bill.
7. You know that you can always rely ....*on*.... me if you need any help.
8. The man sitting opposite me on the train kept staring ....*at*... me.
9. She doesn't eat very much. She lives .,,.*on*.... bread and eggs.
10. When are you going to meet ....*with*.your professor to discuss your paper?

In these sentences put in the correct preposition after **hear**.

11. "Did you hear ....*about*.. the accident last night?"   "Yes, Ann told me."
12. Jill used to write to me fairly often, but I haven't heard ....*from*.. her for a long time now.
13. A: Have you read any books by James Hudson?
    B: James Hudson? No, I've never heard ....*of*..... him.
14. Thank you for your letter. It was nice to hear ...*from*.. you again.
15. "Do you want to hear ...*about*. our vacation?"   "Not now, tell me later."
16. The town I come from is very small. You've probably never heard ....*of*........ it.

In these sentences put in the correct preposition after **look**.

17. When I looked .....*at*....my watch, I couldn't believe that it was so late.
18. The police are still looking ....*for*...the seven-year-old boy who disappeared from his home last week. Nobody knows where the boy is.
19. When we went out for the evening, a neighbor of ours looked ...*after*.the children.
20. I'm looking ...*for*...... Tom. Have you seen him anywhere?

Study this list of *verbs + preposition*:

---

search (a person / a place / a bag, etc.) **FOR** someone/something:
- ■ I've **searched** the whole house **for** my keys, but I still can't find them.
- ■ The police are **searching for** the escaped prisoner.

shout AT someone (*when you are angry*):
- ■ He was very angry and started **shouting at** me.

but: **shout TO** someone (*so that they can hear you*):
- ■ He **shouted to** me from the other side of the street.

speak/talk TO someone ("with" is also possible):
- ■ (*on the telephone*) Hello, can I **speak to** Jane, please?
- ■ Who was that man I saw you **talking to** in the restaurant?

suffer FROM an illness:
- ■ The number of people **suffering from** heart disease has increased.

think ABOUT someone/something (= *consider, concentrate the mind on*):
- ■ You're quiet this morning. What are you **thinking about?**
- ■ I've **thought about** what you said and I've decided to take your advice.
- ■ "Will you lend me the money?"   "I'll **think about** it."

think OF someone/something (= *remember, bring to mind, have an idea*):
- ■ She told me her name, but I can't **think of** it now. (*not* think about it)
- ■ That's a good idea. Why didn't I **think of** that?

We also use **think OF** when we ask for or give an *opinion*:
- ■ "What did you **think of** the movie?"   "I didn't **think** much **of** it."

The difference between **think OF** and **think ABOUT** is sometimes very small. Often you can use **OF** or **ABOUT**:
- ■ My sister is **thinking of** (*or* **about**) going to Canada.
- ■ Tom was **thinking of** (*or* **about**) buying a new car, but changed his mind.
- ■ When I'm alone, I often **think of** (*or* **about**) you.

wait FOR someone/something:
- ■ I'm not going out yet. I'm **waiting for** the rain to stop.

write TO someone *or* **write** someone (*without* **to**):
- ■ Sorry I haven't **written (to)** you for such a long time.
- ■ I **wrote** her a letter.

We do *not* use a preposition with these verbs:

call/phone someone	Did you **call/phone your father** yesterday?
discuss something	We **discussed many things** at the meeting.
enter (= *go into a place*)	She felt nervous as she **entered the room**.

For verb + preposition + **-ing** see Unit 57a.

UNIT 121 Exercises

121.1 *Complete these sentences with a preposition where necessary. If no preposition is necessary, leave the sentence as it is.*

Example: He was angry and started shouting ...**at**....... me.

1. I've searched everywhere .... John, but I haven't been able to find him.
2. Ken gets very jealous. He doesn't like his girlfriend talking .... other men.
3. I don't want to go out yet. I'm waiting .... the mail to arrive.
4. Please don't shout .... me! Be nice to me.
5. We passed Tom as we were driving along. I shouted .... him but he didn't hear.
6. Ann doesn't write .... her parents very often, but she calls .... them at least once a week.
7. Can I speak .... you a moment? There's something I want to ask you.
8. Sally is not well. She suffers .... severe headaches.
9. The police have been searching the woods .... the missing girl.
10. She's a little lonely. She needs someone to talk ....
11. I don't want to discuss .... what happened last night. I want to forget about it.
12. We're going out to eat tonight. I'd better call .... the restaurant to reserve a table.

*Use the correct preposition (**of** or **about**) after* **think**. *Remember that sometimes you can use either* **of** *or* **about**.

13. Before you make a final decision, think carefully .... what I said.
14. I don't know what to get Ann for her birthday. Can you think .... anything?
15. You're selfish. You only think .... yourself.
16. "I've finished the book you lent me."   "Really? What did you think .... it?"
17. We're thinking .... going out to eat tonight. Would you like to come?
18. I don't really want to go out to dinner with Tom tonight. I'll have to think .... an excuse.
19. When he asked her to marry him, she said that she wanted to go away and think .... it for a while.
20. She is homesick. She's always thinking .... her family back home.
21. I don't think much .... this coffee. It's like water.

121.2 *Complete these sentences with one of the following words. Use a preposition if necessary.*

> **phoned**   ~~**shouted**~~   **discussed**   **entered**   **wrote**   **waited**

1. He got angry and **shouted at**..... me.
2. I .... Ann last week, but she hasn't replied to my letter yet.
3. I .... Tom yesterday, but there was no answer. He must have been out.
4. We .... the problem, but we didn't reach a decision.
5. We .... Jim for half an hour, but he never arrived.
6. The children stopped talking when the teacher .... the room.

UNIT 122 Verb + object + preposition (1)

Study this list of *verbs + object + preposition*:

accuse someone **OF** (doing) something (see also Unit 57b):
- Tom **accused** Ann **of** being selfish.
- Three students were **accused of** cheating on the exam.

ask (someone) **FOR** something:
- I wrote to the company **asking** them **for** more information about the job.

but: "**ask** (someone) **a question**" (no preposition)

blame someone/something **FOR** something:
- Everybody **blamed** me **for** the accident.

or: **blame** something **ON** someone/something:
- Everybody **blamed** the accident **on** me.

We also say: "(someone is) **to blame for** something":
- Everybody said that **I was to blame for** the accident.

borrow something **FROM** someone:
- I didn't have any money. I had to **borrow** some **from** a friend of mine.

charge someone **WITH** (an offense / a crime):
- Three men have been arrested and **charged with** robbery.

congratulate someone **ON** (doing) something (see also Unit 57b):
- When I heard that she had passed her exams, I called her to **congratulate** her **on** her success.

divide/cut/split something **INTO** (two or more parts):
- The book is **divided into** three parts.
- **Cut** the meat **into** small pieces before frying it.

do something **ABOUT** something (= do something to improve a bad situation):
- The economic situation is getting worse and worse. The government ought to **do** something **about** it.

explain (a problem / a situation / a word, etc.) **TO** someone:
- Can you **explain** this word **to** me? (*not* explain me this word)

also: "**explain** (**to** someone) **that/what/how/why . . .** " (note the word order):
- Let me **explain to you what** I mean.

invite someone **TO** (a party / a wedding, etc.):
- Have you been **invited to** any parties recently?

leave (a place) **FOR** (another place):
- I haven't seen her since she **left** home **for** work this morning.

point/aim something **AT** someone/something:
- Don't **point** that knife **at** me! It's dangerous.

UNIT 122 Exercises

122.1 *Complete these sentences with a preposition.*

Example: I didn't have any money, so I had to borrow some ..*from*..... a friend of mine.

1. You're always asking me .... money. Why don't you ask someone else for a change?
2. I've been invited .... the wedding but unfortunately I can't go.
3. When I saw Dave, I congratulated him .... passing his driving test.
4. Be careful with those scissors. Don't point them .... me!
5. It's not very pleasant when you are accused .... something you didn't do.
6. The driver of the car was taken to the police station and later charged .... reckless driving.
7. "Is that your own book?" "No, I borrowed it .... the library."
8. It's a very large house. It's divided .... four apartments.
9. Mr. and Mrs. Roberts are on a tour of Europe at the moment. They're in Rome now, but tomorrow they leave .... Venice.
10. The roof of the house is in very bad condition. I think we ought to do something .... it.

122.2 *Use the correct preposition after* **blame**. *Sometimes you have to use* **for**, *and sometimes* **on**.

Examples: Tom said that the accident was my fault. Tom blamed me *for the accident*....
Tom said that the accident was my fault. Tom blamed the accident *on me*........

1. Ann said that what happened was Jim's fault. Ann blamed Jim ....
2. You always say that everything is my fault. You always blame everything.......................
3. Do you think that the economic situation is the fault of the government?
   Do you blame the government ....?
4. I think that the increase in violent crime is the fault of television.
   I blame the increase in violent crime...

Now rewrite sentences 3 and 4 using **. . . to blame for . . . .**

Example: Tom said that **I was to blame for** the accident.

5. (3) Do you think that the government is ....?
6. (4) I think that ....

122.3 *Make sentences using* **explain**. *Ask someone to explain some things you don't understand.*

Examples: (I don't understand this word.) *Can you explain this word to me?*.......
(I don't understand what you mean.) *Can you explain to me what you mean?*

1. (I don't understand this question.) Can you explain ....?
2. (I don't understand the system.) Can you ....?
3. (I don't understand how this machine works.) ....
4. (I don't understand why English prepositions are so difficult.) ....

247

Verb + object + preposition (2)

Study this list of *verbs + object + preposition:*

---

prefer someone/something **TO** someone/something (see also Unit 61):
- I **prefer** tea **to** coffee.

protect someone/something **FROM** (or **against**) someone/something:
- He put suntan lotion on his body to **protect** his skin **from** the sun. (*or*
  . . . **against** the sun.)

provide someone **WITH** something:
- The school **provides** all its students **with** books.

regard someone/something **AS** something:
- I've always **regarded** you **as** one of my best friends.

remind someone **OF** someone/something (= cause someone to remember):
- This house **reminds** me **of** the one I lived in when I was a child.
- Look at this photograph of Carol. Who does she **remind** you **of?**

but: **remind** someone **ABOUT** something (= tell someone not to forget):
- I'm glad you **reminded** me **about** the party. I had completely forgotten
  it.

For "**remind** someone **to do** something" see Unit 53b.

sentence someone **TO** (a period of imprisonment):
- He was found guilty and **sentenced to** six months in prison.

spend (money) **ON** something:
- How much money do you **spend on** food each week?

Note that we usually say "**spend** (**time**) do**ing** something":
- I **spend a lot of time** read**ing.**

throw something **AT** someone/something (in order to hit them):
- Someone **threw** an egg **at** the mayor while he was speaking.

but: **throw** something **TO** someone (for someone to catch):
- Ann shouted "Catch!" and **threw** the keys **to** me from the window.

translate (a book, etc.) **FROM** one language **INTO** another language:
- George Orwell's books have been **translated into** many languages.

warn someone **ABOUT** someone/something (**of** is also possible sometimes):
- I knew she was a bit strange before I met her. Tom had **warned** me
  about her.
- Everybody has been **warned about** the dangers of smoking.

For "**warn** someone **against** doing something" see Unit 57b.
For "**warn** someone **not to do** something" see Unit 53b.

For verb + object + preposition + **-ing** see Unit 57b.

UNIT 123 Exercises

123.1 *Read the sentence and then complete the following sentence with the same meaning. Each time begin in the way shown.*

Example: Many people think he is one of the greatest pianists in the world.
Many people regard *him as one of the greatest pianists in the world.*

1. I don't mind rock music, but I prefer classical music.
   I prefer ....
2. He has enemies, but he has a bodyguard to protect him.
   He has a bodyguard to protect .... his enemies.
3. I got all the information I needed from Sue.
   Sue provided ....
4. I bought a pair of shoes this morning – they cost $60.
   This morning I spent ....
5. Ann said to Tom, "Don't forget your appointment with Mr. Fox."
   Ann reminded ....

123.2 *Complete these sentences with the correct preposition.*

Example: Ann shouted "Catch!" and threw the keys ....*to*....... me from the window.

1. Do you prefer your present job .... the one you had before?
2. They wore warm clothes to protect themselves .... the cold.
3. She's written many books, but most people regard her first book .... her best.
4. Do you spend much money .... clothes?
5. Do you see that woman over there? Does she remind you .... anyone you know?
6. Remind me .... the meeting tomorrow night. I'm sure to forget otherwise.
7. I love this music. It always makes me feel very happy. It reminds me .... a warm spring day.
8. When we went on our skiing vacation last year, the organizers provided us .... all the equipment we needed.
9. Before he went to Seattle, many people had warned him .... the weather. So he was prepared for plenty of rain.
10. He was sentenced .... life imprisonment for the murder of a police officer.
11. Don't throw stones .... the birds! It's cruel.
12. If you don't want to eat that sandwich, throw it .... the birds. They'll eat it.
13. I couldn't understand the letter because it was in Spanish. So a friend of mine translated it .... English for me.
14. I prefer traveling by train .... driving. It's much more pleasant.
15. What do you spend most of your money .... ?
16. She got really angry. She even threw a chair .... me!
17. You remind me very much .... someone I used to know a long time ago. You are really like him in many ways.
18. Some words are difficult to translate .... one language .... another.
19. Before you go into the house, I'd better warn you .... the dog. He likes to jump up on people.

Phrasal verbs (**get up, break down, fill in**, etc.)

a We often use verbs with these words:

on	off	in	out	up	down	away
back	over	about	around	forward	through	along

We often use these words with verbs of *movement*. For example:

get on	The bus was full. We couldn't **get on**.
drive off	She got into the car and **drove off**.
come back	Tom is leaving tomorrow and **coming back** on Saturday.
turn around	When I touched him on the shoulder, he **turned around**.

But often these words (**on/off/up/down**, etc.) give a special meaning to a verb. For example:

- Sorry I'm late. The car **broke down**.
- **Look out!** There's a car coming.
- It was my first flight. I was very nervous as the plane **took off**.
- I was so tired this morning that I couldn't **get up**.

These verbs (**break down** / **get up** / **take off**, etc.) are *phrasal verbs*.

b Sometimes a phrasal verb has an *object*. Usually there are *two possible positions* for the object. So you can say:

　　　　　　　　object　　　　　　　　*object*
I **turned off** the light.　*or*　I **turned** the light **off**.

Here are some more examples:

- Could you ⎰ **fill out** this form?
　　　　　 ⎱ **fill** this form **out**?

- It's warm. ⎰ **Take off** your coat.
　　　　　 ⎱ **Take** your coat **off**.

- The fire fighters soon arrived and ⎰ **put out** the fire.
　　　　　　　　　　　　　　　 ⎱ **put** the fire **out**.

- I think I'll ⎰ **throw away** these old newspapers.
　　　　　 ⎱ **throw** these old newspapers **away**.

- The police got into the house by ⎰ **breaking down** the door.
　　　　　　　　　　　　　　　 ⎱ **breaking** the door **down**.

Sometimes the object of a phrasal verb is a *pronoun* (**it/them/me/you/him/her/us**). These pronouns go *before* **on/off/in/out/up/down**, etc.:

- They gave me a form and told me to **fill it out**. (*not* fill out it)
- Ann's asleep. Don't **wake her up**. (*not* wake up her)
- "What should I do with these old newspapers?" "**Throw them away**."
- Here's the money you need. Don't forget to **pay me back**.

c Sometimes we use a *phrasal verb + preposition*. For example: **look forward to** / **keep up with** / **cut down on**. The object always comes *after the preposition*:

- Are you **looking forward to your vacation**?
- You're walking too fast. I can't **keep up with you**.
- Jack has **cut down on smoking**. He only smokes five cigarettes a day now.

UNIT 124 Exercises

124.1 *Complete the sentences using an appropriate phrasal verb from the box. Use the correct form of the verb each time.*

~~break down~~	**clear up** (= become bright –	**take off**
speak up (= speak louder)	for weather)	**grow up**
turn up (= appear/arrive)	**show off** (= show how good	~~fall off~~
close down	you are at something)	**move in**

1. Be careful on that horse! Don't ..*fall off*......... !
2. Sorry I'm late. The car *broke down*...on the way here.
3. What time did the plane finally ....?
4. There used to be a very good store on the corner, but it......................... a year ago.
5. "We've bought a new house." "Oh, have you? When are you .... ?"
6. Susie is eight years old. When she .... , she wants to be a pilot.
7. I arranged to meet Jim at the club last night, but he didn't ....
8. The weather's horrible, isn't it? I hope it .... later.
9. We all know how wonderful you are. There's no need to ....
10. (*on the telephone*) I can't hear you very well. Can you .... a bit?

124.2 *Complete these sentences as shown in the examples.*

Examples: He told me to fill out the form, so .*I filled it out.*.....................................
He told me to throw away the newspapers, so *I threw them away.*............

1. He told me to put out my cigarette, so I...
2. He told me to take off my shoes, so I...
3. He told me to turn on the TV, so...
4. He told me to call up Ann, so...
5. He told me to give up smoking, so...
6. He told me to put on my glasses, so...
7. He told me to write down my address, so...

124.3 *Complete these sentences using an appropriate phrasal verb from the box. Where necessary use the past tense of the verb. Each time use* **it/them/me** *with the verb.*

look up	~~turn down~~	**wake up**	**shave off**
pick up	**cross out**	**knock out**	**try on**

1. The radio is a little loud. Can you ..*turn it down*.... , please?
2. There was a $20 bill lying on the sidewalk, so I ....
3. The children are asleep. Don't ....!
4. If you make a mistake, just................................. .
5. I saw a jacket I liked in the store, so I went in and ....to see if it fit me.
6. There were a few words that I didn't understand, so I .... in my dictionary.
7. He had a beard for a long time, but he got tired of it. So he ....
8. A stone fell on my head and .... I was unconscious for half an hour.

APPENDIX 1   List of present and past tenses

Simple present   **I do**   (Units 2–4)
I **work** in a bank but I **don't enjoy** it very much.
Tom **watches** television every evening.
Do you **like** parties?
We **don't go** out very often. We usually **stay** home.

Present continuous   **I am doing**   (Units 1, 3, and 4)
Please don't bother me. I**'m working.**
"What's Tom **doing?**"   "He**'s watching** television."
Hello, Ann. **Are** you **enjoying** the party?
We **aren't going** to the party tomorrow night.

Present perfect   **I have done**   (Units 13–15, 17–20)
I**'ve lost** my key. **Have** you **seen** it anywhere?
"Is Tom here?"   "No, he **has gone** home."
How long **have** they **been** married?
The house is very dirty. We **haven't cleaned** it for weeks.

Present perfect continuous   **I have been doing**   (Units 16–18)
I'm tired. I**'ve been working** hard all day.
You're out of breath. **Have** you **been running?**
How long **has** she **been studying** English?
I **haven't been feeling** very well lately.

Simple past   **I did**   (Units 11 and 20)
I **lost** my key yesterday.
They **went** to the movies, but they **didn't enjoy** the film.
What time **did** you **get** up this morning?
It **was** hot in the room, so she **opened** the window.

Past continuous   **I was doing**   (Unit 12)
When I arrived, Tom **was watching** television.
This time last year I **was living** in Brazil.
What **were** you **doing** at 10:00 last night?
The television was on, but they **weren't watching** it.

Past perfect   **I had done**   (Unit 21)
I couldn't get into the house because I **had lost** my key.
When I arrived at the party, Sue wasn't there. She **had gone** home.
They didn't come to the movies with us because they **had** already **seen** the film.
The house was dirty because we **hadn't cleaned** it for weeks.

Past perfect continuous   **I had been doing**   (Unit 22)
I was very tired. I **had been working** hard all day.
He was leaning against a wall, out of breath. He **had been running.**

For the passive, see Units 40–42.
For the future, see Units 4–10.

APPENDIX 2   Regular and irregular verbs

1.   *Regular verbs*

The simple past and past participle of regular verbs end in **-ed**. For example:

base form:	clean	improve	paint	carry
simple past/past participle:	clean**ed**	improv**ed**	paint**ed**	carri**ed**

For spelling rules see Appendix 3.

For the simple past see Units 11 and 20.
We use the past participle to make the perfect tenses (**have/has/had cleaned**) and for all the passive forms (see Units 40–42):

- I clean**ed** my room yesterday. (*simple past*)
- Your English has improv**ed**. (*present perfect* – see Units 13–15, 17–20)
- The house was dirty. We hadn't clean**ed** it for a long time. (*past perfect*– see Unit 21)
- This door has just been paint**ed**. (*present perfect passive*)
- He was carri**ed** out of the room. (*simple past passive*)

2.   *Irregular verbs*

With some irregular verbs, all three forms (*base form, simple past,* and *past participle*) are the same. For example, **hit**:

- Someone **hit** me as I came into the room. (*simple past*)
- I've never **hit** anyone in my life. (*past participle – present perfect*)
- George was **hit** on the head by a rock. (*past participle – passive*)

With other irregular verbs, the simple past is the same as the past participle (but different from the base form). For example, **tell – told**:

- She **told** me to come back the next day. (*simple past*)
- Have you **told** anyone about your new job? (*past participle – present perfect*)
- I was **told** to come back the next day. (*past participle – passive*)

With other irregular verbs all three forms are different.
For example, **break – broke – broken**:

- He **broke** his arm in a climbing accident. (*simple past*)
- Somebody has **broken** the window. (*past participle – present perfect*)
- When was the window **broken**? (*past participle – passive*)

⫸→

3. *List of irregular verbs*

base form	simple past	past participle
be	was/were	been
beat	beat	beaten
become	became	become
begin	began	begun
bend	bent	bent
bet	bet	bet
bite	bit	bitten
blow	blew	blown
break	broke	broken
bring	brought	brought
build	built	built
burst	burst	burst
buy	bought	bought
catch	caught	caught
choose	chose	chosen
come	came	come
cost	cost	cost
cut	cut	cut
deal	dealt	dealt
dig	dug	dug
do	did	done
draw	drew	drawn
drink	drank	drunk
drive	drove	driven
eat	ate	eaten
fall	fell	fallen
feed	fed	fed
feel	felt	felt
fight	fought	fought
find	found	found
fit	fit	fit
fly	flew	flown
forbid	forbade	forbidden
forget	forgot	forgotten
forgive	forgave	forgiven
freeze	froze	frozen
get	got	gotten
give	gave	given
go	went	gone
grow	grew	grown
hang	hung	hung
have	had	had
hear	heard	heard
hide	hid	hidden
hit	hit	hit
hold	held	held
hurt	hurt	hurt
keep	kept	kept
know	knew	known
lay	laid	laid
lead	led	led
leave	left	left
lend	lent	lent
let	let	let
lie	lay	lain

base form	simple past	past participle
light	lit	lit
lose	lost	lost
make	made	made
mean	meant	meant
meet	met	met
pay	paid	paid
put	put	put
read / **ri:d** /	read / **red** /	read / **red** /
ride	rode	ridden
ring	rang	rung
rise	rose	risen
run	ran	run
say	said	said
see	saw	seen
seek	sought	sought
sell	sold	sold
send	sent	sent
set	set	set
sew	sewed	sewn/sewed
shake	shook	shaken
shine	shone	shone
shoot	shot	shot
show	showed	shown
shrink	shrank	shrunk
shut	shut	shut
sing	sang	sung
sink	sank	sunk
sit	sat	sat
sleep	slept	slept
speak	spoke	spoken
spend	spent	spent
split	split	split
spread	spread	spread
spring	sprang	sprung
stand	stood	stood
steal	stole	stolen
stick	stuck	stuck
sting	stung	stung
stink	stank	stunk
strike	struck	struck
swear	swore	sworn
sweep	swept	swept
swim	swam	swum
swing	swung	swung
take	took	taken
teach	taught	taught
tear	tore	torn
tell	told	told
think	thought	thought
throw	threw	thrown
understand	understood	understood
wake	woke	woken
wear	wore	worn
win	won	won
write	wrote	written

APPENDIX 3 Spelling

Nouns, verbs, and adjectives can have the following endings:

noun + **-s/es** (plural)	books	ideas	matches
verb + **-s/es** (after **he/she/it**)	works	enjoys	washes
verb + **-ing**	work**ing**	enjoy**ing**	wash**ing**
verb + **-ed**	work**ed**	enjoy**ed**	wash**ed**
adjective + **-er** (*comparative*)	cheap**er**	quick**er**	bright**er**
adjective + **-est** (*superlative*)	cheap**est**	quick**est**	bright**est**
adjective + **-ly** (*adverb*)	cheap**ly**	quick**ly**	bright**ly**

When we use these endings, there are sometimes changes in spelling. These changes are listed below.

Vowels and *consonants*
a e i o u are *vowel* letters.

The other letters (**b c d f** etc.) are *consonants*.

1. Nouns and verbs + -s/-es

The ending is **-es** when the word ends in **-s/-ss/-sh/-ch/-x**:
match/match**es**   bus/bus**es**   box/box**es**
wash/wash**es**   miss/miss**es**   search/search**es**
Note also:
potato/potato**es**   tomato/tomato**es**
do/do**es**   go/go**es**

2. Words ending in -y (**baby, carry, easy**, etc.)

If a word ends in a *consonant* + **y** (**-by/-ry/-sy**, etc.):

y changes to **ie** before **-s**:
baby/bab**ies**   family/famil**ies**   country/countr**ies**   secretary/secretar**ies**
hurry/hurr**ies**   study/stud**ies**   apply/appl**ies**   try/tr**ies**

y changes to **i** before **-ed**:
hurry/hurr**ied**   study/stud**ied**   apply/appl**ied**   try/tr**ied**

y changes to **i** before **-er** and **-est**:
easy/eas**ier**/eas**iest**   heavy/heav**ier**/heav**iest**   lucky/luck**ier**/luck**iest**

y changes to **i** before **-ly**:
easy/eas**ily**   heavy/heav**ily**   temporary/temporar**ily**

y does *not* change before **-ing**:
hurry**ing**   study**ing**   apply**ing**   try**ing**

y does *not* change if the word ends in a *vowel* + **y** (**-ay/-ey/-oy/-uy**):
play/plays/play**ed**   enjoy/enjoys/enjoy**ed**   monkey/monkeys
exception: day/da**ily**
Note also: pay/**paid**   lay/**laid**   say/**said**

3. Verbs ending in -ie (**die, lie, tie**)

If a verb ends in **-ie**, **ie** changes to **y** before **-ing**:
lie/l**ying**   die/d**ying**   tie/t**ying**

»»→

4. Words ending in -e (**smoke, hope, wide,** etc.)

Verbs

If a verb ends in -e, we leave out **e** before **-ing**:
smoke/smok**ing**   hope/hop**ing**   dance/danc**ing**   confuse/confus**ing**
Exceptions: **be/being**
                verbs ending in **-ee**: **see/seeing**   **agree/agreeing**

If a verb ends in -e, we add **-d** for the *past* (of regular verbs):
smoke/smok**ed**   hope/hop**ed**   dance/danc**ed**   confuse/confus**ed**

Adjectives and adverbs

If an adjective ends in -e, we add **-r** and **-st** for the *comparative* and *superlative*:
wide/wide**r**/wide**st**   late/late**r**/late**st**   large/large**r**/large**st**

If an adjective ends in -e, we *keep* **e** before the adverb ending **-ly**:
polite/polite**ly**   extreme/extreme**ly**   absolute/absolute**ly**

If an adjective ends in **-le** (**terrible, probable,** etc.), we leave out **e** and add **-y** for the adverb:
terrib**le**/terrib**ly**   probab**le**/probab**ly**   reasonab**le**/reasonab**ly**

---

5. Doubling consonants (**stop/stopping/stopped, hot/hotter/hottest,** etc.)

Sometimes a verb or an adjective ends in *consonant – vowel – consonant*. For example:
stop plan rob hot thin wet prefer begin

We double the final consonant (**-pp-, -nn-** etc.) of these words before **-ing, -ed, -er** and **-est**:
stop/sto**pp**ing/sto**pp**ed   plan/pla**nn**ing/pla**nn**ed   rob/ro**bb**ing/ro**bb**ed
hot/ho**tt**er/ho**tt**est   thin/thi**nn**er/thi**nn**est   wet/we**tt**er/we**tt**est

If the word has more than one syllable (**prefer, begin,** etc.), we double that final consonant only if the final syllable is stressed:
preFER/prefe**rr**ing/prefe**rr**ed   perMIT/permi**tt**ing/permi**tt**ed
reGRET/regre**tt**ing/regre**tt**ed   beGIN/begi**nn**ing

If the final syllable is *not* stressed, we do *not* double the final consonant:
VISit/visiting/visited   deVELop/developing/developed
LISten/listening/listened   reMEMber/remembering/remembered

If the final syllable is *not* stressed, and the last consonant is **l**, the consonant
may be single *or* doubled:
travel/traveling/traveled   *or* travelling/travelled
cancel/canceling/canceled   *or* cancelling/cancelled

We do *not* double the final consonant if the word ends in two consonants (**-rt, -rn, -ck,** etc.):
start/starting/started   turn/turning/turned   thick/thicker/thickest

We do *not* double the final consonant if there are two vowel letters before it (**-oil, -eed, -ain,** etc.):
boil/boiling/boiled   need/needing/needed   explain/explaining/explained
cheap/cheaper/cheapest   loud/louder/loudest   quiet/quieter/quietest

Note that we do *not* double **y** or **w** at the end of words. (At the end of words **y** and **w** are not consonants; they are part of the vowel sound.):
stay/staying/stayed   grow/growing   new/newer/newest

APPENDIX 4   Short forms (**I'm/didn't**, etc.)

In spoken English we usually say "I'**m**/you'**ve**/did**n't**," etc. (= I am/you have/did not). We also use these short forms in *informal* written English (for example, in letters to friends). When we write short forms, we use an *apostrophe* (') for the missing letter or letters:

    I'**m** = I **am**   you'**ve** = you **have**   did**n't** = did **not**

Short forms of auxiliary verbs (am/is/are/have/has/had/will/shall/would):

'm = am 's = is *or* has 're = are 've = have 'll = will *or* shall 'd = would *or* had	I'm I've I'll I'd	 he's he'll he'd	 she's she'll she'd	 it's it'll	 you're you've you'll you'd	 we're we've we'll we'd	 they're they've they'll they'd

's can be **is** or **has**:

- He'**s** sick. (= He **is** sick.)
- He'**s** gone away. (= He **has** gone away.)

'd can be **would** or **had**:

- I'**d** see a doctor if I were you. (= I **would** see)
- I'**d** never seen her before. (= I **had** never seen)

We use some of these short forms after question words (**who/what/how**, etc.) and after **that/there/here**:

who's	what's	where's	that's	there's
who'll	what'll	when's	that'll	there'll
who'd	how's	here's		

- **Who'**s that girl over there? (= who **is**)
- **What'**s happened? (= what **has**)
- I think **there'll** be a lot of people at the party. (= there **will**)

Sometimes we use short forms (especially **'s**) after a noun:

- **John'**s going out tonight. (= John **is** going)
- **My friend'**s just gotten married. (= My friend **has** just gotten)

You can*not* use these short forms ('**m**/'**s**/'**ve**, etc.) *at the end of a sentence* (because the verb is stressed in this position):

- "Are you tired?" "Yes, I **am**." (*not* "Yes, I'm.")
- Do you know where he **is**? (*not* Do you know where he's?)

Short forms of auxiliary verbs + **not** (isn't/didn't, etc.):

isn't (= is not)	haven't (= have not)	wouldn't (= would not)
aren't (= are not)	hasn't (= has not)	shouldn't (= should not)
wasn't (= was not)	hadn't (= had not)	
weren't (= were not)	can't (= cannot)	mustn't (= must not)
don't (= do not)	couldn't (= could not)	
doesn't (= does not)	won't (= will not)	
didn't (= did not)		

Note that you can say:
he **isn't**/she **isn't**/it **isn't** *or* he'**s not**/she'**s not**/it'**s not**
you **aren't**/we **aren't**// *or* you'**re not**/we'**re not**/they'**re not**

INDEX

The numbers in the index refer to units, not pages.

Index

back (*in/on the back, in back of*) 112b
bad (*at*) 117
bear (*can't bear*) 54a
bed (*in bed/to bed*) 71b, 113b, 114a
been to 114b
been to and *gone to* 13d
before (followed by the present simple) 9
   before -ing 56b
begin (*begin doing/to do*) 55a
believe (*in*) 119
believed (*it is believed...*) 43a
belong (*to*) 119
better 98a
   had better 62a
blame 124
bored
   bored and *boring* 90
   bored with 117
born 42b
borrow (*from*) 124
both (of) 79
   both...and 79e
   position of *both* 102c
bread (uncountable) 65d
business (*on business*) 116
by
   by after the passive 40a
   by -ing 56c
   by myself/yourself etc. 76e
   by (the time) 111
   by and *until* 111a
   by car/by bus etc. 114d
   by accident/by chance/by mistake 116
   a play by Shakespeare etc. 116

can 25, 30
can't 25, 27, 30
   can't bear 54a
   can't stand 54a
capable (*of*) 118
care (*care about, care for, take care of*) 119
case (*in case*) 38
   in case of 38e
causative have (*have something done*) 44
cause (*of*) 115
chance 60b
charge (*with*) 122
check
   a check for... 115
   by check 116
church (*church/the church*) 71a
college
   college/the college 71a

in/at college 113c
collide (*with*) 119
comparatives 97–9
   comparatives with *any/no* 81d
   comparatives with *even* 105c
complain (*to/about*) 119
concentrate (*on*) 119
conditional sentences (**if sentences**) 9, 34–6
congratulate (*on*) 57b, 122
connection (*with/between*) 115
conscious (*of*) 117
consider (*-ing*) 51
considered (*it is considered that*) 43a
consist (*of*) 119
contact (*with*) 115
continue (+ infinitive or *-ing*) 55a
contractions (short forms) Appendix 4
corner (*in/at/on the corner*) 112e
could 25, 26, 27b, 28c, 30
   could in *if* sentences 34c, 35d, 36c
countable and uncountable nouns 65
crash (*into*) 119
crazy (*about*) 118
crowded (*with*) 118

damage (*to*) 115
dare 52c
decide
   decide + infinitive 52
   decide against -ing 57a
delighted
   delighted + infinitive 96c
   delighted with 117
demand
   demand + subjunctive 33
   a demand for 115
deny 51
depend (*on*) 119
despite 104
did (in past simple questions and negatives) 11c, 47b
die (*of*) 119
diet (*on a diet*) 116
difference (*between*) 115
different (*from/than*) 118
difficulty (*have difficulty -ing*) 58
direct speech and reported speech 45–6, 48b
disappointed
   disappointed + infinitive 96c
   disappointed with 117
discuss (no preposition) 121
dislike (*-ing*) 54b
divide (*into*) 122

Index

Index

Index